# BUSINESS DECISIONS WITH COMPUTERS

## New Trends in Technology

# BUSINESS DECISIONS WITH COMPUTERS

## New Trends in Technology


**Daniel Schutzer**

*Vice President, Citibank*
*New York, NY*



VNR VAN NOSTRAND REINHOLD
New York

Library of Congress Catalog Card Number
ISBN 0-442-31879-0



Printed in the United States of America

Van Nostrand Reinhold
115 Fifth Avenue
New York, New York 10003

Chapman and Hall
2-6 Boundary Row
London, SE1 8HN, England

Thomas Nelson Australia
102 Dodds Street
South Melbourne 3205, Victoria, Australia

Nelson Canada
1120 Birchmount Road
Scarborough, Ontario M1K 5G4, Canada

16 15 14 13 12 11 10 9 8 7 6 5 4 3 2 1

Library of Congress Cataloging-in-Publication Data

Schutzer, Daniel, 1940–
Business decisions with computers: new trends in technology/by Daniel Schutzer.
p. cm.
Includes bibliographical references and index.
ISBN 0-442-31879-0 (hard cover)
1. Decision-making—Data processing. 2. Management information systems. 3. Business—Data processing. 4. Software engineering.
I. Title.
HD30.23.S385 1991
658.4′03′0285—dc20 90-12575
CIP

# Contents

# Preface

Computer applications in business are undergoing important and revolutionary changes. Computer technology is becoming more completely integrated with the business goals and activities. Information technology will grow in importance to business in this next decade to the point that it will become a good business career path to the top. Business managers will need a much better, hands-on understanding of the computer operations within their organization.

By the mid 1990s most companies' cash flow will be on-line; EDI (electronic data interchange) will be the norm, POS (point-of-sale) and electronic payments will be one facet of a company's core services, and technology risks will translate to business risks. Information technology will represent an increasing portion of a business's resources (it is already one of the top four expenses, after salaries, real estate, and interest expense).

The technology is advancing rapidly, offering many new and important products and applications, but making the technological landscape more confusing. Because of the rapid change, many of the new technologies are overlapping and hard to distinguish. But computer applications and computer programming will be more powerful, intuitive, and friendly.

The increased friendliness, coupled with further dramatic advances in cost performance, will continue the move of the computer out of the data center and onto the desktop, where end users will increasingly make computer work part of their daily routine. This will lead to a greater dependence on generic packages.

Computers will be networked, supporting a more distributed work environment and making the business less sensitive to location. Vendor products will become more specialized, but more easily interchanged and interfaced. To make all of this practical, we will make greater use of standards. We will see the rise of the systems integrator, the electronic plumber who puts the information pipes together.

Both the end users' and the computer professionals' skills can be expected to change and blur. Business managers will need to be more knowledgeable about technology, while technologists will need to know more about business. Both will have to be much more flexible.

This book is intended to demonstrate what you need to know in order to plan and prepare for a successful business or data processing career in this new computer-integrated business environment. It aims to educate the reader to the strategic importance of the computer to business, to the relevant technical issues, and to the means for realizing its full potential. If you are already on a career track, it will show you how to help your company exploit these technological changes for competitive and strategic advantage.

The Introduction and Chapters 1 and 2 are directed at clarifying the issues, problems, and opportunities involved in exploiting technology and providing insight into the business decision process and areas where the computer can best contribute. The Introduction describes the challenges and opportunities of the new applications of computer technology. Chapter 1 discusses the impact of these new technology applications on the organization, and describes how to best evaluate, sell, implement, and exploit the new technology. Chapter 2 provides case examples. For those in need of review of fundamental business concepts, Appendix 1 reviews the key business and accounting fundamentals; Appendix 2 reviews the principles of economic theory; Appendix 3 reviews the basic business functions and activities; Appendix 4 reviews the principles of investment management of business finances; and Appendix 5 reviews the principles behind business decision-making.

Chapters 3, 4, and 5 describe the exciting new technology advances and discuss their impact on business. They help you become better prepared and more knowledgeable about relating technology to business needs. Chapter 3 discusses such emerging technologies as expert systems, object-oriented programming, natural language and speech processing, image processing, distributed multimedia databases, CASE (Computer-Aided Software Engineering), hypertext, groupware, neural networks, image processing, parallel processing, and visual programming. Chapter 4 describes the concepts behind the growing move to distributed processing and the client–server model of computing. Chapter 5 provides a glimpse into the future, including such advances as the personal electronic notebook and artificial reality, as well as the technologies of superconducting, optical computers, and molecular computers. As a supplement to these chapters, Appendix 6 provides a review of computer fundamentals; Appendix 7 compares the digital computer to the human processor; Appendices 8 through 15 provide more details for the technological advances discussed in Chapter 3; and Appendix 16 provides details on prevailing computer communications standards.

## ACKNOWLEDGMENTS

This book is dedicated, with my love and appreciation, to my family: my wonderful wife Myra and my terrific children Eric, Richard, and Pamela.

I would also like to thank my editor Dianne Littwin for her thoughtful review and stimulating conversation.

Thanks to all of you out there who like to read and write about computers. Finally, I wish to thank my trusty home computer, which in two senses is truly the origin of this book.

# Introduction

The world is growing smaller. We are currently in the first few years of a global economy where markets, businesses, and consumers are becoming unified across the world. This is occurring to such an extent that less and less of a business's decision-making can any longer be done solely on a national basis.

Along with this global linking, there is accelerating change creating increasing uncertainty and complexity, so projection errors increase and noise and instability increase. For example, practically overnight we have seen the Soviet Union's economy collapse, Germany unify, Donald Trump default on loans, and political scandal in Japan impact interest rates in the United States.

Added to this shrinking world is a demographic explosion. The world population is expected to experience more than 20 percent growth in less than 10 years, reaching 6.3 billion by the year 2000. This sheer population increase can be expected to create great sociopolitical and economic waves. We can expect equally dramatic technology advances, with over 90 percent of all the engineers and scientists who ever lived alive in the world today; their numbers are rapidly growing, promising to further accelerate technological progress. Unfortunately, here in the United States, a recent Workforce 2000 Study predicts that our general population will be inadequately trained to deal with the more complex skills that will be required in this more complex, highly technical world.

These world and business changes are being aided and amplified by dramatic changes in technology. Technology accelerates knowledge diffusion, shrinking the marketplace by increasing the speed at which new products and ideas get introduced and spread around the world. For example, television increases and broadens our vicarious experience. Consequently, the average product life has shrunk from an average of 20 years to only one or two years. It used to be that a company could sell its newer products domestically and, when that market saturated, sell them around the world. Now we can see and vicariously experience, electronically, goods as they are introduced, wherever they are introduced, so we refuse to settle for obsolete products when there are newer, more improved ones available.

As technology explodes, a business threat and competition can often come from new, unexpected quarters, an increased lateral effect. For example, Kodak's chemical film business's main competitive threat now comes from Sony's and Canon's electronic image-making.

As change accelerates, speed becomes the most important competitive factor, followed by flexibility. Businesses now have a smaller margin for error, with less time to react. Delaying or ignoring an opportunity can put you out of business.

Business is changing in response to these challenges, and so is its use of computers. The business hierarchy is flattening, and there is an increasing automation of the decision process accompanying this shift of decision-making responsibility down the management hierarchy. For example, 20 or 30 years ago, the CEO did inventory management; 10 to 12 years ago, middle management took over this responsibility; today, inventory management is handled by first-line management. In addition to its flattening, the business hierarchy is becoming more tangled, more network-like, and more product and less functionally oriented.

This trend is increasing as computers help us bring knowledge and information down from the manager to the worker performing the tasks, down to the point-of-acquisition and the point-of-sale. We are "informating" the workers, providing them with the knowledge and skills, through expert systems, "smart" factory tools and sensors, and computer networks, to enable the workers to react more quickly and effectively. Business is using technology to transfer skills and knowledge, putting them in the hands of the technically unskilled.

Businesses are learning to be more nimble and more innovative, striving for constant improvement. Furthermore, businesses are finding more efficient ways to cooperate and are forming economies of trust and symbiotic relationships with both suppliers and customers, and even, at times, their competition. With these trends, investment in technology and research increases in importance. Business must have appropriate technology to succeed. Organizational motivation and spirit is important, but is insufficient without the appropriate technological support. (For example, in World War II, the Polish cavalry, although of superior spirit, was defeated by the superior technology of the German tanks.)

These changes should soon revolutionize the way both business and computer professionals view and work with computer technology. The seeds of these changes were planted years ago in thousands of small developments that are only now becoming noticeable. By the next decade, these new directions and principles of use will dominate and irreversibly change the computing and business environment. But for the moment, the trends and directions are still not clear. They are obscured by several factors, including:

- The continued persistence and dominance of older applications and systems concepts
- The still highly specialized and technical nature of the subject
- Competing viewpoints, theories, and computer hardware and software solutions
- The vagaries of the economic and political environment

Computer users are currently beseiged by an almost unlimited number of offerings. The field is cluttered with hype and buzzwords such as DOS, OS2, UNIX, SAA, relational databases, and expert systems. All promise great benefits to the user, all profess to be the "true" superior product offering, and all are mostly incompatible with one another. It is difficult to make good decisions in such an environment. But in this great confusion lies the key to your company's continued survival and success, *if* you choose wisely.

Certain trends are already clear:

1. The generalization of many of the older, more mature systems applications (such as accounting, payroll, and financial reporting) as standard packages, forming a foundation upon which other, newer types of applications can be developed.
2. A shift in the focus of computer applications from automating structured tasks in the interest of improving operational efficiency to automating less structured tasks aimed at making users more effective in their jobs.
3. The increased accessibility of computers to the true end user (people without any specialized computer training whose main job function is *not* the design, operation, or maintenance of computers).
4. The wider appeal and improved acceptance of these newer, hands-on, end user desktop applications, resulting from dramatic improvements in user friendliness and reduced costs.

These trends are forcing a fundamental reassessment of how both business and data processing professionals should view, use, buy, and sell computers. The business professional will not be able to ignore computers, or simply delegate the care and maintenance of computer systems to data processing professionals. End users will have to become actively involved in the purchase, justification, and use of computers, because computers will become an integral part of mainstream business activities and operations. The use of computers will have progressed beyond assisting the office worker and business executive in a variety of isolated everyday support tasks such as:

- Word processing and document preparation
- "What if" financial modeling on electronic spreadsheets
- Calendar and schedule management
- Project management
- Personal file and note card management
- Billing and payments
- Payroll and accounting

They will be fully integrated into such primary business processes as planning, decision-making, marketing, sales, product design, manufacturing, distribution, and management control. Computers will become as indispensable to a business as the telephone, the balance sheet, and the marketing plan are today, and will fundamentally alter work patterns and how businesses are organized and run.

The shift in the typical computer user's profile from professional intermediary to lay end user will add strength to viewing the computer as a tool needed to get a job done, and not as an end in itself. This new emphasis will shift the focus of computer system design toward increased functionality, reliability, and ease of use. Furthermore, the end user is interested in minimizing disruption, in preserving and building upon existing applications and functionality, and *not* in keeping up with the most recent advances in computer technology. This will mean an increased emphasis on standardization and commoditization of the computer engine, allowing for greater portability of applications across computer product upgrades and multiple vendor offerings, and reducing the necessity to learn many specialized and arcane system interfaces and languages.

These trends are also forcing a change in the role and purpose of data processing professionals, and in the manner in which applications are developed and maintained. The increasing proliferation of custom and generic software packages emphasizes the role of the data processing professional as a smart buyer rather than a custom builder. Data processing professionals will increasingly be required to work more closely with business professionals as a team, both knowledgeable about business needs and applicable technology.

It will be necessary to grasp the significance of technological trends for the future of business. The design of a computer system application always required knowledge of some appropriate aspects of the business operation as well as the technology. In the future, the succeessful data processing professional will need to master all aspects of the business, to become a full business partner, helping to contribute to the business plans, strategies, and bottom line through the application of technical expertise to the business's goals.

This technical expertise will include knowledge of the various candidate packages' strengths, weaknesses, limitations, required resources, and interfaces. Since the data processing professional will often employ several different existing packages, the needed technical expertise will shift toward the ability to pick packaged solutions and interface, control, and schedule these packages to create a single seamless, integrated business solution. The future software professional will become much more like a hardware engineer who assembles a system from a catalog of standard parts. The existence of these packages will generally lead the buyer to consider software first and then hardware, and often to buy the hardware because of the software application.

This book aims to help both business and data processing professionals to understand these changes and to be more effective in the future through a clear enunciation of the relationship of contemporary trends in business and technology to satisfying the basic goals of business.

# BUSINESS DECISIONS WITH COMPUTERS

## New Trends in Technology

# 1

# A New Role for Computers in Business

Computer systems have traditionally focused on improving efficiency by performing business operations and processing functions more rapidly, with fewer errors and resources than previously needed. Their use has been concentrated in data-processing or MIS (management information systems) departments. A few applications, although modeled on traditional transaction processing activities, have been applied in areas where time constraints are too tight for manual operations. Airline reservation systems are an example. Technology applied to this class of applications is called an *enabling technology* because the application would not be possible without the aid of the computer.

In the 1980s dramatic advances in lowering the cost of computer hardware has led to the rapid growth of a new class of application: Personal computers (PCs) and workstations placed on the individual worker's desk, and equipped with friendly, easy-to-use software designed to support daily clerical, communications, planning, and decision-making activities. For every $2 million spent on computers in MIS today, another $1 million is spent outside of MIS, and this area is growing fast. The MIPS (millions of instructions per second) on the desk first outnumbered the MIPS in the computer center in 1982. At first these workstations were isolated stand-alone devices. Then they were linked together over local area networks (LANs) to share files, printers, and communications lines. Now they are being connected to corporate transaction and operations processing systems. New software developments like artificial intelligence (AI) are being successfully applied to program computers to perform more qualitative and conceptual tasks in addition to the usual quantitative numerical processing tasks.

Today, computers are finally poised to fulfill their potential to improve revenues rather than merely to reduce expenses. Computers can now increase business effectiveness by managing information, by assisting in the planning and decision-making process, and by providing better customer service, through the linking and integration of the personal computer/workstation applications with the older, more traditional operations and transaction processing systems.

In this role, the computer acts as an integral part of the business, as a true partner rather than as a clerk. It is not merely fetching and sorting and preparing, but reducing the bulk of information by reviewing, summarizing, interpreting, and correlating various bits of information to provide the business with a true competitive edge by improving the quality of its products, customer service, and decision-making (Appendix 5 reviews the decision-making process in depth). And with the introduction of this new role, the traditional split between human and machine is shifting, and so is the means of human–machine communication. Consider the following examples:

1. Benetton uses technology to reduce the time it takes to bring a product to market by spotting buying trends at retail stores and reacting quickly to them.
2. Federal Express equips its carriers with digital transmitters and puts machine-readable labels on all its packages so that the company can track and control the status and movement of its deliverables almost instantaneously.
3. Other innovative applications which involve the use of hand-held computers include these (Fuchsberg 1990):
   - Avis agents print customer receipts on hand-held computers to speed up car returns.
   - Frito-Lay delivery people manage orders and feed inventory and sales data to management.
   - Newark police enter license numbers into the central computer to detect lawbreakers.
   - Otis Elevator service workers use radio-powered hand-held computers to get emergency calls and to query service files.

Unfortunately, most managers are not taking full advantage of information technology. After spending millions of dollars on systems, managers are often not achieving the ambitious goals they originally sought (Zuboff 1989). With few exceptions, businesses have been unable to get beyond improving productivity and efficiency. They are generally not using information technology to help create new products and develop new services.

Part of the reason is the lack of acceptable methods to build, evaluate, and validate the impacts of information technology in this area. This is still a relatively new role for information technology. Information technology and computers are still generally viewed as an expense, not as a source of revenue (unless you are in the business of selling computers and computer software). In a recent survey of business executives, 62 percent viewed information technology as an administrative tool and 77 percent as an operational tool; only 38 percent viewed it as a strategic tool. Furthermore, strategic/tactical systems are particularly hard to specify in advance, and complex to build.

There are organizational and cultural barriers as well. The new technology is changing work in a way that makes it difficult for people to accept, and often the result is a negative response to the technology.

## THE ROLE OF AUTOMATION IN THE COMPETITIVE, STRATEGIC, INNOVATIVE ORGANIZATION

The new technology is important to business because it is the key to using technology to make the organization more competitive and more innovative. A competitive system helps to distinguish an organization in its industry, to break away from the pack and to do things differently. There are very few examples of truly competitive systems; American Airline's Sabre System and Citibank's ATM network are two. To be competitive, such a system must:

- Be in a critical part of the business.
- Be an innovative idea.
- Result in a major organizational change.
- Be difficult to reproduce.

A *competitive* system must generate critical behavior changes that result in improved performance. Because of the amount of change involved, it is almost impossible to determine in advance which systems will be successful and which will not. It is also impossible to automate a competitive system successfully without detailed knowledge of what the competition is doing. Furthermore, the market distinctions derived from the introduction of a competitive system often do not remain exclusively with the initiator. The pack can catch up, although a head start can often play a decisive role in establishing an entrenched market share.

*Strategic* systems, on the other hand, are designed to maintain competitive parity over the long haul. A strategic system is not necessarily competitive. It is sufficient for a strategic system to create an environment conducive to the continued generation of innovative solutions and systems. None of the solutions has to be revolutionary or represent a major breakthrough; it is useful just to have an environment that supports the production of a continuous stream of small improvements. With such an environment in place, the business remains vital, innovative, and competitive.

Competitive and strategic systems are obviously vital to the future of a business, but they are difficult to plan. It is hard to know in advance which systems will provide a true competitive or strategic edge, or how much they will ultimately cost to build and maintain, or how to measure their worth to the corporation. The road to employing automation successfully requires good planning combined with a strong organizational commitment, vision, the right sort of corporate environment, and lots of prototyping, feedback, and iterative design.

## IMPACT ON THE ORGANIZATION

As the focus of computer applications changes from efficiency to effectiveness, organizations will be affected in many ways. To realize the full benefits the technology offers, managers must understand the forces of change and ensure that the organization adapts and responds in an appropriate fashion. Calvin Pava of Harvard Business School writes: "Efficiency entails perfecting internal operations under conditions of stability, whereas effectiveness entails bettering the match with one's surrounding environment under conditions of change" (Pava 1983). These goals are often contrary and interdependent, so tradeoffs are often involved. These tradeoffs can involve rethinking the organizational structure itself.

The new technology tends to intellectualize tasks. For example, when an assembly line is automated and a worker is sent into a control room to monitor and control the process through a terminal, that worker is required to do more intellectual work, to interpret data and to detect patterns.

With the help of computer programs that mimic skills that have long set managers apart, lower-level workers can do tasks once reserved for managers; e.g., bank clerks can give investment advice, or grant loan approval. Through technology, workers are gaining access to important information and insights that allow the company to increase the individual's decision-making authority.

This new technology not only automates, it "informates": It generates new information about the organization's underlying production and administrative processes that had been either partially or completely opaque, and it makes this knowledge more explicit and available to the worker. It sets in motion dynamics that could ultimately change the nature of work and the social relationships that organize productive activity. It turns workers into managers. This is an implied threat to the whole structure of authority. And it is not at all what the managers envisioned when they brought in automation: Executives typically approach technology with the idea that smarter technology will make it possible to perform the work with fewer, less educated, less expensive people. But when you use this technology simply to replace people, it falls short of providing the benefits you hoped to achieve.

Consider the classic Harvard Business School case study "Tiger Creek" (Goleman 1988). An electronic expense tracking system is installed in this fictional midwestern paper manufacturing plant. Machine operators have a monitor displaying the exact costs of all the decisions they make. By watching the monitors, the workers gain the knowledge to begin to improve the manufacturing process. For example, they find cheaper chemical mixes. One operator discovers that an expensive new steam hood brought in by management to increase efficiency is actually raising costs. It is removed. Many managers become angry. They feel that innovative cost decisions are *their* responsibility, not the machine operators'.

Richard Walton of the Harvard Business School found that in companies with serious commitments to information technology, corporate activities have become more interdependent. Errors and contributions alike have become more anonymous. News travels faster and farther. When a minor part breaks down, the whole system is affected. Technology tends to flatten hierarchies. Companies that have gone the farthest in using information technology to improve effectiveness have only about half the managerial levels of their rivals. Top-performing companies spend twice as much on information as their rivals and average less than four management layers, whereas poorer performing rivals have eight levels. One British film reduced its management layers from thirteen to four. General Motors has halved its management levels. And these new corporate structures are no longer pyramids; they are becoming more like holograms, with shared information making each person, each part, contain the whole.

So automation is not the issue at all: The issue is what kind of information you are getting and how you use it. In many cases managers have been going after productivity gains when productivity is not the most important thing. What is important is innovation and creativity, the development of products or services or projects or ideas. Take accounting for example. Since the advent of information technology, the number of accountants has increased by about 30 percent. The information being generated has created opportunities for differentiating the accounting practice and developing new kinds of products and services.

With advanced information technology, knowledge becomes shareable. It offers organizations an opportunity to learn more about their business. It provides businesses with the capacity to translate events, objects, or behaviors into data; it provides the capacity for generating information about the underlying company's productive and administrative processes through which the organization accomplishes its work, providing a deeper level of understanding of these activities.

But the technology of "informating" poses a real conflict for most organizations and their employees, and often leads to their rejecting the new technology. In the workplace, knowledge is power. Knowledge that used to be proprietary is now available to whoever knows how to call it up. In that sense, power reverts to whoever can get into the computer. Moreover, by accelerating change and innovation, technology makes jobs obsolete faster. Employees have to learn more on the job. At one company, the time for a worker's skills to become obsolete has dropped from seven to fourteen years to three to five years.

To use and manage these opportunities requires an organizational structure that can exploit the opportunities over and over again, an organization that knows how to learn. In the long run, it may not be important that you can get a new product to market six months earlier than the competition, because the competition will catch up with you there. It is more important that your organization be in a position to keep on creating new products ahead of the competition.

We need organizations that have learned how to create value from information on a sustained basis. The problem is that traditional hierarchical organizations tend to absorb new technology into the status quo, in an effort to preserve themselves. This happens because managers sense a threat to their authority and job security when people at the operating level are given more and better information. Managers should see the change as an opportunity to be more creative. But unless employees are given enough security and freedom, they are unlikely to be able to learn. They will refuse to loosen their grip on their private knowledge sources, to take more chances, and to play with and explore the technology. Dealing with people problems is an important factor in the success of new systems.

## INNOVATIVE DESIGN CYCLE

These strategic and competitive systems are developed in an inherently different way from more traditional systems. With traditional transactional systems, there is usually a good initial understanding of needs even when they are complex to design, so standard life cycle procedures apply. Strategic and competitive systems usually have many unknowns and require more basic research and experimentation. Generally they involve a more evolutionary design cycle. Users want to get going but are reluctant to wait until something is "right," especially since no one is sure what "right" is until they try it. Often prototypes are used.

Prototyping is good when there is a need for learning, but where design complexity is not a serious concern. Unfortunately, today's strategic and competitive systems are both difficult to define at first and complex to design. They often require the integration of many existing systems aimed at helping the business to work differently and better. Therefore, to be successful the project must be a participative design, with the user heavily involved. A major portion of the systems development effort typically involves the integration of existing systems. And here is the dilemma: These systems are too complex to make large initial investments until the need is better understood, yet the system will never be understood until it is tried in an operational environment.

As a remedy to this problem, Michael Treacy (Treacy 1988) recommends what he calls the *innovative design cycle*. His approach is adapted from marketing practices and follows the standard five-phase cycle used for launching a new product (shown in Figure 1.1). The initial stages require very little investment. The first stage, "Basic Research," involves researching what the company and the

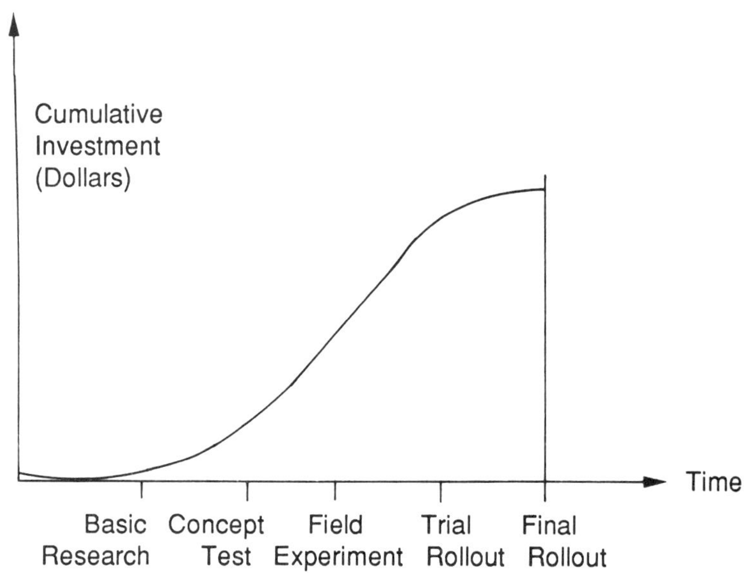


**Figure 1.1.** The Innovative Design Cycle.

competition are already doing. Usually two to four concepts are identified for test and evaluation. The next stage is "Concept Test," the evaluation and measurement stage. It is crucial for justifying the investment, and for using the findings to redesign a better system, since it is rare to get the system right on that first pass. At this point, only about one-third of the budget has been spent.

The next step is "Field Experiment": The system is tried in a pilot mode in the actual operational environment. The system is then rolled out in two final stages. A "Trial Rollout," in which the system is used operationally, but on a limited basis, is followed by the "Final Rollout."

Consider the following example. A bank's market research indicates a strong market for a home cash dispensing machine. Current laboratory research points to several possible designs. Three designs are chosen for further evaluation. Focus consumer groups and surveys are conducted to determine user reaction. The concepts are developed to the point that working prototypes can be tested and evaluated by potential users, who critique the products. At this point the bank has both a measure of the feasibility and cost of implementation of each of the candidate designs as well as a sample of consumer reaction to them. A modified design is selected, developed, and delivered to a few branch offices and homes for use on a trial basis. The results are favorable but indicate the need for further product refinement. The product is improved and then offered for sale in a limited geographic region only. The product's limited introduction is successful; there is strong consumer demand, and a full-scale rollout is planned and executed.

With this type of life cycle, managers can justify a system that is high in cost and high in novelty without incurring the full expense, but still enabling them to have an extensive and complete evaluation period. The more traditional up-front life cycle cost-benefit analysis is best employed to justify high-cost, low-novelty investments.

## MEASUREMENT OF TECHNOLOGY

One of the difficulties with new technology applications is measuring and evaluating their worth. We need new tools to help us plan and justify the cost of these new technologies.

### A Gross Macroeconomic Viewpoint

Gross macroeconomic measures of the worth of information technology to business do not paint a very rosy picture. Since 1973, total U.S. information technology investments have increased continuously, even in the face of a dramatic decrease in the unit cost of information technology. In 1988, expenditures on information technology in the United States were $160 billion, with a $530 billion invested base. Yet this growing investment has apparently failed to benefit business in the aggregate, because during the same period the United States has experienced a protracted period of low productivity, when measured on a macroeconomic scale. The United States is now investing over one-third of its total durables budget on information technology, and it is not seeing productivity gains. The findings seem grim for the future of information technology. Numerous studies, from many sources, support this viewpoint.

For example, a May 1988, 500-page study from the U.S. Office of Technology Assessment reports that, despite a doubling of expenditures for information technology over the last decade,"convincing evidence of productivity growth has yet to be measured" in businesses using information processing equipment (Belitsos 1988). U.S. Bureau of Statistics data show productivity in the information sector of the economy declining steadily since 1974. The study qualifies this finding by further stating: "It is difficult to determine whether this is a transitional effect associated with learning during a period of massive change, a measurement defect, or a real limitation of technology." The study also notes a leveling off of overall expenditure for computers (specifically 14.6 percent average annual growth for 1975–1985, declining to 8.4 percent over the 1985–1990 period, with only 6.6 percent estimated for 1990–1995). This would seem to indicate growing disillusion with information technology.

Loveman of MIT looked at 60 business units in the United States and Western Europe. He measured productivity as the increase in output from an incremental increase in information technology and concluded that the United States would have been better off spending on labor, real estate, or some other noninformation technology.

Martin Baily of the Brookings Institution measured white collar productivity and discovered no significant gain from information technology. He concluded that information technology appears to be a poor substitute for labor. On a more positive note, he does acknowledge, however, that the intangible nature of information technology makes it difficult to quantify its value. Moreover, he points out that the main effects of the price declines on information technology has been to accelerate the introduction of this equipment into the marketing and services area. Since these are relatively new areas, and it takes an organization time to make an effective transition to new technologies, productivity may increase.

Osterman of Boston University analyzed the impacts of computers on clerical and management employment from 1972 to 1978. Although this period was mainframe-dominated and does not necessarily compare with today's desktop revolution, he made the observation that although the introduction of the computer initially led to a great displacement of clerks and a smaller, but noticeable, displacement of managers, two years later the benefits seemed to be offset by increased employment of clerks and especially managers.

Roach of Morgan Stanley (Roach 1987), separates workers into two classes: information workers and production workers. When he measured the productivity of both classes of workers, he found that whereas the output per production worker was increasing, the output per information worker was flat to falling. He concludes that we have "over MIP'd" the information worker. In short, he finds no real relationship between the intensity of investment in information technologies and productivity.

Are these economists right? Perhaps the phenomena they observed are more an effect of demographic and population trends, or business cycles, or a result of increased foreign competition. Perhaps without the use of computers the situation would have looked that much bleaker. Certainly, it seems that many foreign competitors, such as the Japanese, have succeeded in using information technology and engineering to gain a disproportionate share of the international market. Furthermore, the question is not really whether business is currently using information technology inefficiently or ineffectively on the average, but whether a motivated and educated company can succeed in exploiting information technology to its advantage.

## Need for a Better Planning Process

Despite all these negative reports, investment in information technology keeps increasing. Most of us cannot clearly state why we need the new technology; we just know it is useful. So we end up purchasing on faith, without any overall guidance or clear direction or focus in mind. The best example of this approach was the pharmaceutical industry, which in the early 1980s equipped all its sales reps with portable PCs on the theory that they would use these tools to increase sales and profitability.

This same lack of planning and direction is true of many large projects. In a study sponsored by the International Center for Information Technology, Blake Ives and Michael Vitale surveyed 20 American firms. They found that designers and builders of apparently successful systems very seldom make any formal estimate of how much the system will cost, or the benefits it will produce. For example, the American Airlines reservations system, SABRE, began as an automation project with little formal justification. Only later did its true competitive worth emerge. It became a universal customer system, and, until a recent court decision, it always listed American Airlines flights first unless specifically otherwise requested.

This lack of direction and focus is not a good situation. Although 50 percent of information technology executives say that justification of the technology is not a primary concern, they do say they are concerned about how they can convey their contribution. We need some measures of benefit, and we need a corporate view of information technology to guide investment.

## Quantifying Benefit: An Accounting Dilemma

The measurement and management of technology is an important but difficult task. One of the difficulties in identifying and justifying strategic technology investments lies in the fact that much of American business accounting methodology is biased against making such investments. U.S. accounting methodologies tend to view information technology as a cost or capital expenditure, not as an investment. This viewpoint supports a short-term tactical view and places the focus on efficiency rather than effectiveness.

Some criticize these accounting systems as outdated and focused on external reporting requirements (e.g., the quarterly stockholders report), rather than measuring achievement across a forward-looking strategic plan. Current accounting methods are not designed to support the achievement of critical business objectives. Part of the problem is that conventional accounting systems do not really give managers the information they need about the true costs of their products, and therefore provide a skewed assessment. In particular, current accounting practices are attacked as not being suitable for assessment of the newer technologies because their methodologies are not relevant for product costing, for investment justification, or for true total product life cycle cost measurement. With current accounting methodologies, a manager must justify expenditure on information technology in terms of savings in staff and operational costs. But information technology is a poor substitute for labor; it is first and foremost an information and decision-making amplifier. Bob Kaplan of Harvard notes this situation in his report "Relevance Lost: The Rise and Fall of Management Accounting" (Kaplan and Bruns 1987).

Cost measurements are often inaccurate. What is worse, there are few post audits to learn from. Only 10 percent of companies post audit all major projects; 40 percent post audit some major projects. Performance measurements and investment justification need to be better integrated with cost management systems. But benefit measurement is elusive. It is hard to determine how much an improvement in service quality is worth, because it is hard to determine cause and effect. How much of an increase in sales should be attributed to the introduction of a new automated customer assistance system, when during that same time period more salespeople were added, sales training was improved, sales territories were realigned, and new products were introduced? Additionally, current accounting practices are unable to identify and support the costs of intangibles. For example, how do you measure the benefit of using technology to attract, retain, and develop good people? It is difficult to evaluate the importance and measure the benefits of nonfinancial measures. As a result, these practices promote performance measures that often conflict with strategic objectives.

The CAM-I, Computer-Aided Manufacturing International, was founded in an effort to address these problems for the field of manufacturing automation. Its charter is to evaluate the accounting practices of several large manufacturers. The conclusion is that accountants do not assign costs properly to products and processes, particularly products with high unit costs and low life cycle costs. The study concludes that cost and management accounting practices must be rethought.

We need to develop measures of productivity and leverage based on industry and company, and to better link information technology investments to strategic business priorities. We need to develop measures of performance for information technology functions that connect with company performance and convey a clear sense of contribution.

We also need to educate senior and line management on the costs and risks of the system development process. They need a better understanding of the factors and uncertainties associated with system development estimates. Senior management needs to understand the tradeoffs among systems costs, schedules, and functionality if they are to participate actively, as they should, in the selection and implementation of advanced computer system projects.

## Measurement Methods: A Review

It is instructive to review the various methods available for measuring benefit. Measurement techniques are vital if we are to develop a rational strategy toward information technology investments. Properly applied, measurement often produces nonintuitive, surprising results. For example, in a recent study of regional banks, it was discovered that the greatest determinant of market share in the Middle Atlantic region was not level of interest rates or the presence of ATM machines; rather, it was whether these ATMs had access to one of the large banking networks.

There are four methods for measuring benefit: 1. economic, 2. portfolio, 3. analytic, and 4. strategic.

The *economic* method attempts to measure benefit by computing the payback time of the initial investment and measuring the return on investment (ROI) by treating the flow of expenses, revenues, and savings as a form of discounted cash flow from which a net present value can be computed. These are the methods of the accountants and investment bankers, and are presented in more detail in Appendix 4. These methods do not measure intangible benefits.

The *portfolio* method is better suited for the assessment of technology investments with broader impacts and intangible benefits. It incorporates economic measures, mathematical programming models, such as linear programming, scoring models, and advanced statistical and growth models to quantify the value of a technology investment.

The *analytic* method attempts to assign a mathematical value and apply a risk analysis to evaluate the new technology as an investment. It treats a technological investment rather like introducing a new product and attempts to assign worth versus risk taken. This method is better for assessing an investment in technology than the pure economic method. In fact, it suggests capitalizing and then amortizing software for internal use. It is good where there is a high degree of risk. It includes subjective judgments and uncertainty. One such subjective method is to build a small project to serve as a test to see if the company gets the expected benefits, and then expand and extrapolate these results for the larger project.

The *strategic* method is probably the best one for assessing an investment in technology. It includes consideration of technical importance against the business objectives, and the competitive advantages that are likely to result. Questionnaires and surveys are often useful tools in this method. One can also apply a growth option model. Once the base investment is made, one can look at the incremental benefits that result from adding to the investment at a later time. For example, if we make an initial investment, it will not only return some immediate value, but will allow us to build on it at a later time. The growth option model asks the following question: As standards evolve, will we be able to build a platform today that we can add to at a later date? Alternatively, we could ask: If we chose to sell the technology at some later date, how much would it be worth on the open market?

TABLE 1.1. CONVENTIONAL SYSTEMS VERSUS ADVANCED SYSTEMS

| | **Conventional** | **Advanced** |
|---|---|---|
| *Purpose:* | Replacement | Change |
| *Objective:* | Efficiency | Effectiveness |
| *Benefits:* | Tangible | Intangible |
| *Scope Effects:* | Local | Companywide |
| *Organizational Impact:* | Minimal | Extensive |
| *Risk:* | Slight | Substantial |

## CHARACTERISTICS OF ADVANCED INFORMATION SYSTEMS

We conclude that the characteristics of the evolving computer systems applications are quite different from those of their more traditional predecessors. They create new opportunities, but they also present many difficulties in cost justification, development, and successful introduction to the organization. These new information systems can best be summarized by contrasting them with more conventional systems along the six dimensions shown in Table 1.1.

## CONCLUSION

The use of the computer in business has turned from applications that are clerical, transactional, and efficiency-motivated to applications that are motivated toward achieving operational effectiveness as a strategic investment, or for competitive advantage. These new systems applications often use information from, and interact with, the earlier systems. In this sense the new systems would not have been possible without the earlier systems. American business has increasingly designed these newer systems based on the existence and earlier success of the older systems. The dramatic advances in computer technology (improved performance at reduced cost, and new software techniques aimed at representing and manipulating qualitative as well as quantitative data) have helped to make these new applications practical and affordable. In fact, much of the challenge in implementing these new systems lies in the skill with which we can integrate existing systems with newer applications built on one or more advanced programming tools or packages. (Many of these advanced tools are reviewed in Chapter 3).

# 2

# Business-Specific Applications

This chapter attempts to link the previous discussion about business and technology trends through the study of some applications that exemplify these trends in the areas of programmed trading, risk management, and sales and marketing. These examples are representative but not all-inclusive; we could have chosen many other applications in many other business areas.

Each example involves a discussion of the application's evolution; its successes and limitations; the technology employed; the role and use of various methodologies, packages, and commodity products in its development; issues of integration and interfacing with existing databases and applications; the impact its use has had on the targeted business process; and any noteworthy trends and directions in its use.

## TRADING SYSTEMS

This section is concerned with the application of advanced systems to the trading of stocks and bonds: fully automated programmed trading, decision support, back-office operations processing, electronic surveillance, and policing for fraudulent and unlawful trading activity.

### Programmed Trading

Programmed trading has received much publicity since the disastrous October 19, 1987 stock market crash. This application is really not one, but a class of applications. They have been hailed as one of the hottest new money-makers, responsible for improving market liquidity and providing greater investor protection of funds against unpredicted market swings in price. They have also been depicted as the cause of increased market volatility (larger, more frequent, and random stock and bond price fluctuations), as being ineffective in protecting the investor's money in times of dramatic market downturns, and as responsible for the October 19, 1987 crash. In fact, this application has been simultaneously hailed as an indispensable money-maker, and blamed for causing young, headstrong traders to become too reliant upon computer-derived trading signals and recommendations, without tempering these recommendations with experience, common sense, and human judgment. No matter who is right, one thing is sure: These applications, by their very notoriety, have proved to be very successful, in the sense that they are actively used and have profoundly altered the way securities are traded. The applications are a dramatic example of how intertwined and indispensable information technology can become to the heart of business.

Two of the more common programmed trading applications are portfolio insurance and index arbitrage. Both applications take advantage of the linking of markets and the use of information technology to spot important price relationships and permit an instantaneous execution of buys and sells in response.

## Portfolio Insurance

Consider the case of *portfolio insurance*. In theory, futures prices should relate directly to the prices of the underlying securities; for example, the S&P 500 futures contracts traded in the Chicago Mercantile Exchange and the actual stocks traded in New York Stock Exchange. This relationship between futures prices and stock prices allows trading in the futures instead of the actual stocks. Thus, an investor who decides his stock holdings are too risky (likely to drop in price) can *hedge* his position (protect his investment against loss of market value), by selling a number of futures contracts in the proper proportion to the amount of stock in his portfolio. If the stock drops in price, so should the futures contract that the investor sold. The investor can then make a profit by canceling out the futures contracts sales by buying them back at the lower current market price. If the investor's holdings in the actual stock have dropped an equivalent amount in price, he will break even, losing as much in the value of his actual stock holding as he gained in the futures market. The proper proportion to use for this hedge is called the *hedge ratio*, and it represents the ratio between the dollar loss a holder of a futures contract will experience and each dollar lost in the actual stocks. (See Appendix 4 for a more detailed discussion of hedging and investment management.)

Of course, if one's stock holdings increase in value, then so will the futures contract. When the investor covers a short sale in the futures market, he will lose an amount of money roughly equivalent to what he gained in his stock portfolio. So the investor gives up potential gain for protection against loss. Timing here is all-important. The selling and buying back of the futures contract must be timed to avoid getting caught in a large drop in market price, without giving up all opportunity of benefiting from a major market rally. Portfolio insurance is the term applied to a complicated set of methodologies involving the use of this form of hedge.

## Index Arbitrage

Because futures and stocks are traded separately, their prices do not always exactly match. These fleeting variances present an opportunity to the *index arbitrageur,* a trader who seeks to lock in instant profits by simultaneously buying in one market and selling in another. The arbitrageur knows that at the futures contract expiration, the future's price is pegged exactly to the S&P index, which is the actual average of all the prices of the 500 stocks that make up the index. Therefore, if the price of the futures contract ever exceeds the actual stock price by an amount greater than the cost of borrowing sufficient money to buy the stocks and to cover the transaction costs, the trader can lock in an instant profit by simultaneously buying the actual stocks and selling the futures. Conversely, if the futures price drops sufficiently below the actual stock prices, the trader can lock in a profit by borrowing money, buying the futures, and selling the stocks short. If the trader can jump on the spread the instant it materializes and borrow funds at the lowest interest rates, he or she can win no matter which way the markets move. This relatively riskless trade is called an *arbitrage.*The arbitrageur's profits depend on the ability to execute trades in hundreds of stocks—a program trade—before prices change and erase the opportunity.

The net effect of this activity on the markets is to bring the prices of both futures and stocks back into line. Thus arbitrageurs provide a necessary link between the two markets. Of course, the combined action of the portfolio insurer and the index arbitrager can result in amplifying market moves. For example, suppose a drop in a stock's price triggers a large number of portfolio insurers to short (sell) the futures contract. This action will precipitate a large drop in the futures price. If the futures price falls sufficiently below the stock price, the index arbitrager will be triggered into action, selling stocks and buying futures. This will cause stocks to drop in price. A sufficiently large drop in the stock price could trigger another round of the portfolio insurers selling the futures again.

## Dependence on Other Systems

The software designed to compute when and how many futures to sell is not very complicated: It is a relatively simple formula, and not very computer-intensive. The difficult aspect is integration. The programmed trading systems are really part of a much larger system, or rather a collection of people and systems held together by fragile links. The programmed trading systems need to be fed accurate, timely prices in order to make informed decisions. This depends on the price quotation systems feeding it. Next, the programmed trading systems depend on a fast, reliable trade execution system, a system that can receive and act on its orders fast enough to ensure trade execution at or near the quoted price. Finally it needs its trades cleared and processed on time and without error. In 1987, these links and systems began to break down under the strain of the October 19 crash. One of the most significant single breakdowns in the market on October 19 was the "delinking" of the New York Stock Exchange and the Chicago Mercantile Exchange. This occurred because trading on the New York Stock Exchange became so chaotic that arbitrageurs did not dare venture in, even though a substantial spread existed between futures and stock prices.

## Quotation Systems

The exchanges quotation systems processing capacity could not keep up with the volume on October 19 and 20. Trading was taking place at such a pace that there was a great backlog of sells. Prices were plummeting down so rapidly that traders could not be sure they were seeing the real prices. The quote tapes became more than 15 minutes late, and the programmed trading systems could no longer be sure what the real prices were. There were other processing problems as well. ADP's quotation service stopped for about half an hour because the system had been programmed to reject such enormous price swings as impossible. Without an accurate indication of price, arbitrageurs could not be sure their trades would be profitable even if they could be executed. Even if the prices were correct at the time they were received, the traders could not be certain that, with the large backlog of trades, their trades could be executed on time and at the desired prices.

The unusually large spread between the futures and the cash markets had opened in the first place largely because the practitioners of portfolio insurance, seeking to reduce the risk of holding securities in a large downtrending market, had tried first to sell in the futures market. Ordinarily the arbitrageurs, performing their linking function, would then have transferred the large sell off of futures to the stock market by taking advantage of the temporary exceptionally low futures prices relative to the current stock prices. But the arbitrageurs were out of the game for the reasons just noted and the markets were delinked, so the portfolio insurance investors could not find any futures buyers and were forced to go straight to the stock market to unload their securities in a massive program selling in an effort to limit their losses.

## Trade Execution Systems

The trade execution systems also failed under the strain. The New York Stock Exchange's designated turnaround (DOT) processing system had to process 471,513 trade orders on the October 19 and 584,992 on October 20, compared with the previous month's daily average of 138,600 orders (Eichenwald 1988). The amounts exceeded all the system design parameters and many processing bottlenecks resulted.

A bottleneck at the printers caused delays of 45 to 75 minutes in both market and limit orders. To overcome these delays in the future, the NYSE is now switching to electronic displays. The system for routing limit orders came to a halt on three separate occasions because its storage capacity had been exceeded. This caused delays in orders of over 20 minutes. The capacity for this system has now been increased by 40 percent.

The Intermarket Trading System (ITS) also experienced overloads. ITS broadcasts bids from regional trading specialists post to the exchange's specialist's posts, and from the exchanges to the regions, electronically. ITS orders from the regions to the New York Stock Exchange specialist are good for only 2 minutes, and the orders from New York to the regions are good for only 1 minute. On October 19 and 20, the ITS system capacity became so overloaded that it took too long for the orders to reach the specialist's post. Many orders expired before they reached the post.

When these systems backlogged, traders tried to execute trades on the NASDAQ (National Association of Securities Dealers) automated OTC (over the counter) system. They hoped to take advantage of market makers who did not update their quotes quickly enough by running through trades at split-second bargain prices. The NASDAQ system got so heavily loaded that it had to shut down. It could not keep up with the volume. Since then the system has been upgraded from its old capacity of 87 trades/second to 200 trades/second.

## Back Office Processing and Clearinghouse Systems

The back office processing systems also failed under the unprecedented October 19 and 20 volumes (Eichenwald 1988). These are the systems that keep the records and manage the exchange of funds, stocks, and bonds. The systems failed to keep up with the trades, and the specialists' reports were over a day late. Without up-to-date reports on holdings and inventory, specialists could not determine what their financial condition was and what orders they would be able to execute.

These problems carried over into the clearinghouses, which were plagued by a variety of ills due to a lack of integration and coordinated action. Clearing and settlement mechanisms for the transfer of money among brokerage firms, customers, stock and commodities exchanges, and banks usually work smoothly, but during the crash, they proved to be frighteningly fragile and came close to gridlock on October 20.

To understand what happened, we must first review the role of the clearinghouses. After the sale of a stock is executed, a central clearinghouse matches the sale with another investor's purchase. Then the clearinghouse transfers money to the seller and the stock certificate to the buyer. The problem is that the clearing systems of the various stock exchanges have each been set up to meet the needs of the products sold on that particular exchange, with little thought to the impact on the clearing processes of the other exchanges, because in the past these exchanges catered to different people with very different needs. Traders in commodity futures were a separate breed, mostly Midwest farmers who traded relatively independently of the New York Stock Exchange; most investors simply traded stocks. Over the last ten years, with the development of futures on stock indexes and other complicated instruments, many investors began to deal in stocks and commodities futures simultaneously. That is what the programmed trading systems are all about; they treat futures and stocks as one linked, common marketplace. Such linked transactions now account for billions of dollars a day.

When prices fell, people had to meet their margin payments, and clearinghouses called in billions of dollars to cover the growing exposure, even if the investors had offsetting hedging positions in other markets that had increased in value. So, on October 19, the S&P 500 traded sharply down and the clearinghouse telephoned brokerage firms to obtain $200 million in added margin. Next morning, there were margin calls for over $2 billion more. At the same time there were margin calls for over $300 million at the Chicago Board of Trade. Investors who gained in one market while losing in the other were still required to pay the full amount of margin. The clearing process drained billions of dollars out of the market. Much of this was unnecessary because of the offsetting gains the investors experienced in other markets.

These excess margin calls might have been used for purchases that could have slowed the collapse. Instead, investors had to use their cash reserves, borrow, or sell out their positions to meet their margin calls. Additionally, New York banks were slow to commit money for loans. Firms like Goldman and Kidder found themselves $1.5 billion short at about noon that day. This created a further wave of selling, which further depressed prices. The clearinghouses began to fail to keep up with processing demands. First Options at Chicago, one of the clearinghouses that works through the Options Clearing Corporation, was unable to keep up with the demands of matching customer claims and obligations. As a result, officials from many of the exchanges are developing plans for better communications during crises.

## Resistance to Change

Fixes have been recommended to overcome these problems, but to a certain extent they appear to be attempts to preserve the specialist system and the status quo rather than to restructure the system. In an effort to slow things down in times of crisis, a series of coordinated "circuit breakers" has been proposed. Whenever the Dow Jones moves 250 points during a session, the exchanges will be closed for an hour. A fall of another 150 points on reopening would trigger a two-hour halt. Equivalent circuit breakers have been set on the futures exchange side. Furthermore, when the Dow Jones Industrial average moves 25 points from the previous day's close, DOT will give priority to routing of simple market orders (orders submitted for execution whatever the current price) submitted by individuals over institutions, for market orders of 2000 shares or less.

These fixes have been aimed at solving the perceived problems of increased market volatility and dominance of institutional trading while preserving the current organizational status quo through slowing down large institutional automated trading and favoring the individual investor. Although the exchanges have made large investments in automating the initiation of trades, nothing has been done to automate the execution of trades, which remains largely manual, paced by the specialists and the floor brokers. They have not addressed the fact that in the cases of the New York Stock Exchange, the Chicago Mercantile Exchange, and the Chicago Board of Trade, the specialists were required to execute the orders and they could not keep up with the flow and execute the orders in time. Moreover, the market makers on the OTC were often unable to update their quoted prices fast enough to follow the market and not get taken advantage of by the more electronically nimble traders.

## Aftermath

In January and February 1989, both the Chicago Mercantile Exchange's and the Chicago Board of Trade's trading practices came under government investigation (Siler, 1989; Berg, 1989). The FBI had been conducting an undercover investigation on the exchange floors into possible trading fraud for nearly two years. In particular, the government was suspicious of the *broker groups* (associations of brokers who share commissions and expenses) and their practice of *dual trading* (handling customer's trades and trading for one's own account at the same time). The government believes that these practices can and have led to abuses when traders make trades at prices that are not current. Both exchanges were concerned about the investigation and have introduced proposals to add more control, including stiffer fines, banning broker groups, putting new members through stricter background checks, upgrading computer systems designed to track prices during the trading day to check on how many trades that have already taken place were put together, and to assist in detecting suspicious trading activities. Artificial intelligence has been employed to develop computer programs that can monitor executed trades and detect suspicious and illegal activity. Hand-held terminals are being built so that the specialists can electronically record trades faster and minimize the opportunities for illegal price and trade manipulation.

The Chicago Mercantile Exchange had previously entered into an arrangement for Reuters to provide an automated system for trading on the exchange after normal hours. The system, Globex, would provide quotes and automatically take orders and match buys and sells. Interestingly, the Mercantile is now viewing this system with an added plus: It might help ensure that no human fraud can enter into the trading process. As a result of the investigation, the Chicago Mercantile is now looking more favorably on eventually expanding its use of this system. The Chicago Board of Trade has reconsidered its earlier position not to participate in automated exchange trading system. It first proposed a system of its own called AURORA (Shellenberger 1989; Gutierres 1989) but now has joined the Mercantile in using Globex.

Another motivation for the exchanges' interest in this increased level of integration is the threat of competition from overseas exchanges, which are beginning to invest heavily in such automation. Examples include Switzerland's Swiss Options and Financial Futures Exchange (called Soffex), which was introduced in 1988 and is one of the first fully automated exchanges. Germany is planning to open a similar exchange using the Swiss technology. There is also the semi-automated Tokyo International Financial Futures Exchange (Gutierres 1989; Lane 1989). Recently the New York Stock Exchange and the American Stock Exchange have announced automation plans to support all-night trading in response to this competitive threat. Some of the greatest advantages to these automated exchanges are their removal of the restrictions of time and space, and their automated recordkeeping capability, which increases the ability to monitor and prevent fraud and bias.

There is still much debate for and against automated exchanges and programmed trading. Many questions remain regarding the competitiveness of these automated systems with respect to relative cost, efficiency (the bid/ask spread they can maintain and the volume of trades they can keep up with relative to the current open-outcry system), liquidity (some believe that the public nature of the automated systems inhibits traders from executing very large orders through the system and broadcasting their holdings), and the closing off of a useful source of market information (opponents complain that the automated systems will deny them valuable information regarding the full flow of orders that they currently pickup by simply observing activity on the floor of the exchange).

## People and Organizational Impact

The corrective actions that have been taken are based on a belief that many of the problems encountered on October 19 and 20 were due to the large institutional programmed trading activity. The following statistics have been quoted to support this belief: 20 percent of the volume of trading of the S&P futures on October 19 was due to programmed trading, and at three different 10-minute periods, programmed trading accounted for more than 60 percent of the volume. Countering this belief is the fact that the development of the futures market and the use of computers to execute programmed trades and derivative securities was strictly a local phenomenon, whereas the price collapse was a worldwide phenomenon. Richard Roll, professor of finance at UCLA, compared the declines in 23 stock markets around the world (Meltzer 1988). He found important differences in trading procedures, rules, and market organization in the various national stock markets. Roll's findings show that the decline did not start in the New York market. France, Germany, Hong Kong, and Singapore all experienced stock market declines before trading began in the United States, and most of them did not have programmed trading. The real problems appear to stem from increased volatility resulting from increased globalization of the financial markets and advances in the technology supporting the more timely and efficient exchange of information for decision-making.

In the past, each time technology has been employed to deal with the structure of the marketplace, the structure itself has had to change. Consider the history of the New York Stock Exchange. Automation on the Big Board dates back to 1892, when the NYSE celebrated its 100th anniversary with the introduction of the electronic board to page members and to decrease shouting. In 1964 the NYSE introduced a 900 character/minute ticker. But volume soared ahead of the capacity of the ticker to over 10 million shares/day, and trading errors increased dramatically. Then, in 1984, John Phelan, Jr., CEO of the NYSE, spent millions to computerize the Exchange. He installed interactive systems so that specialists could follow the market in real time. This infusion of technology, with its resultant increased flow of information, motivated the brokerage houses to use computers to execute complex trading strategies with new instruments. There is no turning back: "Wall Street's use of computers has moved through three stages," said Mark Smith, vice-president of Stratus Computer. "It went from being an operational tool, to being a competitive weapon, until today it is survival gear."

Some experts are complaining that the accelerating reliance on technology to solve perceived problems, without knowing the impact of these changes on the rest of the trading system, may result in replacing old dangers with new ones. John Bachman, managing principal of Edward D. Jones and Co. and chairman of the Securities Industry Association, said: "We have made so many changes in the last year that we simply don't know yet what they add up to. We don't know where the technology is taking us. " (Meltzer 1988). For example, in response to last October's gridlocked orders, the NYSE super DOT capacity and ticker reports were upgraded from 250 million orders/day to 600 million orders/day in 1988, and can now handle 1 billion orders/day. But this increase in computer capacity could simply put more pressure on the center of the trading sytem. Some scientists say that a system with as many players as a trading system is subject to moments of chaotic behavior that are highly volatile and unpredictable. In a recent study, computer scientists found that when players in a computer model similar to a stock exchange were given more information about the behavior of the other participants, the result was wildly volatile behavior rather than stability.

## TRADER'S WORKSTATION/DECISION SUPPORT

A system that is hard to define and complex to build is a *trader's workstation*. It is instructive to study this application area because of its mixed success. Understanding the factors that have contributed to an application's initial acceptance, success, and failure should help to improve the future success rate.

Typically the trader is charged with daily trading in some subset of the stock or bond markets. The workstation is intended to bring together news, prices, transaction information (trades), and highly complex mathematical analytic tools to valuate the trader's holdings, to quantify exposure to losses due to fluctuations in market price, and to aid the trader in making a profitable transactions. All of this must be displayed in a useful manner, which generally involves tables and graphics. These tables and graphics display both historic price relationships and current changes as they occur. Key prices and price relationships are continuously monitored, and alerts are set off when preset thresholds are crossed. Concern over the trading firm's exposure to sudden large price declines has been heightened as a result of the October 1987 crash.

Many firms are enhancing their existing systems and building new ones to address these needs. This requires interfacing many different systems to bring the information to the traders in one place with a single data access method. Currently traders have to go to three or four or more different places to get the data they need. They get trade and inventory data from in-house systems. They get stock fundamentals, time and sales, from market data vendors like Quotron. They get fixed income and foreign exchange prices from other specialized market vendors like Telerate and Reuters. They often get price, volume, and technical graphs from specialized market vendors like Bridge Data. They get correlations, statistics, and analyses from their in-house research systems and from specialized market vendors like Bloomberg. They often obtain news from still another vendor.

Many Wall Street firms are turning to workstation technology and networking in an attempt to get all these data in front of all the traders in a consolidated fashion, with single common access. Recently there has been a trend to bring all the pertinent data together at a workstation (e.g., a SUN, or high-end PC such as a COMPAQ 386) where they can be commonly accessed and viewed via windows, which can be overlapped, and cut and pasted. Once available in the workstation, the data updates can be extracted and processed locally; e.g., updating spreadsheets, local databases, and local analyses. The technology involves building software that will operate across many heterogeneous systems. A large number of the systems are outside the configuration control of the Wall Street firm. This requires selecting, testing, and then interfacing many off-the-shelf packages (e.g., local area networks, communications bridges, terminal emulators, file transfer systems, database management systems, analytic routines) with one another and a certain amount of custom application work.

A natural extension of this capability is to build an expert system to relieve the user of performing manual repetitive, but "intelligent" tasks required to manage the increasing quantity of real-time data available. The trader's assistant application is aimed at providing assistance to the professional bond and equities trader to monitor the myriad of real-time information that can affect buy, sell, and hold decisions. This involves an analysis of what information to show, and how to process it to reduce the potential flood of data and best present the results.

This is a particularly hard domain for an expert system. In a classic expert system the user initiates the session, but the system then proceeds to dominate the interaction, prompting the user for additional information as required. The system leads the user. Most traders do not have the time or desire to be led by a system; they want to be in control. Moreover, the domain is rich in data, with a continuous stream of information, so the system must be designed to operate on the incoming data as they arrive to adjust to real-time changes in the data, and to provide recommendations with the data on hand. Users are afforded the opportunity to volunteer information if they desire, but they are not required to do so. Finally, the knowledge associated with trading is very dynamic, situation-dependent, and uncertain (for the interested reader, a fuller treatment of decision-making under uncertainty is provided in Appendix 5). There are a large number of cases where even expert traders have judged the situation incorrectly and made losing trades.

## Trader Workstation Examples

Various systems have sprung up to address this area. Although initially highly touted and written about, many of these systems now appear to have fallen into disuse; have failed to spread to any appreciable extent; and failed to stimulate further development. Four of these systems are reviewed to gain a better appreciation of why this situation has occurred. They include an interest-rate swap expert system built by Shearson Lehman; a hedging advisor built by PaineWebber (this system will be discussed later in the section on risk management); an intelligent market filter, called Market Minder, built by Interactive Analytics; and an expert system called TARA (Technical Analysis and Reasoning Assistant), built by Manufacturers Hanover Trust for its FX traders.

### *Shearson's Interest Rate Swap Application*

Shearson's interest rate swap expert system was the earliest attempt of the four to apply expert system technology to the trading community. It was built in 1984 on a Symbolics LISP machine. It attempted to match buyers and sellers of interest-rate swaps. An interest-rate swap takes place when a holder of a variable-rate debt and a holder of a fixed-rate debt swap their debt payments for a fee. At numerous conferences, the system was proclaimed a great success. Shortly after these presentations, the leading advocate and chief user/developer at Shearson left to become a vice-president of sales and marketing at Symbolics. Today, to the best of our knowledge, this system is no longer used at Shearson. The reasons given vary from internal politics, to loss of the leading advocate, to the high cost of maintenance and information integration, to a fundamental change in the way the swap business is conducted (these days swaps are warehoused and both sides to the swap are sold independently, so users no longer have to be identified and matched at the same time).

### *Interactive Analytic's Market Minder*

In 1988, Interactive Analytics came out with a generic trading system software called Market Minder. The software was aimed at providing a real-time, rule-based monitoring system. Current implementations of the tool are based upon specifying complex logical combinations of real-time condition-actions based upon mathematical measures of the intra-day and inter-day price behavior of different stocks (e.g., technical analysis). Although this offering has been on the marketplace for over a year, to our knowledge it has experienced minimal demand.

### *Manufacturers Hanover's TARA*

In first quarter 1989, Manufacturers Hanover Trust announced a foreign exchange (FX) expert trading system, delivered on a Symbolics LISP machine and implemented in LISP and the expert system shell KEE. The system is called TARA, for Technical Analysis Reasoning Agent. Its current version mainly contains knowledge of technical analysis functions and the conditions under which their results/recommendations are meaningful and should be considered. It was designed with close guidance from the head FX trader. It is currently considered to be a great success, and additional workstations are reported to have been ordered for this and other related applications.

## Lessons Learned

What can we learn from these examples? Some of the reasons why many of these systems have failed to gain acceptance is that they have been too simple. They have examined the data from only a single viewpoint (e.g., technical analysis only), and been unable to incorporate such fundamental analysis data as supply and demand or interest rate forecasting, and such qualitative aspects as the impact of news and special events. Traders were often not involved early enough in the project. Sometimes the project depended upon a single trader, whereas there are great differences in opinion, style, and consistency among traders. Often there was a poor integration of the system with the trader's actual day-to-day workflow, making its use awkward and forced. Finally, the system was often not flexible enough; it was unable to adapt to changes in tasks and relationships in a rapidly changing, highly dynamic trading environment.

## RISK MANAGEMENT

Another class of applications is centered around helping the business to assess the risk/reward associated with taking various business actions and recommending when to exercise caution, or take any risk reduction actions. Two examples are discussed. One is closely related to the trading function. It involves assessing the market risk associated with the trading activity. The other application is concerned with assessing the credit risk associated with a counterparty's ability to meet debt obligations.

### PaineWebber's Hedging Advisor

PaineWebber's system, called The Intelligent Hedge Evaluation Assistant, was built in 1988 to advise the equity block trading desk on hedging alternatives. It is part of a larger trading support system that includes trade capture (capture of the trade information as the trader makes the trades), real-time pricing, and analytics. This project was apparently initiated in response to the October 1987 stock crash. There was a lot of concern at that time regarding market volatility and the trader's exposure to market loss. The application was directed toward measuring the potential trading loss should prices drop, and recommending the best *hedges* (offsetting trades that could protect the trader against the potential loss). The system examines a variety of possible hedges using correlated securities, index futures, and options, and comes up with a recommendation. It was implemented on SUN workstations, using the SYBASE database management system, and an expert system shell, CLIPS, to express the hedging "rules." The rules devise ways to decide which analytics to use in structuring and comparing various hedging alternatives. A conventional computer program knows how to evaluate the formulas, but the expert system knows which formulas to use, when, and how to adjust the formulas. Often, the hedging decision is a sequential analysis, but not always.

The programs must be flexible and adaptive. The expert system draws upon a database of security correlations, options valuations, and liquidity data; a library of analytics; and a real-time price feed. It responds to the trader's requests and runs the analytics using the real-time prices and databases information. Typically four ranked alternative strategies are presented to the trader in under 4 seconds. The hedging assistant allows the trader to be his or her own research analyst. It provides advice on how best to execute the trade based on historical experience which comes out of the expert system and databases. But the trader makes the final decision and deals with the execution of the trades for the hedge.

By 1989, this project had been abandoned. Many reasons were given. They included reorganization, the high cost of implementation and maintenance, the return to reduced volatility in the stock market, the lack of acceptance by the traders and the sheer complexity of the task. Managing risk in a large trading house is a very complex and personal activity. Hedging invariably takes away potential profit and is to be avoided unless absolutely necessary. Moreover, even with hedging, one cannot eliminate all market risk; there are no sure hedges.

In the past, PaineWebber and other firms (e.g., Morgan Stanley, Shearson Lehman Hutton) approached hedging on a trader-by-trader basis, with each trader responsible for hedging his or her own portfolio of trades. The results were mixed because some traders do it well and some do not. Also, because many stocks and bonds are correlated (they are likely to experience similar or contra price changes in response to events), each trader's hedging actions could be appropriate for the trader individually, but counter productive to the firm's overall portfolio exposure. Other firms manage risk on a more centralized basis. For example, Bear Stearns reportedly has a few people whose responsibility is to know the aggregate capital at risk to the block desk, and to make hedging proposals on an intra-day basis. Shearson Lehman reportedly has a group talking about implementing risk management firmwide. Not all these efforts use expert system technology, but they all face the same integration problem of bringing a lot of data together from many diverse systems and sources, and combining or processing them to provide some sort of meaningful, consolidated presentation.

## Credit Risk Management

Another related risk management system is the granting of credit. This could be, among others, a financial institution granting a corporation a loan or line-of-credit (LOC), or granting an individual a personal loan, a mortgage, or a line of credit on a credit card. There are many successful applications of these sorts of systems. For example, Arthur Anderson's Mortgage Loan Analyzer (MLA) asks for pertinent information and provides advice and recommendations on individual mortgages. It is a generic package that is customized to the individual companies needs. Syntelligence's Loan Advisor provides advice and recommendations on approving bank loans. It can be customized to meet the individual company's needs. American Express's Authorizer's Assistant reviews a customer's credit history stored on in-house databases and provides advice and recommendations, with explanations, on approving credit card transactions. In this way American Express can give its customers personalized credit approval promptly and efficiently.

These systems have many common features. They typically identify a number of factors that are important to consider when evaluating the financial health of the subject in question, be the subject an individual or a corporation. Figure 2.1 illustrates some of the important factors to consider when evaluating a company. There are three main factors to look into for a company: financial characteristics,

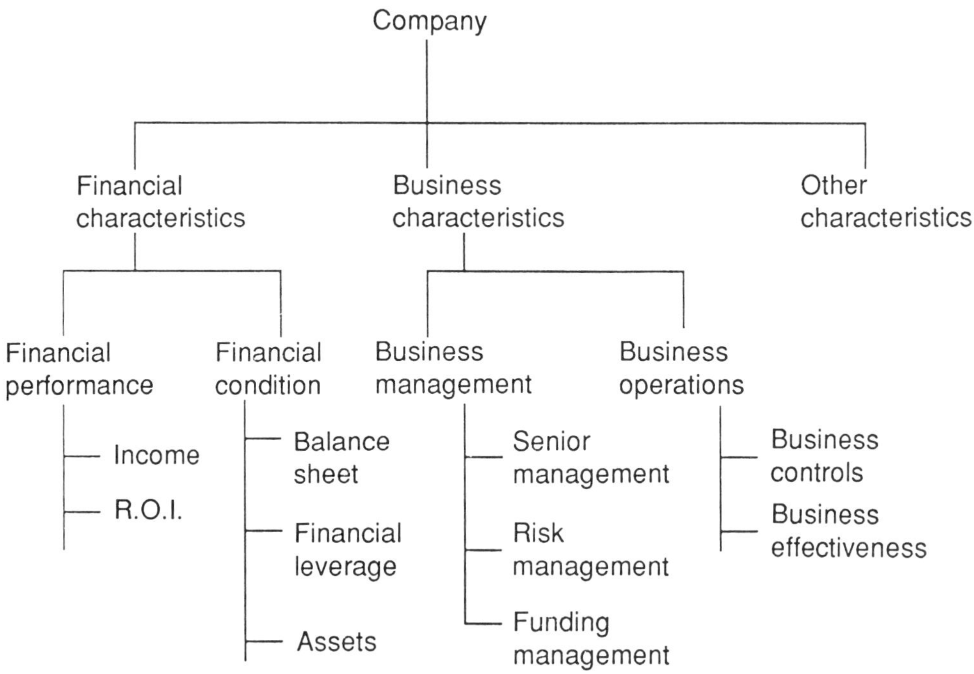


**Figure 2.1.** Evaluation of a Company.

business characteristics, and other factors. The factors in turn are assessed by evaluating a collection of subfactors that pertain to each of these main factors. Each subfactor can be further decomposed into its subfactors, and so on.

This hierarchical decision-tree approach to risk assessment is quite common among the various applications, and generally goes down to at least three to four levels. By replacing a top-level assessment with a larger number of smaller, more specific evaluations, we can obtain a much more consistent, precise, and objective evaluation from analyst to analyst. In many instances, the lowest subfactor often reduces to a calculation, such as one of the key financial ratios (e.g., the quick ratio test) discussed in Appendix 1.

Some areas, like assessment of management's capability, must of necessity be more subjective, based upon past experience and observation of current management actions. Usually the "other" category takes in an assessment of external related events or observations, such as that the firm is currently the target of a takeover, or its product line has not kept up with the competition, that are often subjective and harder to quantify. The analyst or system must then combine each of the relevant subfactors to arrive at an overall assessment. Statistical techniques such as linear regression and credit scoring are quite effective here. Often a single number is not required; a range is acceptable. Usually we leave the final decision to a human who combines other important, more subjective assessments with these quantitative methods. (Appendix 5 reviews statistical and other quantitative and qualitative methods for decision-making under uncertainty.)

Many of the more routine aspects of the analysis can be handled entirely by the computer application, speeding up the risk assessment process and leaving the human expert with more time to concentrate on the finer and more complex aspects of the decision. In a number of cases, expert system technology has been applied successfully to the process of combining the calculations and statistical analyses with the more qualitative assessments; examples include Syntelligence's Loan Advisor, mentioned earlier (Duda 1987).

Obtaining the necessary information often requires collecting information from a variety of sources and media. Some of the data are keyed in by the analyst, but many items are obtained from a collection of electronic databases and textual reports. The electronic databases and reports come from external sources and in-house systems, so a large part of this job is to build the links that can access and interpret the various databases, with their different syntax and data structures and naming conventions, as well as read and interpret hard copy documents. All this information must then be combined and processed into a suitable form for subsequent analysis. Artificial intelligence techniques, notably expert systems and natural language processing (see Chapter 3 for a more detailed discussion of artificial intelligence) are often used successfully in this stage (Wang 1988).

The American Express Credit Card Authorizer is a good example of this sort of integration. To appreciate the complexity of this integration task, note that it only took 8 to 9 months for American Express to develop and refine a prototype, but it took another 18 to 24 months to actually build the linkages and infrastructures to support a production version of this system. As the technology for interconnecting distributed heterogeneous databases and processing systems advances, these applications should get a lot easier and quicker to implement.

Another related field is the underwriting of life, and of property and casualty (P&C) insurance. The life insurance underwriter is concerned with forecasting life expectancy based on an individual's physical examination and health history. The P&C underwriter is concerned with predicting the likelihood of an accident or damage to a property based on the property's measurable characteristics (e.g., location, construction, use, type, owner). As with the credit decision process, a hierarchy of factors and subfactors must be considered. They are, however, quite different from the financial credit-worthiness analysis discussed previously. There have also been a large number of systems fielded in the companion application of insurance underwriting (e.g., Syntelligence's Underwriting Advisor).

Still another sort of risk concern is associated with a company's internal audits. Companies conduct their own independent audits to ensure that they are not conducting any practices or operations in a way that would put the company at risk either legally or economically. It is the auditor's job to review the company's practices and to identify any suspect practices requiring attention. Since not every item can be exhaustively examined, the auditor must intelligently select which items to review. The auditor often has a hierarchy of checkpoints and tests to aid in this selection and examination. Again, systems have been developed to assist in this process. Equitable Insurance's TIARA assists in selecting business units to audit.

## SALES AND MARKETING

The area of sales and marketing represents a class of applications of information technology with a high payoff potential that is likely to see an explosion of applications over the next decade. Sales management is eager and receptive to automation and technology to solve its problems. These managers are looking for new tools, having already tried other approaches such as national marketing, regional marketing, centralized/decentralized distribution, incentive schemes, buybacks, and rebates.

To be effective in marketing and sales, a business must identify the users of its product or services, how to reach them, and what they need. Certainly there is no shortage of data on these topics. In fact, with the increased automation, the amount of marketing data available is increasing at a breathtaking rate (this includes both sales transaction data and data on general buying and saving trends and demographics), and exceeding the capacity to assimilate it. Consider, for example, the impact of the introduction of checkout scanners in most of the nation's supermarkets. They make possible data on customer sales and preferences to an unprecedented level of detail (Schiller 1989).

Buried in this sea of data lies an unprecedented opportunity (for those who can properly digest and interpret these data) to gain a better understanding of why and under what circumstances people buy particular products, to identify underserved market segments, and to refine and sharpen marketing tactics. This is the challenge. A whole new computer application area called "data mining" has sprung up to meet this challenge (Chapter 3 and Appendix 10). Computers make it possible to collect more detail about the purchases and usage of all manner of products and services. They allow us to combine, relate, summarize, and compile vital daily reports based on the results. Properly used, these reports can allow a business to target small markets such as relatively small ethnic or regional or lifestyle market segments more effectively and economically. But there are cautions and associated risks.

If these reams of daily statistics are not properly used, they can swamp the user with information overload, or worse, be misinterpreted and misused. They can create excessive focus on short-term performance. Information is necessary but not sufficient for good decision-making. The geometrically increasing volume of information that managers have to cope with can also increase the chance that crucial facts and insights will be lost. It also could create potential instabilities. If all companies get the same data at the same instant, it could lead to waves of price cutting and product duplication. To overcome these problems, marketing information systems of the future must be able to determine who needs what information and how to allocate decision-making most effectively. Properly directed, technology can allow marketing and sales simultaneously to take advantage of the resultant economies of scale and still act locally, adapting and catering to local and regional needs. Information technology helps to make this possible by helping to collect, and analyze local marketing information, and create more flexible and customized products and sales campaigns.

## Potential Benefits

Technology can be applied to improving sales and marketing in three different fundamental ways:

1. *Bring down the cost of sales and marketing through increased efficiency.* For example, obtaining better customer information to determine the best sales territory plans, or increasing the number of calls made through the use of recordings and/or digitized voice and mailings.
2. *Improve performance of existing sales programs by improving effectiveness.* For example, we can apply automation toward the goal of improving the quality of calls. This is an important but dangerous area: A manager can spend a lot of money automating something that often can be done manually just as effectively. Most automation projects in this area are focusing on improving call planning, improving the quality of sales aids and presentations, increasing the amount of product-related information available to the sales representatives, and improving the allocation of effort (such as helping to ensure that reps are calling on the right people for the right purpose), and territory management systems.
3. *Innovate to create a competitive edge.* One example is American Hospital Supply's ASAP system. Several thousand hospitals that buy American Hospital's products are provided with terminals on their own premises that allow them automatically to enter orders for American Hospital Supply products. This provides the customers with convenience and cost savings if they use American Hospital products and American Hospital's ASAP system. It ties in a unique service around the products American Hospital is selling.

Another type of innovation involves greater vertical integration of the various organization divisions aimed at increasing sales. Today, there is very little integration of sales, marketing, and distribution. Marketing people develop new products; salespeople sell them through promotions and by providing service to retail accounts. With the trend toward regional marketing, where a company creates promotions specific to individual stores or retail chains, there is increasing pressure for better coordination between sales and marketing, for complete integration across divisional lines. Computer automation is a vital component in this process.

## Other Examples

Many sales and marketing activities are a perfect fit for advanced automated systems. Consider the following sales candidate list:

- Lead processing and tracking. Leads can be automatically or manually entered into the system and used to generate direct mail responses or call reports to telemarketers and/or outside sales representatives. Sales progress can also be tracked and monitored.

- Generating call reports to remind telemarketers and salespeople who, when, and why to call.
- Providing an automated ticker system to aid in scheduling and prioritizing important calls and events (calendar functionality).
- Preparing sales quotations, particularly for complex products like computers and insurance policies, which require selecting from among many interrelated components and features.
- Preparing presentations for many formats; e.g., over the telephone, face-to-face, and written proposals.
- Providing call guides, aids to answer prospect and customer questions interactively and overcome common objections.
- Maintaining customer history in a form suitable for unanticipated interactive exploration and ad hoc query.
- Tracking sales performance, which allow sales managers to track progress made toward converting leads into customers on an individual representative basis, on a department basis, or in response to a particular sales promotion.
- Assist in sales territory planning via sophisticated spreadsheet and graphics-based systems that can help sales managers define territories and analyze current and potential profitability.
- Support sales forecasting, so sales managers can integrate historical product performance with industry and market data to project future sales.

And the marketing candidates:

- Direct marketing support, maintaining a database of prospect and customer information that can aid in matching products and services to individual wants and needs.
- Direct mail, permitting direction and customization of promotional mailing pieces to a select group of prospects and customers.
- Creating company/product awareness, automatically sending promotional literature and press releases to customers and/or media contacts for public relations.
- Conducting advertising analyses that permit the analysis and performance tracking of particular advertising campaigns.
- Testing the sensitivity of a given variable to marketing effectiveness (item pricing is an example).
- Performing market research analysis, sorting and analyzing a sales/marketing database to determine such things as the industry/geographic region/type of customer most likely to buy a particular product, and to detect buying pattern changes.
- Conducting competitive analysis, surveying and integrating information about prospects and customers with regard to their current suppliers. Determining a product or organization's competitive standing today and in the future.

### Benetton

Benetton is an example of a successful application of technology to sales (Pepper 1989). The Benetton Group has been one of the great success stories in modern business. It started with a small family-owned sweater-knitting business in a small northern Italian city, Veneto, and turned into the largest manufacturer of knitwear in the world. Today it has 5000 shops in 70 countries, and its 1987 sales were $2.5 billion just from its clothing operations. Certainly the success of this company is due to many factors besides its innovative use of computers, but we will focus on that aspect of its success.

Fifteen Benetton stylists design clothes on video screens using a range of 250 colors. The video terminals are linked by computer to knitting and cutting machines that can turn out a new model within a few hours. Some of these machines are located at Benetton factories, and others are at subcontractors locations. When the product is finished, it is sent to a computerized warehouse. The warehouse is designed to handle 20,000 incoming and outgoing boxes of garments in a 16-hour day. Each box is labeled with a computer-generated bar-coded label preaddressed to the store that ordered it. The flow of boxes into and from the factory and out to waiting trucks is regulated by electric eyes and coded readers. The entire operation is carried out by a staff of sixteen, sitting at computer consoles. The whole operation is integrated with, and driven by, sales. No garment is made until it is ordered by a shop.

Using a computer network, the company takes 80 percent of its orders for its two yearly collections, Fall–Winter and Spring–Summer, nine months before the selling seasons start. Shop orders are relayed to headquarters by 75 company agents around the world who use PCs and Benetton-developed software. The system allows for overnight adjustment of production and midseason reordering, with delivery within 2 to 3 weeks. Data from actual retail store sales receipts are collected and analyzed and used to plan the next collection of designs based upon buyer trends.

Clearly this system requires the integration of many software applications and geographically dispersed computer locations. The applications involved range from CAD/CAM technology for the design, to networking, order processing, and accounting.

### Campbell Soup

Another example of a company that is successful in doing intelligent filtering of market data is Campbell. Campbell is building new systems to highlight exceptional events and report on changes, using inference and analogy and other analytical tools. This interpreted data does not replace the need for the traditional focus groups and in-home interviews. They are still needed, but they are supplemented with computer-processed information. Currently 80 percent of the new products fail. Campbell's hope is that with this added, "intelligently processed" information, it can achieve at least a 50 percent success rate.

### MCI

MCI is the second largest long-distance phone company in America. MCI claims it owes much of its success to its information systems (Bernstein 1989). MCI believes that the long-distance communications business is driven by marketing and customer service, and that information systems help to provide the differentiating factor, assisting the firm in successfully giving customers the products and services they demand. Some of MCI's notable applications include these:

- The Commercial Prospect Advisor
- Pricer
- Netcap
- Integrated Network Management Services

The idea for the Commercial Prospect Advisor came from users during a weekly division managers video conference. It was implemented as a PC-based expert system. It accesses external information sources to provide salespeople with information on prospective customers, such as "How much a prospect is spending on long distance service," or "Who the chief contact is," or "Details about the customer's business." It can also be used for screening and identifying new prospects by answering questions such as "Who in my territory spends over $3000 per month for telecommunications?"

Pricer helps salespeople quickly compose accurate pricing proposals for prospective customers. It centralizes and maintains current tariff rates (which change almost daily and differ from state to state) and allows salespeople to access these rates quickly and to perform what-if scenario analyses on alternative service configurations.

Netcap (for network capability) is a real-time order entry system that lets customers sign up for toll-free 800 service almost instantly, without the need to talk to a clerk. It used to take an average of two days to sort through MCI's 22-page instruction book to set up a new account. Now it is done within 10 minutes of the initial phone call.

Network Management Services is a family of technologies and applications that give users greater control over their voice and data traffic by letting them monitor, analyze, and control their MCI voice and data traffic from a single computer terminal by using IBM's network management system, Netview.

### American Express

American Express charges a premium price to merchants and card members which it justifies by superior service. It uses technology to help differentiate its services from those of other firms, spending an estimated $1 billion per year on information systems. This expenditure represents more than 4 percent of its revenues, which is greater than average, while its information system staff costs are lower than the norm; only 23 percent of the IS budget is used for personnel (Sullivan-Trainor 1989). The Authorizer's Assistant discussed in the section on risk management is an example of American Express technology. It helps agents rapidly evaluate and approve credit transactions on an individual transaction basis, while the customer is waiting.

American Express has also invested in a large, comprehensive future-oriented business plan to address the company's business and technology needs five years ahead. It is called the Genesis Project. Part of this project includes more than $50 million in expert systems to improve customer service.

### Thorn Home Electronics International

Thorn Home Electronics International (THEi) implemented a technological strategy based on flattening the corporate management hierarchy that propelled it from a small group of European home electronics rental businesses to a global consumer electronics rental/retail business, located in over 19 countries with 3000 stores and over 25,000 employees (O'Leary 1989). THEi integrated its organizational, business, and information technology strategies by treating each store as an independent business unit supported by technology that emphasized the local store's needs. To accomplish this objective, THEi built a computer network with applications that allowed the manager of each store to make basic decisions about such things as inventory and credit. Also included were tools to track customer-initiated contract terminations and equipment upgrades. These tools are used by the local branches to analyze patterns of customer behavior, allowing managers to offer customers personalized relationships based on files of their histories and current life styles. All the rental stores send their data back to a central local database linked to Thorn's London headquarters, providing for centralized auditing.

### A. C. Nielsen Co.

A. C. Nielsen, in conjunction with Information Resources and Metaphor Computer Systems, developed "quasi-expert" systems that use retail store scanner data to analyze a product brand's performance within regions and to detail how competing products are doing, which promotions are working, and whether specific store displays are attracting customers. The system generates summary reports, with graphics, that highlight unusual results and market activity.

The system has helped food companies strengthen their relations with supermarkets. For example, Kraft uses data from its system to help chains, such as Kroger and Pathmark, decide how to stock their refrigerated sections most effectively. On the negative side, some marketing consultants argue that these sorts of systems promote bad practices, namely that they create a tendency to focus on short-term gains at the expense of building brand loyalty. Also, they fear we might miss important factors if we look only at the past. Nevertheless, the system has proven useful, has been effective, and its use seems to be growing.

## CONCLUSION

Examples of the new trends in computer systems applications have been provided from the fields of trading, risk management, and sales and marketing. Many more applications are worth noting. They include applications in the areas of:

- Audit and contingency review
- Product and strategic planning
- Forecasting
- Diagnostics and repair
- Detection of illegal or erroneous transactions

All the computer system applications discussed may be characterized in terms of the following five components:

1. Information technology: functions and features
2. Utilization: business functions, embedded knowledge and training
3. Behavioral change: impact and likelihood for personnel and organizational change
4. Performance change: benefits accrued (e.g., increases the chances of success with new products, reduced sales costs)
5. Economic value: profit, ROI.

Most DP systems in the 1970s were not critical to the business, in the sense that the company was not at risk if they failed. Today's systems are increasingly becoming so critical that if they fail, the company's existence may be at risk. These systems therefore demand attention to two contradictory goals. On the one hand, the system must be easy to use, flexible, and responsive to rapidly changing needs. On the other hand, the system must be secure (its data cannot be compromised), must be error-free, and it must have an extremely high system availability. The examples presented employ many of the advanced technologies we discuss next in Chapter 3.

# 3

# The Latest Technological Advances

It is important to understand the new and emerging technologies (both hardware and software) that are shaping and changing the way we develop and use computer systems. There is a lot of controversy associated with many of these technologies. To add to the confusion, these technologies are merging and overlapping with one another. The aim of this chapter is to explain the basic concepts, uses, and issues behind these evolving technologies.

The first section introduces the topic of artificial intelligence. It illustrates how artificial intelligence technology allows the business to use the computer to assist in the more qualitative, conceptual areas of strategizing, planning, design, marketing, sales, risk assessment, interpretation and forecasting, rather than just crunching numbers that measure cost, revenue, production, and sales. It highlights the technology and use of expert systems, natural language and speech processing, and object-oriented programming.

Next we discuss how database management systems are being extended to allow the user to deal with richer media and data structures, including text, sound and images, video concepts, objects, and decision rules, and being made more proactive and "intelligent." Then we show how revolutionary advances in the user interface are making systems more friendly and more end-user–oriented and task-oriented.

Dramatic advances in hardware have been responsible for the continued expansion of computers into our daily activities and for making many of these software advances practical. New hardware architecture and networking concepts like RISC, transputers, parallel processors, and neural computers and high-speed data communications hold the potential for still more revolutionary changes in the future. Image processing is highlighted as a particularly exciting area that holds much promise for useful business applications. Finally, we review advances in the software development process itself, including CASE, reusable software, and visual programming.

These technological advances have made practical many exciting new concepts in the area of decision-making. The ideas emerging from the concepts associated with decision support and executive information systems are followed by a discussion of the concept of groupware, which allows the design of systems that are able to conform to, adapt, and model changing interactions, tasks, and interrelationships among people and organizational units. They help a business accommodate changes in its corporate structure and its product offerings. (Appendices 8 through 15 provide more detail for those who are interested in exploring some of the technical aspects in greater depth).

## ARTIFICIAL INTELLIGENCE

Artificial intelligence (AI) is a field concerned with designing and programming machines to accomplish tasks that, when performed by people, are considered to represent intelligent behavior. Artificial intelligence attempts to understand how humans think by studying the behavior of machine designs and programs that model current hypotheses and conjectures about some aspect of the human cognitive process.

Artificial intelligence technology represents a mind-set, a way of looking at solving problems from a particular point of view, that differs from the more traditional approaches. Much of this difference is traceable to the nature of the problems AI researchers tackle. Artificial intelligence research has concentrated on solving problems that are demonstrably solvable by human beings, but for which no currently well-formulated, computationally feasible methodology exists. This class of problems includes:

- How we learn
- How we play games
- How we communicate with one another
- How we perceive (see, hear, speak, listen, write)
- How we diagnose
- How we plan
- How we create

The approaches to these problems can best be characterized as informal, symbolic, and conceptual rather than quantitative. Of course, where appropriate, formal, quantitative approaches should be integrated with these more qualitative, intuitive methods. The methods employed tend to be nonprocedural (describe what you want done, not how to accomplish it), flexible, and adaptive in nature. Additional knowledge (e.g., facts and rules) can be easily added, deleted, or modified without system design modification. Furthermore, since AI system architecture makes it easy to add, delete, and modify, it facilitates evaluating, examining, and analyzing proposed changes before their permanent addition; thus this technology lends itself to rapid prototyping.

AI knowledge is often expressed in an object-oriented representation. An object-oriented system is made up of objects which are composed of functionally related data, procedures, and rules combined into conceptual units rather than a system of separate data and separate procedure-oriented knowledge representations. Objects communicate through messages. An object can be defined in terms of the properties of other objects. One object can thus "inherit" properties from other objects. (Object-oriented programming is discussed in more detail later in this chapter).

Although AI has much in common with other computer science disciplines, it differs from more conventional computer science areas in the following respects:

1. Viewpoint (plausible and logical reasoning, instead of quantitative calculation)
2. Subject matter (mental activity; very knowledge-intensive)
3. Tolerance for errors and imprecise data; can deal with fuzzy linguistic concepts
4. Symbolic manipulation instead of numeric orientation
5. Evolutionary design principles (nonprocedural, anticipating addition and change)
6. Knowledge-based design
7. Inference and deduction capabilities (It has a line of reasoning and can explain itself.)
8. Heuristic or approximate problem-solving approach

As this technology has become better understood and in more widespread use commercially, it is being integrated into existing products and systems. The best example has been as extensions to database management systems such as SYBASE, INGRES, ORACLE, DB2, as extensions to the more popular languages, such as C and COBOL, and as extensions to vertical market product offerings, particularly in the decision-support area [e.g., spreadsheets, financial and statistical modeling languages such as IFPS, and fourth-generation languages such as FOCUS].

Business and financial problems have some very special characteristics that require a close integration of AI techniques and more conventional programming technology. Most business and financial problems can be characterized by the following:

1. Requires a mixture of numeric and symbolic reasoning
2. Usually has no strong underlying causality models (known as deep models)
3. Involves nonprocedural decision-making knowledge (case data are available but generally incomplete.)
4. Requires a marriage of AI systems and existing, more conventional systems.
5. Usually needs to provide supporting explanation reasoning

Artificial intelligence has a variety of subfields of research activity. The specific areas that have made the greatest inroads and successes commercially in the business world are expert systems, natural language (including speech) processing, knowledge bases (extensions to database technology that endow database systems with inference and self-auditing capability), and object-oriented programming. There have also been important AI applications in the area of manufacturing, robotics, and process control.

One of the most active AI research areas is understanding how to program computers for learning and discovery. This is an activity most often associated with intelligent behavior, and one that offers the greatest potential impact. It holds the promise of overcoming the knowledge engineering bottleneck, the painstaking and time-consuming process of extracting and encoding an area of expertise. Several of the more popular learning approaches include inductive learning, genetic algorithms (Markoff 1990b), and neural networks (discussed later in this chapter).

## Expert Systems

An expert is someone who is recognized as being able to solve a particular class of complex, often ill-defined problems especially well and efficiently (Schutzer 1987). An expert also usually knows the limits of his or her expertise. An expert system attempts to mimic the problem-solving activities and performance of an expert. Expert systems are typically used for problems dealing with complex diagnosis, scheduling, forecasting, monitoring and control, or data analysis and interpretation.

One remarkable thing discovered by artificial intelligence researchers is that human expertise can be fairly well emulated by a rather simple straightforward reasoning structure and a lot of detailed domain-specific knowledge. For example, rule-based expert systems encode all knowledge in terms of simple "IF . . . THEN" rules. If a set of attributes satisfy a given condition, then a conclusion can be reached and a set of actions can be taken. The difference between rule-based and traditional programming is that there are just IF . . . THEN statements and no ELSE statements; the control strategy is not embedded in the program logic, but is a separate independent component known as the *control strategy*. These rules can be used to solve problems through one of a number of relatively simple control strategies.

One popular technique, called *backward chaining,* involves guessing a conclusion, searching the rule set for a matching conclusion, attempting to verify that the preconditions are satisfied by matching it with a known fact, or finding another rule whose conclusions would satisfy the condition, and then continuing on in this manner until a complete, consistent logical path is found from facts to conclusion. Another example would be *forward chaining,* where observed facts trigger rules and their conclusions, which in turn lead to new rules and new conclusions, and so forth until no further conclusions can be inferred.

An important aspect of the control strategy is called *conflict resolution,* which includes the knowledge of which rules to try first when more than one is applicable. The control strategy itself can be expressed in terms of rules known as *metarules* (rules about how to prioritize the order in which to process rules).

Clearly, if we have a system with a large enough number of rules, it pays to structure these rules into rule sets, and control which chunks we try when in a broader strategy. *Frames* and *objects* are concerned with packaging, structuring, and logically linking these rules along with facts, (data) and procedures, for efficiency and ease of update. This becomes important when the knowledge (the number of rules) grows large (over 10,000 rules). Since it has been determined experimentally that most human experts employ 70,000 "chunks" (a "chunk" can be loosely related to a production rule) of information, give or take a binary order of magnitude (e.g., ± 20,000), to solve a real problem, this is a valid design concern (Reddy 1988; Schutzer 1987). Furthermore, these rule-structuring approaches match well with our understanding of how experts solve a problem (see Appendix 8).

The typical expert system architecture is pictured in Figure 3.1. It consists of a separate knowledge base and inference engine. The knowledge base stores the explicit knowledge in the form of facts, rules, and objects. The inference engine stores the control strategy (the procedural knowledge) for using the knowledge base to solve a problem. In addition, there generally is an explanation facility which reveals the line-of-reasoning in response to a user's query by explaining why the system reached a certain conclusion. The system can be used in two ways:

- Interacting with the expert during the knowledge acquisition stage
- Interacting with the user during a problem-solving (decision-making) session

During knowledge acquisition, the system prompts the expert, acquiring and organizing the knowledge, editing and checking for logical consistency, and testing against a prior set of cases.

During problem-solving, the system attempts to reach a conclusion, prompting

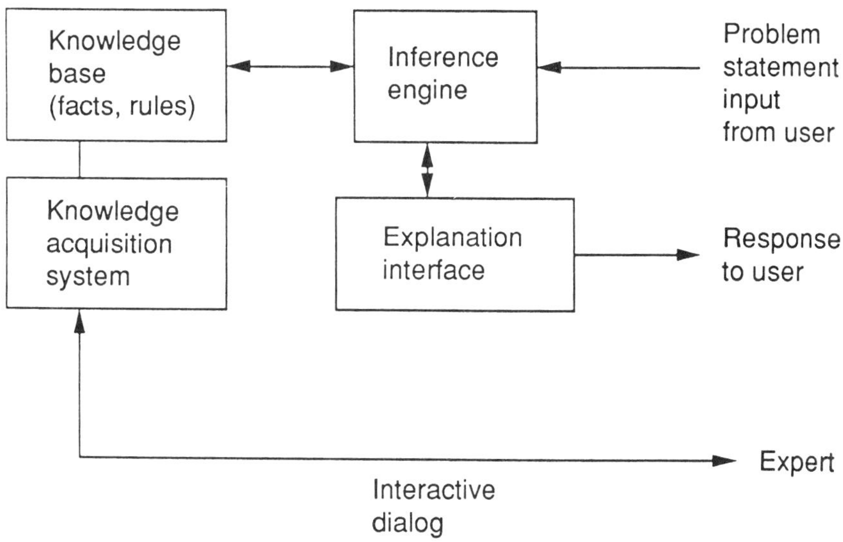


**Figure 3.1.** Expert System Architecture.

the user for additional data as required. Generally if the requested data is not known or provided, the system will still attempt to make a recommendation, even though it is based on incomplete data.

Several goals motivate us to want to build an expert system rather than just hiring experts when we need them:

- Increase productivity (computers work faster, without fatigue)
- Increase profitability (computers can work more efficiently)
- Improve training and education (by making the knowledge more explicit, it serves as an educational tool to train new employees)
- Improve the quality of customer service (enhances availability to customers by making it more cost-effective to extend service to lower-volume customers, and by making expertise available on a more timely basis and at inconvenient hours and locations)
- Enhance competitive advantage (can apply scarce expertise to wider audience and to a broader range of products, and make advice more consistent and more customizable)
- Increase ability to operate under tight time constraints (for complex problems with many conflicting aspects and variables, the expert system approach, although not optimum, is often less computationally intensive and therefore more likely to find a solution within an acceptable response time than a purely algorithmic approach)
- Increase tolerance to missing or incomplete information (expert systems technology, like human experts, is designed to work in an environment where much of the available information is suspect and uncertain, whereas more formal algorithmic solutions tend to fall apart or produce misleading results)
- Can handle complex, ill-defined tasks (often this technology offers the only possible means of finding a solution)
- Can handle confusion and misunderstanding (there are too many conflicting objectives with too many unclear tradeoffs to apply another more rigorous methodology)
- Overcomes lack of perseverance (the task is too overwhelming, too boring, too tiring, or other things have a higher priority for a human expert)

Based upon a Cooper and Lybrand study, it was determined that some 43 percent of the major financial services institutions are using, developing, or actively researching expert systems applications. More than one-quarter of this active group has systems in use. The expert systems activity is primarily motivated by a desire for strategic or competitive advantage. Fully 90 percent of the firms using or actively developing expert systems believe the systems will be crucial to the success of their organizations.

The same conclusions can be extrapolated to the general business community. Engineering and scientifically oriented businesses are the most advanced in their use of expert system technology, but the general trend is clear: Expert systems activity is expected to grow significantly and to become more fully integrated with the entire computer sciences discipline. Almost one-third of the firms not yet involved in expert systems plan to become involved by the early 1990s. (Some examples of applications of expert systems to business are provided in Appendix 8.)

### Expert System Shells

Many expert system shells are currently being offered commercially to assist users in developing expert systems. An *expert system shell* consists of a collection of expert system building tools, such as rule editors and rule searching logic, designed to minimize the amount of specialized knowledge and engineering and programming skills required to build an expert system. For example, most expert system shells have a user-friendly interface that, in the building mode, accepts knowledge in the form of English-like rules, frames, or object-oriented structures. Most offer an integrated environment with the popular databases, spreadsheets, and graphics packages. Neuron Data's expert system shell NEXPERT interfaces with, among other things, the ORACLE database and LOTUS 1-2-3 spreadsheet. The expert system shell KEE interfaces with the database IBM DB2 and ART with LOTUS and ORACLE. (A listing of some current expert system shells is provided in Appendix 8.)

Another recent trend is the appearance of *inclination shells*. These are customized reasoning schemes developed for a vertical market (e.g., insurance, accounting, or investing) rather than just a generic expert system shell. Syntelligence's SYNTEL and Arthur Anderson's Mortgage Loan Advisor are two examples of inclination shells. Many business expert system applications have been developed as standard packages and are now being offered for sale (see Appendix 8).

## Natural Language and Speech Recognition

Language, written or spoken, serves as our basic vehicle for thought and communication. By actively engaging people in conversation, the "intelligent" machine can more properly infer their wants. Natural language—any language people use to converse among themselves, such as English, French, Japanese, or Russian—although richer, more expressive and more concise, is much more ambiguous and ill-structured than the artificial languages invented to deal with machines and specialized fields of study, such as FORTRAN, COBOL, LISP, algebra, and music. So natural language is far more difficult to understand and requires considerable cognitive activity and background context to be interpreted properly.

The ambiguity that pervades natural language helps to make it rich, expressive, and interesting. The ambiguity exists in many forms:

- In word meanings (Is "saw" a tool for cutting wood, or the past tense of "to see"?)
- In adjective modifiers, noun-noun modifiers, and modified attachments (Is "fruitfly" a kind of fruit or a type of fly?)

- In pronouns (Who does "he" refer to in the sentence?)
- In ellipsis and substitution (There are incomplete sentences such as "has the sales quota been met in Naples? And in New York?")
- In anaphoric references (where a sentence or word makes a reference that can only be interpreted in terms of earlier sentences, phrases, or words, such as "John took a test. He was nervous about the results.")

There is also ambiguity due to incorrect usage or grammar and the many possible sentence structures. Even after all these other areas have been resolved, there still can be ambiguity in overall sentence meaning. Does "Print all unfilled sales orders in the New York region on Tuesday" refer to all the outstanding orders generated on Tuesday, or to all the outstanding orders to date on Tuesday? Despite these difficulties, there are successful commercial natural language processing systems using AI techniques (see Schutzer 1987) that, used in properly constrained applications, provide great benefit. After all, most information is still communicated with words and not numbers.

Natural language processing systems are concerned with both the generation and presentation of results to the user, and the interpretation and understanding of user input text. They are directed at making it easier and more natural for the user to communicate with the computer. They include applications such as front-end to databases, news filters, front-end to help system, front-end to an expert system, and text browsing.

The future holds the promise of further advances and successful applications in more complex domains. But it is important *not* to use a natural language processor without also providing the system with some minimum capability for logical reasoning and deduction. Generally when one uses a natural language system, he or she automatically expects a certain minimum level of intelligent behavior. After all, we are communicating to the system as if it were human, so why shouldn't it think and respond like a human? For example, if we ask the system to determine the best-performing sales region and the system was previously told that monthly sales volume is a measure of performance, we expect the system to know enough to rank the sales regions by monthly sales. If the system is told that Frank Smith moved to the Chicago office, it should realize that Frank is no longer at the Los Angeles office where he previously worked. So a natural language processing system must have "smarts" to be successful.

A natural language processing system works best with the casual but informed user. A routine user might prefer to learn how to use a few cryptic commands or key strokes. The learning time spent is well worth the subsequent savings in what is probably a daily routine, or one performed many times during the day. The casual user, on the other hand, uses the system infrequently and would find it difficult to remember a bunch of awkward, unnatural commands that must obey a strict unforgiving grammar. For this user it is much easier and faster to type instructions in "English." But the user must still have a good general understanding of the system's functions and data content or will not know how to start, or what to expect from the system. The completely naive user is probably best off interacting with a system of prompts and menus.

The combination of speech recognition with natural language processing makes for a particularly effective interface. The system learns the user's language, and the user is not required to type in large amounts of text. Speech communication has been shown to be the most effective form of human communication for many tasks.

Speech understanding is much more difficult than natural language understanding because it must cope with speech recognition at the acoustic level. Here are some of the difficulties:

- Many words and word groups sound the same.
- Words are often spoken in a run-on manner that makes it difficult to recognize where one word ends and another begins.
- Great variations in pronunciation exist among people.
- Regional accents can involve extreme differences in pronunciation.
- Women generally have higher pitched voices than men.
- Some people slur their words or drop endings.
- Stress and intonation patterns vary.
- The same person's speech may vary from day to day as a result of a cold, stress, or some other external influence.

A speech-understanding system must be able to separate linguistically significant variations in speech signals from insignificant variations such as pronunciation differences. Background noises can contribute to aural confusion and to the likelihood of misclassification of speech sounds as well. These difficulties combine to create considerable ambiguity in the speech detection and understanding process.

Current state-of-the-art systems possess capabilities that are still far from a human's speech understanding capabilities. Most systems have one or more of the following limitations:

- They are speaker-dependent. Each speaker must go through a training session in which he or she repeats the words the system must recognize.
- Discrete speech. The word phrases to be recognized must be separated by a few seconds' pause.
- Limited vocabularies. Typical speech processors can handle only several hundred to several thousand words. [A 500,000 word vocabulary is typical of the average high school student (Carrol 1971).]

As we relax some of these limitations, such as allowing for speaker independence (no speaker training required), and/or continuous speech (no pauses required between utterances of word/word phrases), we tend to see increased error rates, reduced vocabulary sizes, and greater cost. Some of the more expensive systems are capable of continuous speech for a limited (usually less than 1000 words) vocabulary. Current prices for these systems range from a few hundred dollars to tens of thousands of dollars. One major problem is that not enough standards exist for testing and evaluating these systems, so it is still difficult to compare them.

Speech synthesis is a companion technology to speech understanding, just as text generation represents a companion technology for natural language understanding. Speech synthesis is an easier problem to solve, and the technology is much further along in its development, with many more commercial offerings and applications. Early speech response units consisted of recording spoken human phrases. The difficulty with this method is that the output speech is relatively inflexible, so the recording speech cannot be easily combined and pieced together and still sound natural. Synthetically constructed speech, on the other hand, can be used to articulate computer-generated text, allowing the system complete freedom in selecting its chosen response under program control. The quality of the speech generated depends upon the coding scheme. These involve a tradeoff between output rate and memory requirements.

As speech processing systems grow in capability at reduced cost, they offer great potential for making the user interface friendlier and more natural to the user. Speech processing is expected to become a billion-dollar industry in the 1990s.

## Object-Oriented Programming

Object-oriented programming (OOP) is an important programming technique that has been shown to produce programs that are particularly easy to read, maintain, and reuse in new applications. This style of programming involves building objects rather than discrete applications, where collections of interacting objects perform the functions that would be considered an application.

Objects are self-defining components that incorporate data and descriptions of their behavior and their relations with other objects. Objects can come into being, create other objects, and then disappear or be stored permanently (persist). Objects consist of bundles of functionally related procedures, data, images, screen layouts, and so on. The state of the object is described by the values of its attributes. The behavior of an object is defined by its procedures, also called methods. Objects interact by exchanging messages requesting data or methods to be performed and results returned. Objects can respond to a given message in various ways; this is known as *polymorphism*. An example is a document object which acts differently on a PRINT command than a graphic object.

Objects allow the separation of specification (e.g., display video in a window) from implementation (display video at a particular resolution on a certain monitor type).

*Object class* is an important concept. An object class is all those objects with the same attributes and methods. The system builder can create new objects by selectively inheriting the behavior and attributes from previously defined objects or object classes. In inheritance, an object class can retain some characteristics of the parent (inherited) class. New objects can be reconfigured, generalized, or specialized from existing classes. Suppose there are ten different Treasury bonds. Without the notion of class, we would require ten Treasury bond yield procedures, one for each object. With a Treasury bond class, all the Treasury bond objects can inherit actions from their class definition, and we require only a single class Treasury bond yield procedure. This class concept can be augmented by allowing a hierarchy of class definitions. Objects can also have multiple inheritance, where they accept attributes from multiple classes.

Many object-oriented systems also permit the existence of a *metaclass*. Metaclasses give the user control over the basic operations of the system itself. For example, a metaclass definition may alter the semantics of inheritance and default. Depending upon the object-oriented implementation, these classes and inheritance may be statically defined and compiled prior to execution, or can be dynamically linked during execution. (See Appendix 9 for more detail on object-oriented programming.)

With the object-oriented approach, a lot of low-level work is hidden in the object, transparent to the rest of the application. This is of great benefit for incremental development and debugging. It allows internal representation and procedures to be altered and optimized transparently to the program as a whole. Consider the following example: Different types of bonds have their yields computed according to different formulas. Some base their computations on a 30-day month, others use actual days in the month. With object-oriented programming, each bond knows how to compute its own yield when asked. When an accounting object wishes a bond's yield, it sends a message to the appropriate bond-objects asking them to compute their yield and return the result.

A more conventional system would need to incorporate logic to determine which yield subfunctions to call under what circumstances. With object-oriented programming, each bond type object maintains its own rules and procedures for computing yield. When the rules and regulations change, we merely need to update the appropriate object. All objects interacting with that object will then be assured of receiving the new corrected yield computations.

With object-oriented programming, experts would still be needed to write software. But once written, users can easily adapt the software to suit their needs by just rearranging objects rather than rewriting software; e.g., each object could represent a step in a bank transaction.

As an example of what can be done with object-oriented programming, Arthur Anderson has used Smalltalk to create a simulation program for visualizing business practices. Arthur Anderson is also applying object-oriented techniques to large business applications like billing systems and accounts receivable.

Some people claim that nothing can be done with object-oriented programming that cannot be done using conventional techniques, just as many people claim that rule-based systems are just large CASE statements, or that LISP can be replaced with assembly language. These claims are valid in the sense that they are based on the theoretical equivalence of computing automata. However, these claims ignore the importance of programming convenience, and the power of using the proper representation set in problem-solving. The object-oriented concept is now spreading to all aspects of the software life cycle. There are four major areas of object-oriented activity: languages, databases, operating systems, and environment. Object-oriented programming languages embody the object-oriented programming principles just discussed. There are two types of object-oriented programming languages (OOPL's):

- Self-contained (e.g., SMALLTALK, ACTOR)
- Extensions to traditional third-generation language (e.g., $C^{++}$, Objective C)

The NEXT computer uses Carnegie Mellon's Mach, a UNIX derivative that will likely be adapted by the Open System Foundation as its operating system. Mach supports object interaction in a distributed environment. Macintosh's operating system has used object technology for some time. Hewlett Packard's New Waves adds an object manager on top of Microsoft Window.

Object database management systems deal with storing and maintaining objects. They address the problem of maintaining object version control, providing each object with a unique identifier, determining and effecting optimal storage structure to support the update and retrieval of a large collection of objects, providing concurrency control to allow multiple users to query and update a common set of objects without corrupting the database, implementing a user authorization scheme, and providing a user query language. The best solution to these needs for objects with their inheritance hierarchy is not obvious. How can you employ lock-out for concurrency control with an object hierarchy? Do you to lock out the entire hierarchy? How do you handle version control with an object hierarchy? Which object inherits what version?

Object-oriented database technology is still quite new, and there are still very few working models. Examples of object-oriented databases include Gemstone by Servio Corp. and POSTGRES by Berkeley. Gemstone was the first pure database. Servio Corp. is now working with Sybase to build an object frontend to their relational database. POSTGRES is another example of an attempt to link object techniques with the relational database model. Other object-oriented databases that are currently commercially available are VBASE by Ontologic, ORION by Artemis Technology, and Statice by Symbolics. By 1995 we should expect even more to be available. Object-oriented databases are being built by Innovative Systems, Object Databases, and as part of Hewlett Packard's IRIS project.

There are also object-oriented analysis, object-oriented structured design and CASE (see the section called "Software Development Technologies"), and object-oriented databases (see the section called "Multimedia Databases").

## MULTIMEDIA "SMART" DATABASES

There are several important trends in the database technology area. First, databases are increasingly being applied in areas beyond the mere management of records. Future databases, like humans, will be concerned with managing (storing, retrieving, logically relating, and maintaining) the universe of information in all its varied forms—data, test, graphics, image, voice. Furthermore, database technology is becoming capable of more "intelligent" retrievals and deductions, and of linking this information to other applications and proactive triggers/alerts through AI techniques.

### Proactive, Intelligent Databases

Users want to be alerted to interesting information patterns and trends as they occur or become noticed. This suggests the need for a database that not merely maintains information, but is knowledgeable about content, can spot relationships, and can control and check for data integrity. The database must also be capable of understanding how the user intends to use this information in the context of the task or application, through questioning and inference. It should not have to wait for tasking, but can voluntarily prompt and suggest interesting items. Smart database systems are based on a blend of database management and artificial intelligence. They attempt to imbue a database management system with the ability to capture the knowledge relating to the application of the data and not just store the data.

For example, a database system has intelligence if we impart it with the knowledge that if company A is a parent of company B, then company B is a subsidiary of company A, and that a company is taxed on the combined earnings of all its subsidiaries. Then when the system is queried regarding the corporation's taxes, the system examines its knowledge base of rules to determine that to compute the tax it must look up all the individual subsidiaries' taxes and find the total. It does not have to store a separate total tax entry for the entire corporation. This knowledge can be represented by semantic networks, rules, and objects (see the section called "Expert Systems" for a discussion of rule-based reasoning, the section called "Object-oriented Programming" for a discussion of objects, and Appendix 10 for a review of current methods and technologies including semantic networks) (Schutzer 1987).

Ultimately, databases will possess the intelligence to employ statistical, logical induction and advanced heuristic learning techniques to search for and discover otherwise "hidden" trends and relationships. This is called "data mining," and it is becoming an active research area, with commercial products already being offered (see Appendix 10).

## Multimedia Databases

Information needs to be stored, managed, and manipulated in many different formats or representations (e.g., spreadsheets, documents, tables) in order to match the organization's needs and work flows. Spreadsheets are a natural electronic representation of financial management and budgeting information. In spreadsheets, each item, usually a number or a formula, is associated with a cell (an intersection of a row and a column). Often the columns represent time (months, years) and the rows represent financial entities (revenue, expenses, profits, tax).

Document representation is an appropriate representation of an organization's communication of ideas—the firm's reports, forms, and memos.

Relational tables are an appropriate format for maintaining data records—data on employees, sales, and products.

There are many other natural forms of information, such as graphics, images, time series and so on.

Each representation, taken by itself without a link to a database management system, is limited in several respects:

- It represents information from only one particular viewpoint.
- It doesn't store data in a single location where it is available to multiple users.
- It tends to duplicate data in many files.
- It forces users to create large files that use up memory.
- It provides insufficient data security.

Therefore, each representation should be a window on data stored in a database management system. The link should be bidirectional, giving users an easy way to use data in the database, and to put updated information back in.

Having a database management system integrated with all of the various representation schemes brings:

- Flexibility to combine data in meaningful ways.
- Data integrity: Since the data are centrally maintained, we are assured that we are always getting the most current and up-to-date data.
- Data security: Provides access control.

A truly integrated and effective data management system should be capable of administration and management of all the forms of information fundamental to a company's work. This includes the ability to receive and deliver data, to attach these data to spreadsheets, documents, and reports, and to control their disposition. In other words, a full-function integrated database is used in conjunction with all the possible representation systems.

## Database Developments

Next we discuss some of the advances being made in developing databases capable of managing information in all its various forms and representations more intelligently, efficiently, and proactively.

### *Text-based Management Systems*

Unlike traditional database management systems (DBMS), which deal only with structured information, text-based management systems (TBMS) are able to manage free-form text. While word processors can only create and edit text, TBMSs can use text as data, and text entry can be connected to several applications. There are many different implementations of TBMSs and each handles text in a different way. Some pertain solely to text and some handle both text and images. They go by different names: information management system, text retrieval package, text-based management system. Many TBMSs file and retrieve facts in the form of text, with related information linked by hypertext (see below for more information on hypertext); others use key word searches; still others employ AI and natural language processing technology to select files by "reading" or "browsing." Intelligent Technologies produces a TBMS product that incorporates extensive artificial intelligence functionality.

One example of a TBMS is the Lotus Agenda. Agenda accepts any information the user wants to enter up to 10 pages in length. Once entered, Agenda helps the user to organize the data. Agenda allows decisions on how to organize data to be made and changed at any time during the life of the file. A special utility program allows the user to import a variety of text data formats into a structured Agenda file. Agenda also uses artificial intelligence techniques for organizing and retrieving text files. Appendix 11 illustrates the concepts behind text-based management systems through a more detailed description of Agenda and other popular product offerings.

Two systems that support adding and linking documents, building files of documents, creating hypertext links, and support quick search through text for the occurrence of words are AskSam by AskSam and ZyIndex from ZyLAB. AskSam can search 15 Mbytes in about 10 seconds; ZyIndex, 25 Mbytes in 5 seconds. Both are PC-DOS based, link with commercial word processors, and are popular with legal firms.

### Hypertext

Hypertext is a marriage of both document and database systems. It manages information in much the same way that people manage and file their own information, through connections and semantic associations (Tazelaar 1988). For example, we are reading an economic forecast and we see the word "dollar." We highlight the word and request more information with a mouse click or a few keystrokes. Suddenly graphs of the historical dollar-yen and dollar-mark exchange rates are presented, as well as a picture of the U.S. dollar. What we have experienced is a Hypertext link, which is like an electronic footnote.

Hypertext was originally designed to support a single user on a workstation, but it is now available on the PC. Hypertext goes under many different names (hypercard, hyperlink, hyperpad plus) and many different implementations, each designed to support a number of different tasks (text editor, graphic editors, database, and browsing tools for 3D viewing). Many implementations use a "point" to show where there are links in the document. A "point" is a single character (or token or icon) that indicates the presence of a link. There are graphic browsers that provide a structural diagram of the network of nodes to help guide the user in finding desired data through a kind of graphic roadmap. Some provide a default path through the database to guide or direct the user to follow a particular path through the data.

We can categorize the current hypertext implementations in terms of the type(s) of applications they have been optimized to address. Here are the basic systems (The hypertext concept and its applications are discussed further in Appendix 12.):

- On-line help
- Problem resolution
- On-line browsing
- Library or literary exchange and interactive publication
- Personal knowledge organizers
- Workgroup collaboration
- Multipurpose/hyperverse

The hypertext technology is still immature, and problems exist with using it. It is difficult to create a sound underlying data model that can be maintained. Its facilities work well as long as the user follows the hierarchical structure of the hypertext system. However, if the user continually jumps sideways from one topic to another, it is easy to get lost. Methods for controlling the jumps and helping the user to navigate and remember where he/she has been are still in the research stage.

At present, hypertext works best for new application development on static or growing information bases. It is possible to delete information from a hypertext system, but this breaks down the structure established by the links. Inaccurate and out-of-date information is better kept as a historical record and linked to a chunk giving the correction.

Another problem with hypertext is that the specialized form of its data organization is not always applicable. It is often difficult to break a thought or a segment of information into nodes; themes or thought could be tightly interwoven in a document.

### Distributed Databases

Databases are becoming increasingly distributed and shared across different locations and different machines; many are specialized for a specific use. This trend has prompted a user-initiated drive for a more standard and integrated OS/database/networking environment. Database vendors are responding to these needs by forming strategic alliances and jointly developing integrated product sets; e.g., IBM OS/2 Extended Edition combined with Microsoft presentation manager, 3 Comm local area networks, and Sybase's relational database manager; the UNIX operating system, the Oracle relational database, and Novell networks. (This trend toward distributed databases and distributed processing over a network of computers is discussed more fully in Chapter 4).

## ADVANCED USER INTERFACES

Advanced multimedia workstations that combine sound, video, graphics, animation, text, and data are likely to become the next generation of workstations. They will have access to vast archives of CD-ROM (compact disc–read-only memory) storage. They will also include all the advanced man–machine interaction devices, such as mice, track balls, tablets and bit pads, and speech input.

They will include application of the latest knowledge of the human cognitive process to the design of interfaces. This includes such advanced techniques as context-sensitive menus; pop-up windows; "what you see is what you get" (WYSIWYG) interaction; the ability to memorize, replay, and edit past sequences of commands and interactions; proactive prompting; and other advanced techniques. The workstation will learn and adapt its interface and explanations to an individual's style and skill level, and grow with the individual as he/she increases in skill level. When integrated with reusable software and object-oriented programming concepts, this should allow the end user to perform almost all his/her programming needs, once a rich enough library of routines exists through visual programming by modifying and linking object icons and screens through pointing and clicking and overtyping. A hint of things to come was unveiled by Steve Jobs in October 1988 when he presented his new company's computer, appropriately named NEXT, and its user environment, NEXTSTEP. It is implemented on top of an object-oriented programming environment and possesses many of the features of the multimedia workstation of the future.

Peridot, an experimental user interface management system, is still another illustration of the direction user interface design is taking (Myers 1988). Peridot is used to create highly interactive, graphic manipulation interfaces. It allows designers to demonstrate what they feel the interface should look like by drawing a picture on the screen and then demonstrating how the interface should respond to the end user's actions by moving the mouse and other input devices. It combines the techniques of visual programming and programming by example. It uses artificial intelligence techniques (case-based and plausible reasoning, discussed in Appendix 8) to infer general-purpose parameterized procedures from specific examples.

## HARDWARE TRENDS

Several hardware trends hold the key to dramatic changes in the computer landscape. Some of the key areas include these:

- *RISC technology* (Reduced Instruction Set Computer), which has ushered in the age of the workstation, already accounts for almost 30 percent of the computer market, and is the fastest-growing segment of the computer hardware industry. It is responsible for a realignment among computer makers and the emergence of several important new computer manufacturers.
- *Special purpose processing hardware* are exemplified by the transputer. These machines, optimized to perform very specific operations (e.g., vector processing, database engines, image processing) and to take advantage of parallelism, are also growing in popularity and may add still further change to the computer architecture landscape.
- *Parallel processing machines* have exploded onto the commercial market. They are typified at one extreme by superminis and high-powered workstations like CONVEX and Stardent, Intel's IPSC/860 supercomputer, and at the other spectrum by the Thinking Machine. The progress in parallel processing is not restricted to the hardware, but has involved advances in the systems and applications software supporting and exploiting it.
- *The neural network computer* is perhaps one of the most intriguing and controversial developments in parallel processing. Its design is inspired by the architecture of the brain. This class of computer architecture has

begun to gain much publicity and some limited success, particularly in areas of human perception, such as speech, handwriting, and vision perception.

- *Advanced scanner devices and image processing* has recently seen tremendous improvements in cost and performance, opening the door to many important new business applications that were previously impractical.
- *Advanced, high-definition TV* promises to combine with computer technology to revolutionize the entertainment and information services areas.

All these technologies are discussed in more detail in the succeeding sections (those with little background in computer systems should read Appendix 6, "Introduction to Computers," first).

## RISC

RISC (reduced instruction set computing) stresses a simple, streamlined instruction set. New instructions are added only after careful consideration. In RISC, the entire hardware system must be capable of processing a new instruction and transferring data on each clock cycle. While the instruction set is simplified, the hardware needed to maximize concurrency and integration is quite complex. Software is a key RISC component. Compilers must be written to take advantage of the streamlined instruction set and RISC architecture.

RISC has been shown to possess a key performance advantage, so we are likely to see RISC play an important role in future computing technology. Currently, graphics and imaging systems, robotics, fault-tolerant computers, and engineering workstations (SUN, MIPS) are the major users of the RISC hardware, but the list of applications is expected to grow. RISC-based engineering workstations are expected to be selling 1000 MIPS for under $15,000, with voice and image I/O, in the 1990s. Most of the leading traditional computer manufacturers (IBM, DEC) now offer RISC machines. In February 1989, INTEL and Motorola joined the RISC bandwagon, announcing new, more powerful, more cost-effective chips based on RISC technology.

INTEL's current RISC chip is a million-transistor microprocessor incorporating graphics and number-crunching components into a single chip. It has gained the endorsement of IBM, AT&T, Prime, Olivetti, and Microsoft. Motorola's chip will be used by Data General for its new 17 MIPS workstation, starting at under $7500. Its adoption by workstation vendors is expected to grow. As RISC is married with faster bus architectures and more comprehensive I/O capable of driving large banks of secondary storage and terminals comparable to mainframes, we can expect this technology to grow in dominance across the entire computing spectrum.

However, some new architectures may eventually supersede RISC. VLIW (very long instruction word) machines are designed to better exploit opportunities for parallelism. VLIW machines have a big processor with $n$ arithmetic units that connect to the same register file. The instruction word is made $n$ times longer so that it can tell each of the $n$ arithmetic units what to do. Intel's 80860 ("Cray on a chip") implements one of the main VLIW design tenets—the ability to start more than one instruction at the same time. Many of the concepts that guide VLIW design are extensions of the RISC philosophy. But the VLIW machines need more sophisticated and complex hardware. Some people think that a super-RISC chip (the next generation, much faster than today's crop) could achieve close to a VLIW machine's performance at much lower cost, so the jury is still out on VLIW.

## Transputers

The transputer is a specialized processor suited for performing parallel and concurrent numerically complex operations, such as speech processing, image processing, and robotics control. Transputers are designed to operate in networks and support multiprocessing.

A current transputer network is based upon the Evergreen transputer distributed control system (XP/DCS), engineered in conjunction with the Yale Robotics Department. Each processor component is a 32-bit T800, equipped with a fast RAM, a fast hardware interrupt capability, and four DMA (direct memory access) serial interprocessor communications links. It comes with its own high-level language, Occam, which supports parallel processing, as well as the TDS (transputer development system) that assists in writing, distributing, and debugging code. The transputer handles the interprocessor communication and software development support, letting the designer concentrate on customizing the computational "identity" of particular nodes with special-purpose hardware.

## Parallel Processors

Parallel processing architectures, often comprised of thousands to millions of processors are beginning to dominate the supercomputer and superminicomputer with their ability to perform complex, time-consuming mathematical operations and data searches across many data items in parallel.

Many of these machines employ techniques such as *vectorizing* (performing the same operation on multiple sets of data simultaneously) and *pipelining* (breaking up a computation into a set of smaller independent operations and performing different stages of many instructions simultaneously). These parallel processors are often classified as to whether they are SIMD (single instruction, multiple data; they execute a single instruction across many data items in parallel), or MIMD (multiple instruction, multiple data; they can execute different instructions against many data items in parallel).

Until now these computers have been big, expensive, and hard to program and slow to load data, often requiring a conventional processor as a front end. We are now seeing great progress on all these fronts. The superminis and workstations, and specialized vector processing and array processing chips that can attach to conventional processors, are making supercomputing more affordable to a greater number of users. Novel, more distributed secondary storage techniques, where the storage is often associated with the processors, is beginning to solve the I/O bottleneck. Extensions to conventional programming languages (Fortran, Pascal) have been developed that allow them to compile code that will take advantage of the capability for parallel execution. New application algorithms designed to take advantage of parallel processing are being developed and sold as generic software modules for use with these machines.

Part of this wave of new parallel computer architectures is the rise of the neural computer, a controversial architecture patterned after the human brain.

## Neural Networks Computer

Neural networks, as the name suggests, attempt to model the human brain. Neural computers consist of layers (also called slabs) or arrays of processing elements: an input layer, an output layer, and one or more intermediate (or "hidden") layers. In an analogy to the human brain, the processing units can be thought of as neurons and the connections as synapses. Each layer's processing units can be connected to any other unit, although they are most often just connected to units of neighboring layers. Typically, each unit is connected to a large number of input units and outputs to an equally large number of units. The processing elements combine their inputs nonlinearly.

A neural network learns by adaptation; you don't program a neural network, you "teach" it by giving it examples which it attempts to "learn." It adjusts its processing elements thresholds and input weights in response to some measure of its success rate in order to improve its processing accuracy. The knowledge in a neural network is in its connections, their weights, and the learning algorithm by which the neural network adjusts its weights to match its responses to a stimulus.

Every time you use a high-speed modem, you are using a single-neuron, many-synapse neural network developed in the 1950s by neural network pioneer Bernard Widrow of Stanford University. This tiny neural network uses adaptive signal processing to learn and eliminate some of the problems, such as echoing, that may occur.

Artificial neural networks can be implemented in software, in hardware, or in a combination of both. Most systems today simulate neural networks in software, and most run on personal computers. Examples include The TRW Mark V; Martingale Research's SYSPRO, which runs on PCs, IBM mainframes, and the VAX; and SAIC's UNIX-based common LISP neural network simulator. Of course, simulation is much slower than with a hardware implementation. There are two neural network hardware types: (1) accelerator boards to speed processing on conventional computers; and (2) specially designed neurocomputers (a computer with an embedded artificial neural network implemented either in hardware or software), such as the TRW Mark II available to the Department of Defense.

Today many neural network products are commercially available. The oldest and one of the most successful neural network developers is Nestor of Providence, Rhode Island. Other successful neural network companies include Hecht-Nielson and SAIC. Nestor was founded in 1975 by Leon Cooper, a Nobel Prize winner, and Charles Elbaum, a fellow Brown physics professor. Cooper and Elbaum patented the RCE (Restricted Coulomb Energy) neural network configuration, and used it to develop a character recognition system that, after training, converts letters handwritten on a digitizer pad into ASCII. The product is called the Nestor Writer. It consists of 15 interacting neural networks and can detect 97.2 percent of the characters correctly, misidentifying only 2.56 percent, when forced to identify all patterns. They also built a Japanese kanji version that can recognize some 3000 different written characters.

There are already many reported neural network applications. Examples include a production line quality inspection system that is indifferent to changes in the ambient light or object orientation; a check signature forgery detection system with 97 percent accuracy; a system for the State of New York to identify corporate candidates for sales and use tax audits; a claims processing and underwriting system for Blue Cross/Blue Shield; a pattern classification system to analyze and detect abnormal heartbeats monitored by an electrocardiograph; a pattern recognizer that distinguishes between sonar pings and background clutter that outperformed a Bayesian classifier; and an adaptive communications line conditioner balancing the frequency in a long distance call. Other applications include evaluating bank loans; reading handwritten Japanese characters; distinguishing between a submerged rock and a cylinder; teaching machines to read different styles of print; inspecting goods in a manufacturing process; recognizing enemy aircraft from video images; looking for desirable trading situations by analyzing daily and intraday price fluctuations; scanning a database of mortgage applications and loan officers' decisions to come up with mortgage loan approval recommendations.

All these applications have certain factors in common: They are less amenable to solution by either traditional algorithm or rule-based expert systems, and they usually require human perception skills and/or intuitive reasoning, but do not require a complete explanation of how the decision was reached and what it was based on.

Current neural networks are still a far cry from the human brain. The human brain has $10^{15}$ interconnections that fire off electrical impulses at a rate of $10^{16}$ connections per second. Even the brain of a common housefly processes at $10^{9}$ connections per second. In contrast, one of the most powerful neurocomputers, the TRW Mark V neurocomputer, which runs on a $150,000 VAX, has only $10^{7}$ interconnects and a firing rate of only 16 million connections per second. The 80286 Intel computers, where most of the neural simulations take place today, are capable of only 30,000 interconnects and a fire rate of 25,000 connections per second. Moreover, the artificial neural network nodes are much less complex than a real neuron, which has over 42 different distinguishing attributes. (See Appendix 7 for a more detailed comparison of the human brain and both conventional computer systems and advanced parallel processing computer system architectures.)

There still is much work to be done, and the decision on the usefulness of neural networks is still to be made. Most of the applications implemented to date are quite simple, requiring only a little over 100,000 connections. Many practical applications, however, such as analyzing radar and other sensor data, require millions or billions of interconnections. This is orders of magnitude greater than the current technology can provide. We are still not sure that the technology will improve. There is difficulty determining what type of neural network is best for what type of problem. The choice of a neural network architecture for a given problem is still more of an art than a science. There are over 40 different neural network architectures, and the choices keep growing. Table 3.1 lists some of the more popular architectures. Choosing an architecture involves "tweaking" the number of nodes in each layer, the strength of the transmitted signals for input and output, the threshold, the number of elements, the number of layers, and the learning algorithm (the rules by which the thresholds and input weights and biases are adjusted). In many cases, the best neural network architecture may be a hybrid of several of the alternative neural network architectures.

There is also difficulty in determining the proper number of training sets to be presented to the system, and the number of iterations required before the training can be considered done. Recently there have been breakthroughs in the analysis showing that various neural networks can be equated to a network realization of nonlinear regressions analysis, approximation theory representations, and stochastic optimization algorithms such as simulated annealing. These insights may put neural networks on a sounder scientific footing and provide greater insights into their design. (Appendix 13 discusses these issues and the concepts behind neural networks in more detail.)

## Advanced High-Speed Networks

Another trend is to increase the speed (bandwidth/capacity) of computer networks to enhance the ease of file and application sharing over a network to the point where distributed processing can be performed transparently to the user, as if all the files and programs are located in the same machine environment. This becomes particularly important as the concept of distributed processing spreads and networks grow larger and more comprehensive.

In the past, all the files an application needed resided in a single machine. Now these files can be distributed over thousands of locations. Without any computer network speed constraints, we could swap files instantaneously, send messages and run programs at widely separate computer sites. For all practical purposes, the network, from the programmer's and user's perspective, would begin to disappear.

IBM and Carnegie Mellon University have built such an experimental high-speed computer network with these goals in mind (Markoff 1988c). The system

TABLE 3.1. NEURAL NETWORK ARCHITECTURES

| | |
|---|---|
| ADALINE | Hopfield/BAM |
| Adaptive Resonance | Marr/Albus/Gilbert/Pellionisz Cerebellatron |
| Avalance | Neocognitron |
| Backpropagation | Perceptron |
| Boltzman Machine/Cauchy Machine | Probabilistic Neural Network |
| Brain State in a Box | Restricted Coulomb Energy |
| Counterpropagation | Self-organizing Map (Kohonen) |
| Graded Learning Machine | Steinbuck/Wallshaw/Palm Learn Matrix |

is called the Andrew File System (AFS), after Andrew Carnegie and Andrew Mellon. It runs under both IBM's UNIX and OS/2 operating systems. Its software protocols allow different computers to exchange files automatically.

AFS is designed around large file chunks rather than smaller units as its basic element of data transfer and storage. Workstations on the network cache these partial files on a local disk and write modified files back to the file system in their entirety. This requires very high-speed transmission lines. Computers are now connected by medium-speed networks (7000 characters/second, or 56,000 bits/second). This experimental system will replace these lines with communications lines over 30 times that speed (1.5 Mbps, the speed of a T1 line).

IBM is also porting AFS to its MVS operating system as part of a project with the University of Michigan for the National Science Foundation. (Schatz 1988). They are using this system approach to upgrade a portion of the NSF network that links five national supercomputer centers and eight regional network hubs, connecting up to twenty university/research sites. The nodes are IBM RTs and IBM PS/2 under 4.3 UNIX. It uses IBM's Netview network manager, runs on two IBM 4381s, and is managed by the Merit Computer Net, a consortium of eight Michigan State University sites. Their communication lines are being upgraded from 56,000 bits/second to 448,000 bits/second by employing digital microwave and fiber optic technology. Even at these speeds, a typical 1-million-byte file transfer will take between 5 minutes and half an hour during busy periods. For this reason, they plan further upgrades, first to 1.5 million bits/second, and ultimately, in the 1990s, to 45 million bits/second, a speed they estimate is the minimum required for the satisfactory transmission of real-time graphics.

Steve Wolff, networking division director of NSF, thinks a substantial portion of commercial information systems will be using ultra-high-speed links by the end of the 1990s (Schatz, 1988). Several years from now, we will see a half-million users on gigabit per second links.

Still more revolutionary is David Farber's research project. Farber, currently of the University of Pennsylvania, initiated the MEMNET project as a "way of removing the overhead found in distributed operating systems by taking advantage of the ultra high-speed network through a radically new way of looking at the structure of computer systems, instead of tweaking the current protocols." It may mean a rethinking of the protocol layering concept (see Appendix 16 for a review of this layering concept). Farber attempts to convert ultra-high speed (greater than 400 Mbps) computer networks into what he calls memory networks, or MEMNETS. When computers function as MEMNET nodes, they relate to each other as components of a giant virtual computer, each computer using its normal access mechanisms and simply reading and writing to memory addresses.

Farber draws an analogy between his current project and the MIT MULTICS project, one of the first timesharing operating systems. MULTICS was the first system implementation where external storage media were viewed as just an extension of the processor's memory-addressing structure. One advantage of this approach was program simplicity. Farber hopes to take a similar approach for distributed processing.

In his early work on the development of the distributed computer system (DCS) at the University of California at Irvine, Farber extended the interprocess communications of the message-based operating system across the new distributed token ring network. It achieved the equivalent of a shared-memory single-bus multiprocessor by treating ring controllers as I/O control devices. Now he hopes to further simplify this process.

Farber has been responsible for revolutionary new breakthroughs before. He co-developed the first electronic switching telephone system, the SNOBOL Language (a string-manipulating language that was a predecessor of the popular artificial language, LISP), the first eight-bit FORTRAN, the Program Design Language, probably the first distributed computer system, and a few early messaging systems.

## Optical Scanners

Recently there have been radical breakthroughs in the world of scanning and converting drawings, photographs, and text into computer files at affordable prices (Lewis 1988; Markoff 1988b). At the August 1988 Macworld, a new Apple scanner, along with a software package called Omnipage from Caere Corp., was introduced for under $2500. The Apple scanner scans and captures information from a page as bit-mapped graphics, black and white dots. The Omnipage software can read and store text of mixed font, typewritten or typeset. Its software uses advanced character recognition algorithms to read any font, including headlines up to an inch tall, photo captions, and body text, with a consistent accuracy of over 95 percent. PC versions are also available as software and plug-in board combinations from Caere, Palanter Corp., and Kurzweil for about $2500.

These functions previously cost in the $10,000 to $30,000 range. Of course, the more expensive versions run on industrial-size systems and powerful workstation computers. They also are based on older techniques that try to decode and recognize a character at the same time, whereas the newer technologies are based on a series of methods to examine an entire page, making assumptions about the content of the document before attempting to recognize individual characters. Caere's program will first look for dense areas of the page and apply tests to determine if these areas are filled with graphics or text. The system then tries to recognize individual columns, paragraphs, and line spacings. Only after determining where each character lies on the page does it try to identify the individual characters.

## Image Processing

Image processing should become increasingly popular in the 1990s as the technology improves and the prices fall. International Data Corporation, a market research firm, estimates that document image processing will show a compound annual growth rate of 81 percent from 1988 to 1992. The 1992 installed base is expected to exceed 21,000 systems, with finance, government, health care, and manufacturing comprising 87 percent. Other potential industry users include utilities, oil/chemicals, and information services. Temple, Barker, and Sloane, a management consulting firm, predicts a 54 percent annual increase in the electronic imaging market, with growth from $800 million in 1988 sales to $6.8 billion in 1993.

Ninety-five percent of today's information is still stored on paper, according to a study by the Association for Information and Image Management (AIIM). For example, today only 10 percent of banking business information is stored on-line on data processing equipment, while 85 percent of a typical bank's information (checks, charge slips, application forms) is stored on paper and another 5 percent on microfilm. Image processing can capture the majority of information on-line and integrate it with data and text, resulting in both a dramatic reduction of operating costs and improved customer service. This represents a lot of money in paper and storage.

### Benefits

Image processing helps reduce these costs and allows for more convenient and rapid storage and retrieval of these archival off-line files. Consider the experience of Christopher Poole, director of the MasterCom program at MasterCard International, Inc. Government regulations protect a customer from illegitimate charges by allowing a customer to refuse to pay a disputed charge if the merchant's bank cannot supply the customer's bank with a copy of the charge slip within 21 days. Without image processing, when the customer's bank requests a copy of the slip over a terminal, the merchant's bank must locate and mail a copy. The process is costly, about $10 per request, and time-consuming—it normally takes about 14 days for the slip to reach the customer's bank, and sometimes it arrives too late. Poole estimated that 20 to 25 percent of the transactions charged back to the merchant result from late receipt of the charge slip. MasterCard International deployed image capture and communications equipment at member banks to reduce these administrative costs and the possibility of a late sales slip. The system is estimated to save over $200 million annually. Additionally, this new MasterCom system makes the customers happy, because it lets MasterCard handle their retrieval requests much faster. There are many other applications, including the storage and retrieval of student loan documents, bank transactions, engineering drawings, and legal documents.

### System Aspects

The components of an image processing system include scanners for automatic input of text and data; workstations to review, edit, and process the input; indexing systems and databases for storing and retrieving the data; optical disk drives with massive storage capabilities to match the high capacity required to store images; networks and communications devices to exchange the images among work groups, including FAX machines and image compression techniques; and output devices to convert the images back into paper form when necessary.

There are several systems now on the market. IBM announced the ImagePlus family of image processing systems in June 1988, and a future High Performance

Transaction System in April 1989. Wang introduced its Wang Integrated Image Systems (WIIS) in April 1987. It includes an entire architecture with application programming interfaces (APIs), image access protocols, and a family of image servers. Digital Equipment Corporation provides its workstations to Eastman Kodak for use in the Kodak Image Management System (KIMS). In June 1989 Kodak announced faster scanners (can capture 3000 letter-size documents per hour and scan microfilm images), and higher-capacity optical disc subsystems, including a jukebox that can hold more than a terabyte (a trillion bytes) of data with 150 6.8-Gbyte 14-inch optical platters on-line. Kodak also has a low-cost personal computer line. The software lets IBM PC-AT and PS/2 users call up images stored on the DEC VAXstation-based KIMS system.

Other vendors also offer low-cost add-on products. The Hewlett-Packard ScanJet scanners work with Intel 80386-based workstations. Summit Software Corporation in Atlanta offers a system that includes a PC with a 80 Mbyte hard disk, laser printer, high-resolution monitor, scanner, two optical drives, and all the requisite software. Sony Corporation of America's imaging system works with its Sony News Unix workstation and the Unify database management system for indexing. In addition there is Intergraph and other Unix workstation vendors; Bell & Howell's Data Search 8000 Computer-Assisted Retrieval System; Xerox Imaging Systems; Apple scanners; and Microtek scanners.

More advances can be expected in this area using systems based on arrays of common programmable processing elements, such as the AT&T pixel machine, as well as DSP (digital signal processors) and other special-purpose processing elements. To date, much of the work in image processing has centered around the preprocessing stage, which takes raw visual information as input and prepares it for higher-order, more abstract processing. Image acquisition, noise reduction, edge enhancement, and motion detection are examples of preprocessing. Higher-order processing is more complex, generally using artificial intelligence software techniques or neural networks.

## Advanced or High-Definition Television

Television is a primary source of entertainment, and to a lesser but still significant extent, education. Many computer-based games and educational packages are delivered using the television set as a computer screen. The biggest problem with using the television set, rather than a special computer monitor, has been that the television picture is of somewhat marginal resolution quality. All this may change, however, if high-definition television (HDTV) takes off.

These advanced television sets not only provide a much higher-quality picture (35 mm screen image quality in wide screen) but include many more features and functions. They use low-cost workstations and ultrasmart terminals to connect the home to both outside databases and entertainment centers via two-way fiber optic cables or some other high-bandwidth transmission media such as direct satellite broadcast. Various HDTV proposals call for 1050, 1125, or 1250 scanning lines, in contrast to the 525 scanning lines in American and Japanese television today, or the 625 lines in current European TV. They will thus generate a picture that is almost like a photograph.

The ratio of width to height, the aspect ratio, approaches that of a movie screen (typically 16 wide by 9 high, in contrast to current 5-to-9 ratios). This aspect ratio most closely matches the aspect ratio of the human eye, and therefore appears most natural and compatible with our experience. The first HDTV sets will have screens of at least 30 inches on the diagonal. Today's engineering workstations have comparable or better resolution than an HDTV display, but are expensive and smaller, and have a different aspect ratio.

HDTV includes such features as a picture-in-picture (PIP) display, which allows you to select and view 1, 3, or 9 PIP images on the screen at once. You can also store, edit, swap pictures, and make adjustments using controls displayed on the screen. To achieve this functionality, HDTV will use state-of-the-art electronics. This is the reason it is viewed by many as a strategic market. Potential HDTV sales are predicted to total $40 billion a year worldwide by 2010, with $11 billion in the United States alone. Some 10 percent of U.S. households are predicted to own one or more HDTV sets four years after their introduction in 1993, and 25 percent by the year 2000. By 2003, HDTV is estimated to hold a 32.5 percent market share of all color television receivers sold. If it sells at this level, it will provide a massive production base for leading-edge semiconductors, microprocessors, microcontrollers, and application-specific integrated circuit (ASIC) devices. It is feared that whoever captures this market will capture the future markets for these key electronic devices as well. Japan has spent over $1 billion over the last 15 years, and is currently building and selling these high-definition television sets domestically and intends to export them in the near future. European manufacturers (Siemens, Phillips, Thomson-CSF) are also pursuing this new technology. Europeans will spend $200 million per year in a crash catch-up program.

Until recently, the United States has had no large entry in the field. In March 1989, Zenith and AT&T announced a joint project aimed at producing a high-definition television. They hope to combine the research and semiconductor expertise of AT&T with the manufacturing capability and television expertise of Zenith. They are targeting to produce a receiver at a price of $1000 to $2000. This is less than the $3000 initially targeted by several Japanese firms. The possibility also exists for a joint U.S.–European effort (European TV and U.S. microprocessors and ASICs) to counter the Japanese introduction. An analysis by the American Electronic Association Advanced Television Task Force predicts grim consequences unless U.S. chipmakers win a major share of the HDTV market. American companies currently hold about 70 percent of the world's PC market. They can hold onto that share if they grab 50 percent of the HDTV market by 2010. But the PC market share will drop to 35 percent if they obtain 10 percent or less of the HDTV market. For this reason, the Defense Advanced Projects Agency has agreed to spend $30 million for HDTV research. American HDTV pioneer William Glenn of the New York Institute of Technology feels the only way the United States can regain leadership in this field is through a radical technology shift, like flat panel displays, that would make existing plants obsolete, just as the transistor killed the vacuum tube industry.

There is some dispute about the outcome of HDTV. The consumer is probably not asking for HDTV. Indeed, other consumer products, such as quadriphonic sound, have been rolled out with great expectations, only to be rejected by the marketplace. There is also the issue of possible interference due to HDTV's very wide bandwidth, and the need to protect the investments of millions of TV owners. People should not be forced to scrap their current sets just to be able to continue to watch TV; TV broadcasts should be able to support both the old and the new receivers without interference. A coalition from the U.S. broadcasting and television industry has launched the Advanced Television Test Center in Alexandria, Virginia, to test and evaluate the many proposals for HDTV advanced transmission systems. Proponents of advanced TV systems are invited to submit their systems for technical and subjective tests devised in cooperation with the Federal Communications Commission's advisory committee. The tests will measure quality, resistance to interference, and operating characteristics of the new system in the electronic environment.

Many critics of HDTV claim that the current generation of high-resolution workstations will become the preferred device, capable of interactively displaying TV and computer-generated images and responding to user commands. (As currently proposed, HDTV does not accommodate digital information.) Not surprisingly, many of these critics include the current leading computer and workstation manufacturers. Apple Computer believes that the U.S. standard should accommodate digital information, improving the link between computers and video. So, television has the potential of growing into a multipurpose appliance.

A recent move in this direction occurred when the popular video game manufacturer, Nintendo, joined with AT&T to offer an interactive videotext service based on using Nintendo's computer-based game device as the interactive intelligent interface between the phone and the TV.

Ultimately, the entertainment and home computer markets will merge and create endless possibilities, including an integrated home entertainment and service center with the following components and features:

*Components*

- TV
- Stereo
- Home alarm systems and security monitors
- Computer
- Telephone
- Laser printer
- Videodisk

*Features*

- The ability to download books, movies, and games from electronic libraries
- Interactive TV with joystick, keypad, and/or keyboard for entering text and data to support:
  - video games
  - home banking
  - on-line gambling
  - two-way game shows

participative town hall meetings
televideo shopping
home editing

This increased functionality includes the eventual blending of photographic quality images, digital audio, compact disk, digital phones, ISDN, "smart" phones that can display the number of the calling party, a combined facsimile-copier-printer machine, and a data processor. High definition television (HDTV) could accelerate this trend.

## DECISION SUPPORT AND EXECUTIVE INFORMATION SYSTEMS

There is a lot of confusion and overlap between EIS (executive information systems, also called executive support systems and executive decision support), DSS (decision support systems), MIS (management information systems), and office automation. These systems differ mostly in the level of the decision-maker, the repetitiveness and structure of the decisions made, and the extent to which the system is data-intensive versus model-oriented.

It is important to understand the business decision-making process in order to appreciate how these support systems can help in decision-making (the decision-making process is discussed in Appendix 5). It is also useful to understand the nature of the different basic business activities in order to appreciate the types of decisions people must deal with in business (Appendix 3 discusses these basic business activities).

EIS is designed to support the top management—the CEO and senior managers reporting directly to the CEO. EIS contains elements of all the various support systems just discussed, but because of the nature of the jobs, interests, and tasks of senior management, EIS is more communication-oriented, deals more with softer, less quantitative, objective information, and is more data-oriented than model-oriented. It is designed to enable the executive to monitor, disseminate external information, perform a liaison function, coordinate, motivate, and lead.

DSS is concerned with more complex, longer-term decisions. Accordingly, DSS not only uses data, it includes forecasting, modeling, expert systems, and sensitivity analysis in support of planning and decision support. DSS analyzes the effects of future actions in order to establish a decision, policy, or rule of behavior. MIS tasks are focused to assist the decision-maker in the more operationally-oriented decision tasks. It is therefore characterized by summary reporting of such information as sales, order status, production, and inventory in support of management control. It is used to analyze current status, given a decision rule or policy, to determine the degree of compliance with some standard of performance. Office automation tasks are characterized as word processing, electronic mail, calendars, and personnel scheduling. These tasks use the computer to effect office-oriented transactions often related indirectly to decision-making.

DSS, MIS, and office automation are well-established applications that have frequently been written up and discussed. Accordingly, we will concentrate on the newer concepts of executive information and the related concepts of systems groupware and visualization. Groupware is a relatively new concept. It is software designed to enhance group problem-solving, decision-making, and task collaboration. Visualization involves the use of advanced interactive graphics to assist in problem-solving and decision-making. As we will see, none of these newer concepts really involves a new technology, but rather combines and adapts many existing technologies to support a new user or user concept.

## Executive Information Systems

The idea of executive information systems was first introduced by Rockhart and Treacy in their 1981 *Harvard Business Review* article. It was later expanded on by others, including Scott Morton and Peter Keen. EIS uses elements from DSS, MIS, and office automation, but with a different orientation and emphasis. It is more unstructured, with more emphasis on external data than MIS, more data-intensive, with more built-in reporting structure than DSS, and more communication- and schedule-oriented than office automation.

Top managers are most remote from the firm's operations so they need status information to keep track of the firm's performance. Their focus is more strategic, dealing with planning and analysis activities that are less well-defined, with longer time horizons, less structure, and often involving conflicting measures of performance. Therefore, their information needs are more qualitative and subjective and require a lot of external data on competitors, regulatory, political, and social factors. Hands-on access is not important for a successful EIS. What is important is the need for the executive to identify for him or herself what information should be available, through what medium, in what format, and with what frequency.

The growth of executive information systems is controversial. Some think it is only a short-lived craze, while others think it is a fundamental management trend. There have been many failures, and top managers remain split in their opinion on the need for and importance of EIS. Edgar Schein of the Sloan School of MIT and research associate Diane Wilson surveyed 71 CEOs with respect to their attitude towards EIS. Fifty-seven percent see potential benefits, but they also see the potential for major problems, including hidden costs, technical difficulties, and organizational resistance. The results were mixed: 19 percent were ambivalent, 22 percent were extremely positive, 2 percent were skeptical, and 34 percent said that they made some use of computers (DeLong 1988). IBM is betting on EIS and recently entered into a joint venture with Comshare to market Comshare's products.

Today only 10 to 15 percent of businesses' senior managers regularly use computers, but experts like Robert Berlond, vice-president of IBM applications systems division, forecasts that in ten years more than half will be using them (DeLong 1988). Computers are becoming an integral part of the way more executives run their companies. They use it to check on the competition and to communicate with subordinates. Charles Harper, chairman and CEO of Conagra Corp., a $10 billion food and agricultural products company, uses the PC to check grain prices, to look at updated economic forecasts from Washington, to scan the Dow Jones service for analysts' views on the earnings prospects of a company he wants to buy, and to review weekly profit estimates for some key operating divisions. He also gets 70 percent of his internal correspondence through his computer. He can meet weekly with senior staff and the presidents of his business units, even though they are physically apart, because they are linked by phone and computer terminals. In this case, as in many others, the applications and computers used are hardly noteworthy, but the user is (DeLong 1988). The user is what most vividly defines the EIS system.

Other examples of EIS systems abound (DeLong 1988; Rockhart and DeLong 1988). Robert Wallace, president of Phillips 66, says: "Companies that are reluctant to move electronic information into the executive suite are naive, . . . and [this will be] a significant limitation on their managerial and competitive ability in the 1990's." E. James Ferland, CEO of Public Service Enterprise Group, a Newark-based utility holding company, checks the daily output of his power stations and monitors the news services. Thomas Plaskett, chairman of Pan Am, uses computers to track his airline's service, its dependability, and the reasons for any late flights. James Orr III, chairman and CEO of UNUM Life Insurance Company, uses computers to check the daily claims activity and staffing levels. He likes the fact that the whole staff looks at the same data; he finds that this cuts through discussions quickly.

Beneficial Corp.'s CEO likes electronic mail. He finds that it improves the speed of decision-making because messages no longer languish in interoffice mail or the in-basket. He now gets responses to questions within hours, not weeks as previously. CEOs say they want help with the tasks of communications and analysis and monitoring of business performance and the external environment. The most common use of computers by executives today is for monitoring purposes.

This increased usage of computers by senior executives is being brought about by several factors. One cause is the advent of more powerful PCs with more user-friendly software designed for executive use. These software packages can combine text, graphics, and numbers in customizable formats. Examples of this type of software include the Pilot's Command Center and Comshare's Commander EIS. Another reason is the natural progression of younger middle managers, who were schooled in a different era and are computer-savvy. They are getting promoted, and they are bringing their skills and interest in technology into their new offices.

A most important point, agreed to by many CEOs, is the increasingly uncertain political and economic climate. This climate has made business more complex and competitive, and is requiring more information to be provided more quickly to the executive. This increased need for more timely information has come at a time when there has been widespread corporate downsizing in order to stay competitive. There are fewer staff analysts to do this increasingly more complex analysis and more computer support is needed.

One benefit of EIS is that it seems to help break down hierarchical structures and to permit more rapid response to the marketplace in more global, volatile, and uncertain times. EIS is leading to a new type of infrastructure, and to a new breed of computer usage patterns and applications that are specifically designed for these patterns. When executives start using computers, a common result is that it begins to shift and change the management process. In the past, we used computers to support individual management. Now, with software products like Groupware, software is being structured to support management teams.

Xerox redesigned its strategic planning process as a result of the introduction of computers in the executive suite. Under the new process, each business unit submits its business plans in a five-page format to corporate management over the company's electronic network. To see how this new process works, consider the following hypothetical situation. Imagine that the West Coast unit submitted a plan that Paul Allaire, Xerox's president, considered too risky. He tells his managers to find alternatives to cut the resource requirements and lower the risk. A new set of strategic options is developed and sent over the network. Then a video conference is set up to hash out the revised strategic plan. Plans developed this way are more thoughtful, gain the involvement of a much larger group of executives, and are produced in a shorter time.

## Groupware

Groupware is not really a new technology; it is a concept that combines and adapts many existing technologies to conform to the user's organization and way of doing business. Groupware is software for a group of people working together. We should all be familiar with electronic mail and bulletin boards. Electronic mail has several unique attributes that distinguish it from most other communications vehicles. It bridges distance and time zones, allowing users to send and receive mail at different times and locations, and it tends to flatten the hierarchical lines of communications.

Groupware builds on top of these communications and computer concepts to help groups of workers do their jobs better. Groupware is a collection of software, systems, and services that works in two ways:

- Regulating work content
- Controlling workflow

Groupware manages data actively, classifying, presenting different views to different users, and combining data from different sources into more meaningful shared information.

Groupware is also concerned with who has what files (text, image, data) and who should have them, monitoring the assignment and completion of tasks.

Groupware understands that there are different kinds of users, with different views of data, that there are different sources of data, and that work may flow in different ways from user to user. Groupware maintains a knowledge of people and their various functions, roles, locations, and information-sharing needs.

The intention of groupware is not to automate the data-intensive, person-intensive tasks formerly done by clerks and operators. Groupware is aimed at professionals for whom a large part of their job is interaction and coordination. Their work, although routine in its outlines, is different in each instance, requiring a varying combination of persons and machines to get the job done. Groupware is aimed at improving the effectiveness of these less structured work group activities, and may ultimately change how people work. Another name for Groupware is collaborative computing, because it is an extension of the natural interchange that goes on between people in the workplace. It is aimed at modeling and adapting a system to a business's unique operations—its internal flows, channels of responsibility and lines of communications, including exceptions as well as recurring events. Whereas the initial focus of the PC and workstation was task automation, the initial focus of groupware is to automate the flows of information between individuals, work groups, functional groups, divisions, and countries.

Groupware models the organization by having the system build its own files (storing parameters, subroutines, and rules), and maintain a directory of its users with passwords, roles, privileges, plus the databases for the applications it manages. Communications management is a cornerstone of the concept. Messages, directories, and processing tasks are organized, prioritized, scheduled, controlled, and routed according to the organization's lines of communication and the procedures they are to support.

In order to use groupware, all users must use the same syntax and the same uniform system structures. Groupware is a relatively new and still unproved concept; there are no standards. Several different systems have been built around different visions:

- A data and forms orientation
- An agent-centered orientation
- A work center orientation
- A transaction-based orientation

The data and forms approach manages paper flow through the organization. This is accomplished by following a piece of actual paper through its life cycle. An example of this type of implementation is FCMC's Staffware. The agent approach divides the work among people and assigns them each a role (e.g., Hewlett Packard's New Wave). The work center approach looks at combinations of tasks that are performed in concert by department or work groups (such as Coordination Technologies' BCOS/Orgware). The transaction model maintains a careful status and history of all the work items opened and closed (e.g., Action Technologies' Conversation Manager.)

Paul Saffo describes one revolutionary application at the University of Arizona's Decision and Planning Lab, where groupware software is used to assist in making business meetings more efficient and effective, even when all parties are in the same room (Saffo 1990). It provides tools designed to facilitate meetings. They are broken into the following five groupings:

- Brainstorming
- Issue analysis
- Prioritizing
- Policy formation
- Stockholder identification

Although you might question the need and usefulness of computer communications tools for people meeting in the same room, this paper presents some surprising results. For example, an IBM study reports a personal savings of more than 50 percent, and a 92 percent reduction in time to complete a project through the use of these tools. (These systems and other examples of groupware are discussed in more detail in Appendix 14.) Groupware is still in its infancy. Many commercially available products are naive and do not properly reflect the work setting. Other groupware products, such as Lotus Notes, a group communications tool, have received rave reviews.

## Graphics for Scientific Analysis (Visualization)

Another advanced form of decision support involves the interactive use of high-resolution, multidimensional graphics. Graphics are beginning to be used in unconventional ways to supplement applications that have traditionally been associated more with number crunching, like engineering and scientific calculations. Researchers are using pictures and movies to simplify the presentation of their answers and to gain new insights (Markoff 1988d). People generally have a much easier time getting intuitive insights from pictures than they do from numbers and tables of formulas. They can gain insights and deeper understanding faster by manipulating design parameters and instantly seeing the results in graphic and/or pictorial form.

The user can explore a design or concept by interacting directly with a picture or graphic—rotating, translating, or changing its parameters. For example, engineers now design cars, airplanes, and computer circuits by interactively manipulating three-dimensional graphic images. Wolfram Research, Inc., is using this technology to develop software tools to permit mathematicians to view equations as three-dimensional images with its product MATHEMATICA. University of Illinois scientists visually modeled a transistor to watch it switch on and off, and also developed a three- and higher-dimensional model of a thunderstorm. Medical researchers at the University of Colorado are modeling human cadavers. Physicists at Los Alamos National Laboratory are viewing the progress of the solution of partial differential equations with three-dimensional models. They can control the program by directing the computer to focus on certain portions of the solution. Neurobiologists at the University of California at Berkeley modeled a single neuron in a cricket's brain. To accomplish these objectives, scientists have begun to use supercomputers, like the Cray III, with high-resolution graphics.

More recently, a class of smaller desktop supercomputers has been designed specifically to display graphics for this sort of application. These desktop supercomputers are built by companies like Pixar, Inc., and Stardent Computer.

The use of images instead of numbers to aid in problem-solving and scientific analysis has the potential to produce a fundamental change in the way researchers think and work. It should allow scientists to spend more time thinking purely about their sciences and less worrying about the mechanics of experiments. These technologies should present similar opportunities in other areas. In the financial community, they should allow "financial engineers" to focus on the business transaction concepts rather than the computational details.

## SOFTWARE DEVELOPMENT AND MAINTENANCE

Software development and maintenance is big business. An International Data Corp. study sponsored by the federal government estimated the 1985 worldwide bill for workers who design and code software at $139 billion (Feder 1988). Maintenance requirements grow with each new application. The cost is growing, and there are not sufficient programming personnel to do all the work.

In addition, good information systems are becoming a more important and integral part of a business's goals. Many large banks have literally staked their futures on their ability to deliver and maintain complex software packages on time and within budget in order to gain a competitive advantage. So it is important that software (a) not fail, (b) keep up with the changes in the business, and (c) is reliable and free of error. A vivid demonstration of the key role software plays was the breakdown of the AT&T long-distance service on Monday, January 15, 1990 (Barron 1990). Because of a flaw in a new release of computer software for the switching system, half the long-distance, international, and toll-free 800 class calls dialed on its network were not completed. At one point, the network was described as "chaotic and almost out of control" by a company technician. This failure hurt AT&T, which advertises its reliability against its chief competitors, MCI and Sprint. It also hurt many businesses that rely on the network, like hotels, airlines, travel agencies, home shopping services, telemarketers, and computerized information-retrieval services, to name a few.

Yet software development remains a lengthy, manpower-intensive, error-prone process. These deficiencies must be overcome if business is to achieve its future goals. Technology advances are approaching this problem on several fronts:

- CASE: Providing automated assistance to the traditional life cycle development process
- Reusable software: Making it easier to share and build on existing software modules and packages
- End-user programming: Simplifying the programming process until the original goals of the early fourth-generation languages (FOCUS, RAMIS) are finally fully met and the end user can program without the need for any special training, or the need to have a sophisticated understanding of computers and computer software.

### CASE Technology

Computer-assisted software engineering (CASE) technology promises to alleviate the software development bottleneck. The CASE field is still relatively immature and unproved, although it is growing in popularity, and a track record is slowly being built. Approximately $100 million in CASE products were sold in 1987, and International Data Corp. expects that figure to reach over $1 billion in the 1990s. CASE was further legitimatized when IBM made the CASE products part of its AD/Cycle SAA strategy in 1990.

There are several testimonials both for and against the technology. CASE is promoted as making software products that are more consistent, of better quality, easier to maintain and reuse, and that support prototyping. For example, du Vair of Irving Trust states: "Software written with CASE has a useful life of 3 to 4 times that of human [produced] software" (Feder 1988). However, there are many who feel that CASE is still relatively unproved. Peter Levin of Gartner Group states: "CASE suffers from protracted immaturity" (Feder 1988).

The concepts behind CASE, plus its products, are summarized in Appendix 15. CASE tools can be directed to assist in one or more of the three classic phases of software development, namely:

1. *Front-end tools* (also known as Upper CASE), to help in the analysis, design, and document phases of systems development
2. *Back-end tools* (back-end CASE), to automatically convert program specifications into code like COBOL or FORTRAN
3. *Life-cycle tools,* to help document and maintain existing code

Unfortunately, most current products fail to satisfy all three needs. A few life cycle packages have truly integrated front and back ends (I-CASE or Integrated CASE). They include: Texas Instruments' IEF; Knowledgeware's ADW/IEW; CGI Systems' Pacbase; Anderson's Foundation; Software AG's Predict; CASE's Natural; and Seer's HPS. Most of the leading front-end CASE products employ an open architecture, making it relatively easy to create bridges between the front and back ends. Maintaining these bridges, however, requires user effort. One drawback is the lack of industry standards that would allow various CASE products to be designed to work together. Strongly associated with CASE is the concept of a Repository, a library of tools and data definitions that would be used and maintained in conjunction with CASE products.

Most CASE products require fundamental changes in current software management practices that will sharply curtail programmer freedom. The use of CASE often leads to dramatic changes in the way we organize to build software. With CASE, programmer teams get smaller, and the same people tend to manage a project from start to finish. Additionally, contrary to their reputation, some CASE products are not that easy to learn and master.

Today, over 50 to 60 percent of effort goes into maintaining old software rather than developing new software. Currently, 85 to 90 percent of business applications are written in some version of COBOL; this adds up to over 80 billion lines of COBOL code. CASE tools have focused almost exclusively on the design and coding of new software. This is a significant shortcoming, but the task of reverse engineering and retrofitting old code to the new CASE technology is a difficult problem.

COBOL dates back to the 1950s. It is one of the worst languages to maintain because it is easy to change the meaning of a portion of code by modifying or inserting software somewhere else in the program, perhaps thousands of commands earlier. Furthermore, different programmers have vastly different ways of expressing themselves in COBOL, so there is usually little consistency in the code. The result is what is often termed "spaghetti code," and it generally requires restructuring before it can be maintained manually. Certainly restructuring is required before there is any hope of using a more automated maintenance tool. There are several restructuring products on the market that lend automated assistance to this effort. They include Language Technologies' Recoder and XA/System's Structured Retrofit. A problem with restructuring is that it perpetuates conventional third-generation manual programming. A better approach would be to reverse-engineer the old codes so that they would be interpreted in terms of front-end CASE design documents and graphics, and to make future changes from that foundation.

Reverse engineering is still in its infancy. It is a hard problem and only a handful of CASE companies have begun to attack this retrofitting problem. They include Language Technology, Inc.; Viasoft, Inc.; Adpac's PMSS; XA System's DataTec; Bachman Information System's Reverse Engineering Product; IBM; and Peat Marwick. They all work slightly differently. Language Technologies' product, Recorder, analyzes the structure of the COBOL program and then rearranges it. Viasoft's ViaInsight highlights one part of COBOL and asks to see the other parts it interacts with. Bachman provides tools to restructure the databases. It allows the user to insert data and see how it would change the diagram of the data structure.

Most existing CASE products are targeted toward the large mainframe market. According to a study by Focus Research Systems, 21.3 percent of IBM 309X sites and 12 percent of IBM 308x sites (these are the large IBM mainframes) use CASE tools, whereas only 5.7 percent of all IBM mainframes and compatible sites are using CASE tools. The conclusion is that large sites are currently the most likely to adopt CASE.

This emphasis on new mainframe software development may be a mistake. CASE cannot yet retrofit old code, and businesses are increasingly turning to developing new applications on smaller networked machines. Traditional CASE tools still generate mostly procedural COBOL applications that execute on mainframes and communicate in screens or panels (e.g., Query Management Facility in IBM's OS/2 extended database manager). Even though many CASE products are built on top of workstation technology and exploit many of the latest advances in human–machine interaction in their own use, they do not yet implement the new, more interactive applications and human–machine paradigms (discussed in this chapter and in Chapter 5) like group coordination, rich data structures and graphics, heterogeneous environments, cross-system communications, and proactive system-initiated exception handling). In the design products they produce, CASE systems could include these new advances; the obstacles preventing this are cultural, not technological. In the mid 1990s, however, several workstation-based software vendors (primarily database and fourth-generation language) have begun to incorporate CASE functionality with the advanced interface features into their products.

## Reusable Software

The concept of reusable software is closely related to CASE and automated programming. Some problems get solved over and over again. These include such areas as laying out displays, managing user interactions, trading data and sharing files, sharing work, managing and manipulating calendar and date functions, and arranging schedules and trips. For software to be reusable, we need to be able to link subroutines for sharing across multiple programs. Several techniques exist that will do this. The first is the original concept of the macro, where a programmer can specify a routine within a program in a shorthand that is expanded at compile time. LOTUS 1-2-3 introduced a different sort of macro. Lotus macros allow the user to create macros by recording actions, or commands, and then editing the listing. These commands can also be developed in response to a series of prompts, or written as a listing from scratch.

Command languages or shell procedures (e.g., JCL, Exec and REXX on IBM) allow a user to address the operating system and the applications directly, conditionally controlling the scheduling of applications, inputting variables, and the like. Another technique uses templates, or code structures with variables or parameters left empty or easily changed, allowing for customization without recoding.

"Frontware" is a term coined by the Gartner group. It refers to a class of tools for building GUI (graphical user interface) front ends to existing unmodified host applications. They include WYSIWYG (what you see is what you get) GUI generators with screen mapping parameters from the GUI to the appropriate terminal emulator response. Terminal emulators supported usually include 3270 and VT100 terminals. Examples of these products include:

*For DOS machines*
- EASEL (DOS and OS/2)
- Mozart System's Mozart
- MultiSoft's Superlink

*For Macintosh*
- MITEM's MitemView

Object-oriented programming concepts offer a particularly attractive technology for enhancing the reusability of software (see the section on object-oriented programming for a fuller treatment).

All these techniques can be combined to form "standard" user interface libraries of reusable subroutines. Templates can be maintained for user interface constructs, command interpreters, menus, prompts, and graphic objects.

## End User Languages

One way to reduce the cost and time associated with software development is to let the end users do their design and programming. In this context, end user means someone who does not program for a living. The end user fourth-generation languages on the mainframe (FOCUS, RAMIS) greatly increased programmer productivity, but failed to provide a truly universal end user environment. Only the sophisticated, computer literate end user actually programs in these languages.

The PC toolkit (dBIII+, Paradox, LOTUS) has gone still further toward the goal of end user programming. The marriage of these PC tools with a large library of reusable software; a nonprocedural problem specification language (where you tell the computer what you want, not how to do it); an artificial intelligence logic inferencer; and an advanced user interface that transparently integrates software and data across distributed heterogeneous processors through an intuitive, easy to learn, visually oriented user environment (programming by point and click, selection and moving of icons, names, boxes, and links) finally holds the promise of achieving the original goal of do-it-yourself end user programming. Steven Jobs' NEXT computer's programming environment, NEXTSTEP, and the METAPHOR software environment recently licensed by IBM, come close to achieving this goal.

## CONCLUSION

Many of the key advances in computing show a general trend toward more direct end user involvement and interactive use, a greater integration of the various types of applications, interfaces and information media, and an extension of the role of the computer toward greater assistance in the actual decision-making process. Some of these advances include expert systems, where computers are programmed to capture and mimic human expertise; object-oriented programming, which lends itself to user-directed programming through manipulation of icon representations of objects; natural language processing and speech processing (both input recognition and output generation), making the computer interface more natural, intelligent, and human-like; hypertext, which organizes information to more naturally conform to the way humans think and associate; and multimedia databases, which address the integrated management and control of all forms of information: data, text, image, sound. There are also advanced user interfaces, which combine various media and advanced programming techniques to make the computer easier, more natural, and more fun to interact with and to instruct; groupware, which networks computers together to more naturally support the kind of work group/team problem-solving structures so common in business and in society; executive information systems, which are designed to support that most difficult and demanding customer of all, the CEO; neural networks, where the computer parallel-processes, adapts, and learns patterns in much the same manner as we believe the human brain does; and high-speed networks that promise simpler and revolutionary new ways of interfacing remotely distributed computers to share and cooperate in processing tasks.

# 4

# The Current Status of Technology

Current computer applications can be classified in terms of the following categories: number crunching, text processing, symbolic reasoning, image processing, speech processing, database utilities, entertainment, and education. All these categories can be shown to have applicability to the business world. In each category, there is a clear trend toward greater ease of use and the expansion of the role of the computer to that of a problem-solving assistant. These applications and their trends are discussed in the following sections.

Additionally, we see a trend toward greater standardization, linking, and integration of the different application specialties. Larry Smarr, an astrophysicist who directs the National Center for Supercomputing Applications, envisions a laboratory where technologies like high-resolution graphics, artificial intelligence, voice recognition, and supercomputing will come together to produce the ultimate scientist's apprentice (Markoff 1988c).

This can be achieved through networking. "The central computer facility used to be the heart of an information system, and its networks and terminals were considered peripherals. Today the heart of the information system is becoming the intelligent network, an integrated system of communication and business applications" (Frank 1990). The network peripherals have become an array of attached PCs, file servers, special processors, and mainframes. The computer age is quickly becoming the network age.

Accompanying this growth of the network is a growing demand for a common architecture, across different machines, that can provide the user with a single environment which can manage and coordinate multiple concurrent processes. This desire for greater integration, linking, and sharing of special resources has been accompanied by two trends: distribution and sharing of various specialized resources across a network; and greater standardization of the basic hardware and software component building blocks.

This latter trend results in two benefits: It becomes easier for various distributed (often specialized) heterogeneous computing processors to talk, to cooperate, and to share tasks and information; and basic computer hardware and software components become "commoditized" (commodity-like), resulting in increased vendor competition and thus further acceleration of the trend toward cheaper, high-performance, easy-to-use components. Finally, we see a transformation of the software applications from custom-designed turnkey solutions (addressing a specific problem) to (1) more generic product software (addressing a class of problems); and (2) a software environment that serves as a toolkit for building custom packages for vertically tailored environments in which the user can do his or her own exploratory problem-solving without prior computer expertise.

This reflects an emerging philosophy toward software—characterized by the following quote: "Don't give the user a hammer and boards to build a house, but don't give the user a finished house either. Let him custom design his house and then build it automatically with pre-fab parts. And make sure that the plumbing in the bathroom uses the same kind of pipes as that in the kitchen" (*Release 1.0,* December 30, 1987).

## NUMBER CRUNCHERS

Number crunchers includes computer models, analytics, simulators, statistical analysis packages (SAS, SPSS), spreadsheets (LOTUS, EXCEL), special mathematical languages and packages (interactive matrix-based languages such as APL; mathematical optimization routines such as MPSX; symbolic mathematical packages such as MACSYMA and MATHEMATICA); and business-specific packages (financial accounting). There is a clear trend toward augmenting and improving these packages with respect to their human–machine communications and their problem-solving capability, as well as toward introducing specialized hardware like vector processors and math co-processors to speed up and support ever more sophisticated and demanding calculations. The evolutionary upgrade of the popular LOTUS software illustrates this trend. Over the years, LOTUS has been augmented by the addition of natural language and speech input modules, improved graphics output, links to other application packages such as database and word processing modules, and the inclusion of goal-seeking, problem-oriented commands.

## SYMBOLIC REASONING

Artificial-intelligence-based packages add an additional specialty, systems optimized for qualitative symbolic reasoning and logical inferencing. This capability for reasoning about words, concepts, and relationships is being integrated into all the various application areas. For example, mathematical packages such as MACSYMA and MATHEMATICA include the capability for reasoning about mathematics relationships and formula manipulations. Many text processors are adding the capability for limited text understanding.

## TEXT PROCESSORS

Text processors include word processors and desktop publishing systems. There is also a clear trend toward augmenting and improving text processors' human–machine communications and problem-solving capability. Some systems are even beginning to provide a limited capability for text understanding. Word processors now come with spelling checkers, grammatical and style correctors, and outlining and indexing capabilities. Desktop publishing includes layout planning assistance, and provides control over the processes of producing typeset commands, including the production of multiple fonts, multiple copies, two-sided copies, binding, and compatibility with most of the graphics and printing standards, such as Postscript.

Consider the following examples. Microsoft's Word for Windows combines advanced "what you see is what you get (WYSIWYG)" style interaction, word processing, desktop publishing features, an easy-to-use graphic command structure, and powerful tools for customization. It can create dynamic links with other applications such as Microsoft's EXCEL. For example, it can create a "hot link" so when you input data in an EXCEL spreadsheet, it changes the corresponding linked data, formulas, and graphs in the word document file.

Data Conversion Lab provides software to use for editing headlines, for boldface, for extra spacing, and for providing cues in organizing material, including reading and analyzing indexes.

## IMAGE PROCESSORS

Image processing, which is concerned with the capture, enhancement, manipulation, storage, display and management of images (textual, graphic, and pictorial), has become more affordable and practical. It does not necessarily involve the reading and understanding of the image, just its faithful replication and storage. Many of these systems are being integrated to provide other related capabilities, such as fax transmission, optical character recognition software, and document management systems.

Image processing includes animation, 3D modeling, and graphics packages which vary from mainframe-based graphics packages such as TELEGRAF and SASGRAPH to numerous PC- and workstation-based products. Here the trend is toward more interaction and more capability in the problem-solving area. Assistance is provided in art layout and planning, translation of desired screen graphics and artwork to any number of printers and plotters, both color and black and white, reduction and magnification, and cut and paste. PCs are now even capable of producing photo-realistic images. Pixar provides Renderman, a language for describing how images are to be shaded and drawn. For 3D images it is analogous to Postscript, the software developed by Adobe Systems for describing how a printed page should look.

Image processing is also being incorporated into other packages such as desktop publishing and video processing. We can now purchase computer hardware and software that allow us to add computer graphics to video presentations, both directly on TV screens, on computer monitors, and on video recorders. Current product offerings in this area include Computer Friends for the MAC II and Truevision Inc., for IBM-compatible PCs. Television and movie sequences can now be recorded on optical disk and driven by software to produce integrated output superimposed with text, graphics, and animation.

## SPEECH PROCESSORS

Speech has important advantages as an input medium. It remains the most natural form of human communication. Studies have shown that speech can be the most efficient form of communication for handling many problems. Casual users with relatively little training could access a computer that was capable of receiving speech input. Speech is the fastest mode of communication (about twice as fast as the average typist). Speech input allows free use of the hands and eyes for pointing, manipulating a display, flying an aircraft, controlling a device, watching a quote screen, making a bid, or making a repair.

As speech recognition and speech generation systems grow in capability at reduced cost, they should increasingly be integrated into all systems that interact with the user. Speech offers great potential for improving and making the user interface friendlier and more natural.

## DATABASE UTILITIES

Database utilities store, retrieve, and maintain all manner of data. Traditionally this has meant numerical or formatted text, but more recently database management systems have been extended to include freeform, spreadsheet, text, and graphics (pictorial) information. Database utilities have also become more user friendly, and extended to manage distributed databases and intelligent retrieval. Intelligent retrieval includes the integration of natural language interfaces, expert system technology, and improved output specification and generation (e.g., Query By Example). Database-oriented languages, such as FOCUS and ADABAS, have been extended to include artificial intelligence and natural language capabilities.

## ENTERTAINMENT AND EDUCATION

Games have been the chief source of computer-based entertainment. These include games of manual dexterity like Pac-man; games of mental skill like Adventure; and simulation games like Flight Simulator, which demand both mental skill and manual dexterity.

Computer-based education started out as little more than electronic textbooks. Soon animation and game-like qualities were added to increase user interest; simulation games geared toward modeling aspects of the subject matter were developed. If the subject were French, for example, we would find ourselves in the middle of Paris, stopping people and trying to find a good restaurant, or rather "un bon restaurant." If the subject matter were human anatomy, we would be exploring and dissecting a computer-generated model of a human body.

More recently, efforts have centered around analyzing the student's interactions and answers, using these responses to create a model of the student's needs and learning abilities, and tailoring future system responses, questions, and lessons on this model. There have been similar attempts to modify and adjust the difficulty of the game to fit the perceived model of the current players and their abilities.

Many of the features and ideas originally developed in the entertainment field are also proving useful for business systems. For example, Interactive Video Disk Technology (IVDT) is part of a touch display system at Disney Epcot Center and the World Trade Center, which is used to order and pay by inserting a credit card. Advertisements in electronic form can be scanned and selected. IVDT is a particularly efficient storage medium where 1 laser disk is equal in capacity to 60,000 floppy disks. People enjoy interacting with this system because it is like an extension of a video game.

## A CASE FOR STANDARDS

Today most of a business's systems are incompatible, resulting in the multiple appearance of data in inconsistent or inaccessible forms, a prohibitively high cost of updating mission-critical data and applications, awkward manual interfaces, and little systematic support for ad hoc decision-making. This often becomes a roadblock in any effort to achieve important strategic objectives requiring integration and linking of these systems. To help overcome these problems, it is important to move toward standards and open systems.

Open systems will allow users to take an architectural approach, opening up the list of permissible systems that may be purchased. With an open systems architecture, users will no longer need to restrict themselves to the purchase of a short list of allowable vendor's hardware. This increases in importance as the useful life of the hardware platforms grows progressively shorter (often less than three years), while the useful life of an application can be as long as fifteen years. It becomes important to preserve a software investment when shifting hardware platforms. This is expecially important as the need to integrate, link, and interface the various applications just discussed grows and software costs become the dominant systems costs.

Open systems promise to eliminate much of the redundant effort involved in maintaining today's plethora of operating environments and having to build many one-to-one links between them. Not only must these standards address the operating system and communication data exchanges, they must also address interactive access to remote databases, human interface (both graphic and character-based), security, and multilingual support.

However, it is not easy to achieve this desired level of integration and standardization. The existing computer and communication systems are a mirror image of the organizations that created them. Organizations generally consist of compartmentalized structures with multiple computer-buying bureaucracies that do not communicate with or trust one another. Incentive systems reinforce some of the organization's goals in some functions, but not in others. And there is generally no widely shared understanding of the end-to-end corporate information flow. Adding to these difficulties are the political aspects of integration. Because information is power, any suggestion of changing the status quo implicit in the existing structure and computer-based systems will undoubtably meet with resistance. Integration is not something a corporation can buy. To make the technology work, management must work on the whole system and address the environment, the people, the culture, the incentives, and the organization along with the technology. Unique solutions must be developed.

## Merging of Application Categories

There has been a gradual merging of the different application categories. As the problems addressed become broader and more ill-defined, it is becoming increasingly important to take advantage of the best features that have evolved in all the application specialties, mixing media of presentation and form of computation to provide the best, most unconstrained environment for effective problem-solving. Furthermore, advances in an application area makes its tools and specialized hardware useful in areas where they were previously impractical to apply. The increased motivation to integrate these separate application areas has put added emphasis on the importance of standardization. Standards make interfacing and integration of software and hardware modules much easier. Adherence to standards also makes it easier to reuse and build upon existing software.

## Reusability

With the large base of existing applications, there is a desire to be able to build upon existing functionality, not to have to redo and redesign perfectly acceptable existing systems. In the past these sorts of capabilities could be achieved only by adhering to an individual manufacturer's proprietary products, and requiring centrally controlled, compatible systems (preferably all from the same manufacturer). Today these constraints are becoming unacceptable. Users want to take advantage of the rapid advances in personal computers, workstations, and the growing list of available third-party software for them. Users don't want to be tied down to a single manufacturer or other similarly narrow choice. They often find the need for a range of equipment, from supercomputers to desktop machines, to satisfy their computing and communications requirements, and they prefer to be free to select each device from a different vendor. Today, these seemingly conflicting objectives can be accomplished through advances in technology targeted toward the use of open systems. Open systems are systems that adhere to universal standards and apply new distributed processing concepts that support this increased flexibility and heterogeneity. In such a distributed, open environment, processing takes place across the network in parallel on many nodes, rather than in one node. This is why there has been an increasing emphasis on distributing data and functions, and on creating systems capable of flexible interprocess communications and data exchange.

## Commoditization

A key motivation for this standards-conscious, open systems attitude is *commoditization*. The idea here is that many segments of the computer business are becoming more competitive as hardware and software products become commodity-like. With this approach, central processors are beginning to be bought on the basis of $x$ dollars per MIP, and disk storage on the basis of $y$ dollars per megabyte, just like we buy tomatoes or potatoes. Commoditization is moving into the software arena, with UNIX-like operating systems, SQL-access database systems, and LOTUS-like spreadsheet systems. This trend toward open systems, open software, open everything leads to computer clones, disk clones, spreadsheet clones, laser printer clones, all at lower and lower prices. Therefore users have begun to associate standardization with modularity and lower prices.

The goal is to agree upon common human-machine interfaces, common application program interfaces, and common rich data structures that are the same whether the entities being interfaced are co-located on the same system, or remote from one another and located on different systems. If this is achieved, then applications can communicate and share data and tasks, and avoid redundancy of data and programming effort. In such a system, workstations will be replaced by media servers and work will be accomplished not on a single workstation, but on the network. In such a system, any client (a user, a display, or an application) has concurrent access to multiple servers (e.g., computational, application, file, peripheral). This situation is illustrated in Figure 4.1.

There are two ways to achieve this level of coexistence and cooperation among applications across heterogeneous systems: (1) through an extra layer that sits on top of the operating system such as windows; and (2) through use of common constructs across and within applications. The second approach is better with respect to processing efficiency, but hard to retrofit. Both approaches require some level of adherence to standards.

## American Airlines SABRE System

The SABRE system literally runs American Airlines. It schedules the planes, runs the flight operations, sells the seats, issues the tickets, and even coordinates the catering. American Airlines would not be able to operate if SABRE were down for an extended period. It is so essential to the airlines that its datacenter is buried and protected.

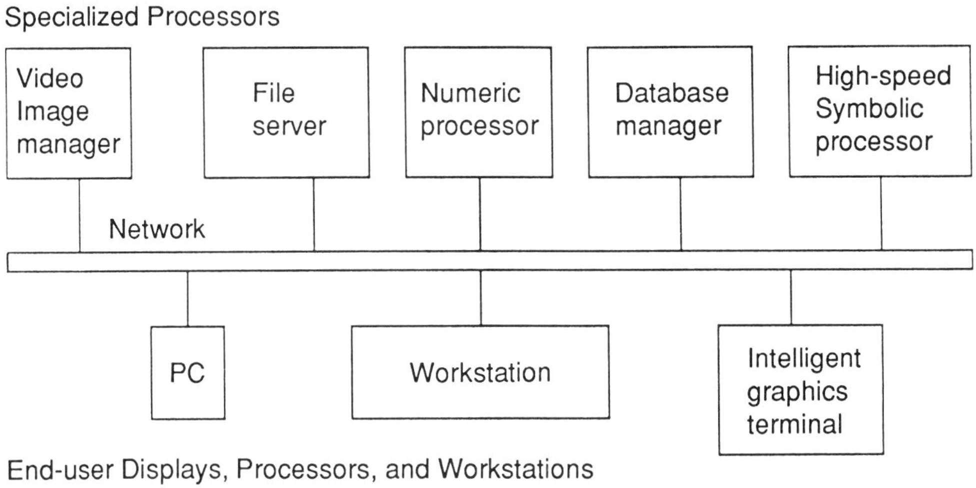


**Figure 4.1.** Distributed Processing Concept.

SABRE is a closed system. It runs under an IBM operating system called Airline Control Program (ACP) and programmed in Assembler. It now has to be reprogrammed under the new IBM operating system, the Transaction Processing Facility (TPF), in order to keep up with increased volume of transactions and host hardware and software upgrades.

The closed system presents many other problems. It is hard to get at the 7 million customer profiles to support innovative uses and analyses. It is difficult for other in-house systems to link with SABRE and access its data. These systems include the corporate office automation systems, which consist of IBM, Tandy, and AT&T PCs linked to HP minicomputers. American also has a telemarketing system which uses Digital computers, a hotel reservations system which uses Sequent, the CAPTURE travel expense control system running on SUNs, the ADS travel agency accounting system which uses a Data General, and an operations control system which uses Macintosh and MIPS computers. This great diversity of systems came about as a result of acquisitions and past purchases driven by specific application needs.

The closed SABRE system also makes it difficult to provide new services to customers who need applications to interface seamlessly with their installed systems, which are often incompatible with the American Airlines systems. For these reasons, American is now considering moving to an open systems architecture (Lytton 1990).

## Some Negative Aspects

There are several cautions against becoming too standards-conscious. Standards can freeze a system architecture prematurely, preventing one from taking advantage of an unanticipated future revolutionary advance that is incompatible with the standards.

Standards are often achieved by an increased abstraction and layering of services, which results in the sacrifice of system resources and performance through the additional processing and storage overhead that generally results. However, with the dramatic advances in computer hardware, this latter penalty does not seem so big a penalty to pay.

The recent outbreak of computer viruses and worms presents another concern. Viruses are programs maliciously or accidentally inserted into a system that succeed in penetrating the system's security and erasing, destroying, or otherwise impairing important programs and data that the user should not have had access to. For example, in November 1988, a Cornell student, as a prank, succeeded in penetrating a number of university, industrial company, and U.S. laboratory computers running the Berkeley 4.3 version of UNIX and connected to each other on a U.S. government packet-switched network called the ARPANET. These computers were crippled by the student's program as it traveled down the network, entering computers, where it began to consume all the computer's resources. Computer theft and embezzlement, where the computer system penetrator uses unauthorized entry into system files to transfer funds and/or manipulate information to their advantage, represents another side to computer system vulnerability.

No system, to date, is completely free of weak spots that are subject to penetration by some knowledgeable user. Whenever we allow computers to be accessed by users located in physically nonsecure areas, we run the risk of the system contracting a virus, or being penetrated and manipulated by an unauthorized user.

The more standard the software, the greater the likelihood that someone will know and understand the system's strengths and weaknesses and be able to exploit them. And the more widespread the standard, the greater the number of systems that become vulnerable to the same viruses and security loopholes. Thus, with the growth of standards, it becomes more important than ever to protect a system against virus and security infringements. Accordingly, computer system security should grow in importance.

## A REVIEW OF TRENDS IN STANDARDS

### Operating System Standards

The emergence of the IBM personal computer and its hardware architecture as a de facto standard, with Microsoft DOS as its de facto standard operating system, spoiled the user and the software developers. Suddenly, there was a universal standard buyers could compare against and developers could write programs for. The personal computer hardware and the software applications built on that architectural base became commodity products from which we could pick and choose from competing vendors solely on the basis of cost, reliability, performance, and service. Users have benefited greatly from this situation and naturally wish to preserve it.

Unfortunately, the DOS operating system has drawbacks that prevent users from staying with it if they wish to take advantage of the newer, more powerful offerings. The DOS operating system was designed assuming a single user who does a single task at a time; it cannot handle multitasking and/or multi-users. Furthermore, the operating system was built with a 640K byte restriction on the amount of space a program can occupy in main memory.

On the surface, this may not seem like much of a restriction, but it rules out some of the advanced human–machine innovations that allow a user to perform multiple tasks through multiple windows displayed on the computer screen, sharing data and results among tasks and windows. It also provides an inhibiting constraint on implementing networking applications that allow a program on a local personal computer to interact with programs on other computers, interrupting tasks and exchanging information and results in real-time. There are workarounds, but they are awkward and limiting. Thus, if we wish to implement more advanced applications that take fuller advantage of increased, affordable computer power, we need to migrate our personal computer or workstation to a new operating system.

Recognizing the strategic importance of being the next accepted personal computer/workstation (this comprises the fastest-growing computer area) operating system standard, several advanced operating systems are competing for this position, notably UNIX and IBM's OS/2. There is no clear winner yet, and indeed a peaceful coexistence may result. Of course vendors differ with respect to whether a standard operating system is necessary for having an "open system." Some vendors require users to move to UNIX to get the benefits of interpersonal computing, whereas others (HP with New Wave) offer heterogeneous system-integration facilities that allow users to bridge the multiple operating environments they are currently using. However, the latter approach is much more complicated and does not fully address the problem of porting or developing software applications across multiple vendors' hardware.

### UNIX

The UNIX operating system is the oldest and currently the most popular of the candidates. Developed at Bell Labs and offered as a public standard for a minimal licensing fee, it initially caught on in academia and the engineering and scientific community. With the spread of RISC workstations and the newer, more powerful 80286 and 80386 Intel microprocessors, UNIX has spread dramatically as well. In fact, it has become the de facto standard operating system for most high-powered workstations, particularly the RISC-based ones.

UNIX has grown in popularity with the rise in popularity of the RISC computers and their superior cost-performance ratio. In fact, many computer firms that have tried to stand behind their proprietary lines and avoid opening up their installed bases to new competition have been forced to join the move to standard systems. Examples include Wang and Tandem, which have announced support for UNIX; Data General, which switched to its AVIION RISC product line under UNIX and related standards such as TCP/IP and X Windows (more detail on these standards is provided in subsequent sections of this chapter); Unisys, which acquired Convergent Technologies and is purchasing Motorola's 88000 RISC MPU (multi-processing unit) under UNIX; Hewlett Packard, which set plans for phasing out its Micro 3000 proprietary lines running under its proprietary operating system MPE XL in favor of an open system architecture running under UNIX; Prime, which is also focusing on UNIX; and even DEC, with its license to sell MIPS RISC UNIX-based workstation under the DEC label; and IBM, with its RISC work-station, the RT, running under its version of UNIX, AIX.

Because UNIX is generally written in a higher-level language, C, it is more portable (easier to port to different hardware) than most other operating systems. We can run multiple MS DOS graphics applications on top of UNIX through utilities such as VP/ix from Interactive Systems and DOS Merge from LOCUS computing. But with this approach, it is necessary for each DOS application to use the whole display, so simultaneous execution is possible, but simultaneous viewing is not. Only one application can be seen at a time; the rest must run in background. Even graphic applications developed for the Macintosh Plus and SE must run full screen when executing under the initial version of Apple's UNIX operating system, AUX, rather than under its own proprietary operating system.

There are many variants of UNIX on the market. The most popular include AT&T's UNIX System V and Berkley's UNIX version IV; Microsoft's Xenix, which runs on 80286 and 80386 systems; and ULTRIX, which runs on DEC VAX computers. With the spread of UNIX throughout the commercial business marketplace, there has been a concerted effort to improve the human–machine friendliness, the performance, the robustness, and the security of UNIX.

Two major competing upgraded versions are currently being promoted as the new UNIX standard. One standard, UII (UNIX International), is promoted by AT&T, SUN, Amdahl, and Wang. The other standard is sponsored by the Open Software Foundation (OSF), a cooperative formed by over 70 member companies, notably IBM, DEC, and HP, which do not want to conform to a standard developed by their leading UNIX competitors, SUN microsystems and AT&T. Both versions of UNIX are more alike than contenders would care to admit. Both offer similar distributed system processing extensions, real-time capabilities (current versions of UNIX are time-sliced and not interrupt-driven), increased security, and a friendlier user interface. Both can accommodate a variety of hardware systems. Furthermore, both comply with POSIX (a vendor-independent operating system standard) and SVID (the System V interface device standard). Both have joined X/OPEN, a European-American consortium that is trying to provide a common application environment. It includes POSIX, SVID, C, and SQL standards. Both have agreed to comply with X Windows standards. X Windows is a layered interface separating the terminal or workstation (called the server in X Windows terminology) from the specifics of the host processor where the executing program resides (called the client). It allows for multiple sessions on a workstation with various heterogeneous processors.

The OSF is considering standardizing on AIX (Advanced Interactive Executive), a variant of AT&T's System V UNIX developed by IBM, or MACH, a recent Carnegie-Mellon University version of UNIX. AIX currently runs on PS/2 personal computers, IBM 9370, IBM 4300, and IBM 3090 under the operating system

VM/370. AIX is also planned to be increased to a B-1 security level. OSF plans to use Apollo's Network Computing System (NCS), DECwindow's Application Programming Interface, X Windows version 11, developed at MIT, and for the user interface, Microsoft's Presentation Manager's functionality combined with Hewlett Packard's three-dimensional Motif's "look and feel" and interface builders' toolkit.

The AT&T/SUN UNIX is based on an upgrade of the current AT&T System V to System V version 4 with a B-1 security rating, SUN's Open Look user interface, SUNS & AT&T's Network File System (NFS), Remote Procedure Calls (RPC), and compatibility with X Windows version 11. With AT&T's decision to sell its UNIX Software Division to a neutral organization, and with the early successful implementation of System V version 4, it will most likely be accepted as the single common standard by both factions.

### *OS/2*

IBM's entry for the next standard operating system for personal computers is OS/2. The latest version at the time of writing is OS/2 Extended Edition with Presentation Manager, an advanced user interface (Lewis 1989). Presentation Manager contains more than 1 million lines of code, including a relational database manager, concurrent communication sessions, multitasking, the ability to expand beyond the 640K memory limits of DOS, local area network (LAN) management, and the Presentation Manager interface.

The Presentation Manager interface increases the power of the PC, giving the user a common query language to simultaneously and transparently access many different machines and applications, getting and generating information, letters, and electronic mail from any PC or mainframe to any other. OS/2 requires a lot more system resources than MS DOS or UNIX, 22 megabytes of hard disk, 6 to 8 megabytes of RAM, at least a 80286 and preferably a 80386 processor.

## Database Standards

Database management systems (DBMS) have evolved as an additional layer of software between file access software and the application software. A DBMS forms a central place where all data files are managed and accessed, and through which all applications can access data, independent of the physical structure of the data or the physical access method (sequential, direct, or indexed direct). Database management systems manage the physical storage and access of the data, and maintain the logical views presented to the user and to the application programs. Database management systems perform the following functions:

1. Minimize the redundancy in data collected, stored, and processed
2. Assist in integrating information
3. Reduce the difficulty of establishing and modifying integrated files
4. Make it easy to accommodate changes in data elements and their relationships with minimum impact to existing applications

5. Reduce the complexity and enhance the maintainability of the application program
6. Improve database integrity and security

Most modern database management systems also have a user friendly query language (a fourth-generation language, usually nonprocedural; you tell the system what you want, you do not tell it how to do the task), that supports ad hoc data requests and makes it easy for the end users themselves to query the database and prepare reports. The query language allows the user to locate, retrieve, and store data in terms of their content and their defined relations.

Database management systems present one or more of the following common logical views: (1) hierarchical, where the data are organized in a tree structure, like an organizational chart (IBM's IMS); (2) network, where the emphasis is on explicitly representing sets of data records and the linkages between them (Cullinane's IDMS); (3) relational, where data are organized in terms of logical sets or relations (IBM's Structured Query Language/Data System); (4) object-oriented, where data are organized in terms of objects (bundles of data, procedures, and rules).

The object-oriented and relational databases represent the highest level of abstraction because they do not assume any particular linkage, logical or physical. In the relational model, the user is required only to show which data elements are logically related to one another by defining relations, where the columns represent the related data items and the rows represent instances of the relation. A data item can be associated with more than one relation.

In addition to a query language, some relational databases support a facility for the user to specify data requests by providing an example of the desired query. This method is called "query by example." Since relational databases are so completely implementation-independent, a relational database query became the natural choice for standardization across different hardware and software systems, and IBM's sequel data query language (SQL) has become the de facto standard database query language.

An object-oriented database system is a persistent and sharable repository and manager of objects defined by an object-oriented model. Whereas a data model is a logical organization of real-world objects (entities), constraints on them, and relationships among them, an object-oriented model extends the data model to include rules for grouping objects into a class, and for expressing aggregation, generalization, and specialization relationships between classes of objects. In the object-oriented model, the user queries and updates the objects by means of messages.

The object-oriented database is a much newer concept, with no clear standards yet. Many of its features are being incorporated into the more popular relational databases as an extension of SQL. For example, POSTGRES at the University of California at Berkeley is based on the extended relational approach. It starts with a relational model of data and a query language and extends them in various ways to allow the modeling and manipulation of additional semantic relationships and database facilities.

## Communications Standards

Communications standards are essential for heterogeneous computers to exchange data and information among themselves, or to run applications that are distributed among several computers. Currently there are several network standards. The best known and widest in use are three de facto standards: IBM's Systems Network Architecture (SNA), DEC's DECNET, and the Transmission Control Protocol/Internet Protocol (TCP/IP), which was developed originally to ensure interoperability among U.S. Defense Department networks, but has expanded to all UNIX platforms as well as to many PC local area networks. More recently, the Open Systems Interconnection (OSI) standard has been proposed by ISO, the International Standards Organization.

All these systems follow a similar architecture, a multilayering of protocol levels (see Appendix 16 for details.) They differ in their actual implementation and in the number and boundaries of the various layers. For many of these architectures, each layer may possess more than one possible standard within that layer. By breaking up a communications architecture into discrete layers or levels, users can interface different networks with different layer protocols at different layers.

Because of these multiple standards, a number of companies, including Apple, Apollo, DEC, Hewlett Packard, and Sun, have decided to bring their products into compliance with at least two, and sometimes three, protocol standards to match their customers' needs. For example, Digital supports distributed filing and processing across VMS (DEC's proprietary operating system for the VAX), ULTRIX (DEC's version of UNIX), MS-DOS, OS/2, and Macintosh environments, including gateways to IBM's SNA and TCP/IP.

As transmission speeds increase, new, improved, more streamlined communications hardware, protocols, and standards are evolving. With the introduction of SONET (Synchronous Optical Network) communications backbone, speeds will increase greatly from today's standard 56,000 bps and 64,000 bps and T1 speeds of 1 to 10 million bps. By 1993, we will have the following standard SONET backbone speeds:

| | |
|---|---|
| OC (Optical Carrier) - 1 | 51 million bps |
| OC - 3 | 155 million bps |
| OC - 12 | 620 million bps |
| OC - 24 | 1200 million bps |

(Note that 51 million bps provides sufficient capacity to support 135,000 calls/second.) The National Research Education Network has a capacity of 3G bps.

These increased speeds are needed to support some of the new applications. Consider the area of scientific visualization discussed earlier. To transmit animated high-resolution graphics, even with 50 to 1 compression, requires 15 million bps (1024 vertical × 1024 horizontal × 24 color × 30 frames/second × 1/50 compression).

These increased communication needs and advances in communication capacity have led to new protocols. At the data link level (level 2), we see the emergence of CCITT Standard Link Access Procedure—D (LAPD, Q.921), also known as Frame

Relay. Frame Relay is closely related to LAPB (Link Access Procedure Balanced) level 2 protocol of High-Level Data Link Control (HDLC) for X.25 links. It supports variable length packets and a more streamlined, fast-packet switching protocol, with less protocol processing by minimizing error checking and flow control overhead.

At the physical level (level 1), we see the emergence of the Cell Relay Standards. Namely, there are two related standards:

IEEE 807.6, otherwise known as Distributed Queue Dual Bus (DQDB) for MANS (Metropolitan Area Networks)
ATM (asynchronous transfer mode) for WAN's (Wide Area Networks)

Cell relay supports a 48-byte data packet (includes a 5-byte header). With these new, more streamlined protocols and communication advances, we will see by the middle of the decade a broadbased ISDN based on ATM switching and SONET access and transmission. Even today, we are beginning to see 100 million bps campus area networks over FDDI (Fiber Distributed Data Interface) and 45 million bps MAN's over SMDS (Switched Multimegabit Data Services).

## The Client–Server Model

A new architectural model, the client–server, has emerged to address the need for linking many diverse heterogeneous computers across the organization (Pollack 1989). When the processing is distributed among many processors across a network, it is desirable to have these processors cooperating, sharing resources, and interacting. Cooperative processing is where two or more programs interact on two or more machines. The client–server model is one of the configurations supporting cooperative processing. This model permits the user to take advantage of the rapid advances in hardware, adding the latest models as they become available, or to buy specialized processors that can be shared by many users on the network. It allows the user to connect existing and previously incompatible computer systems so that they can share resources and data. It allows a program to be run across many different interconnected systems, such that the data may reside on one system, the programs executed on other systems, and the results displayed on still other systems. It is based on the idea that one program or resource, the client, may call upon another resource, the server, located somewhere else in the network, without regard to system software, communications protocol, or physical locations.

## Windows

As business and government automate every facet of their organizations, they find that different users require different systems and applications for their varied needs. These systems will have to be interconnected and support information exchanges. Networks of the future will therefore be comprised of many different types of workstations, processors, and operating systems that must talk together. Standard application programming interfaces, display commands and toolkits, graphic user interfaces (GUIs), and desktop managers help to achieve this goal. A key part of these standards is known as the windowing system. It allows the user to write standardized programs that can interface with a variety of existing hardware and software display systems without any rewrite or special customization, and to build an application using an existing library of graphic user interface routines and iconics. In particular X Windows, a popular standard from the MIT, Microsoft Windows, and IBM's OS/2 Presentation Manager comprise the primary windowing systems of the 1990s. These systems are designed for integrating diverse hardware software application systems (for example, PC DOS, UNIX, DEC VMS) under one common, intuitive, graphic user interface.

Windowing is closely coupled to the management of applications; it is not concerned just with the physical display of images. The concept of windowing is to insulate applications from the physical pecularities of the display device by separating the application processing from the physical management of the presentation device. In this way the display device specifics are transparent to the applications designer, who communicates to the display through a standard window interface. This allows the same application program to work under a variety of display devices. The window system receives the results and is responsible for managing the display of the image on the selected physical display device. It has to size windows and to display only the viewable portions.

The concept of a windowing system originated at Xerox Park. Its first version was implemented in the object-oriented language SMALLTALK. Early commercially successful versions were Apple's LISA and Macintosh, and SUN's Windows. These window systems are tightly coupled to the operating system. Microsoft introduced this concept into the PC DOS world with its Microsoft Windows product. The X Window standard is a product of MIT's Athena project. It was developed as an extension of the windowing concept to enable applications processing to be run across remote, distributed heterogenous environments.

### *Microsoft Windows*

Unlike MS-DOS, where programmers wrote directly to the screen buffer and to the registers of the graphics hardware, Microsoft 386 Window's virtual monitor program traps all interrupt requests and transfers them to a virtual monitor. This allows several programs to be run and viewed in separate windows concurrently. The virtual monitor can handle only one request at a time, so multiple screens can be viewed simultaneously, but cannot be refreshed simultaneously. They cannot be updated on a real-time basis if there are multiple updates for multiple programs occurring at the same time. X Windows, SUN's window system, NEWs (Network/Extensible Window System), and Apple's proprietary operating system do not have this limitation.

### *X Windows*

The X Window standard was developed at MIT to achieve hardware and operating system independence. It is based on the client–server model previously discussed, which is supported on a variety of UNIX and VAX VMS-based hosts. X Windows shares a similar architecture to SUN's NEWS. Both have a controlling server for each physical display, with client applications communicating over a reliable duplex byte stream (see Figure 4.2). This architecture allows for device independence and transparency across the network and from one hardware configuration to another. The server becomes the base window system, carrying out its duties as traffic cop between server applications and actual hardware, providing hooks to needed resources for whatever user interface the client uses.

The communications protocol between clients and servers makes no references to hardware configurations, so the addition of new display types does not require changes to existing applications. The server may be placed in the kernel of the operating system to increase performance, but the typical approach is to maintain independence and run it as a user process.

Companies have tried to run MS-DOS programs under X version 11, but they have experienced the same problems as when running these programs under Microsoft Window's monitor program. MS-DOS programs are often ill-behaved, in that they directly access the video display adapter and physical console. The XDOS package attempts to trap direct accesses made by MS-DOS programs and translate them into X.11 service calls.

## Distributing Data and Processing

A further trend in the open systems client–server model is the development of a standard environment that can allow the exchange and processing of files and programs across remotely located heterogeneous computer systems. This concept

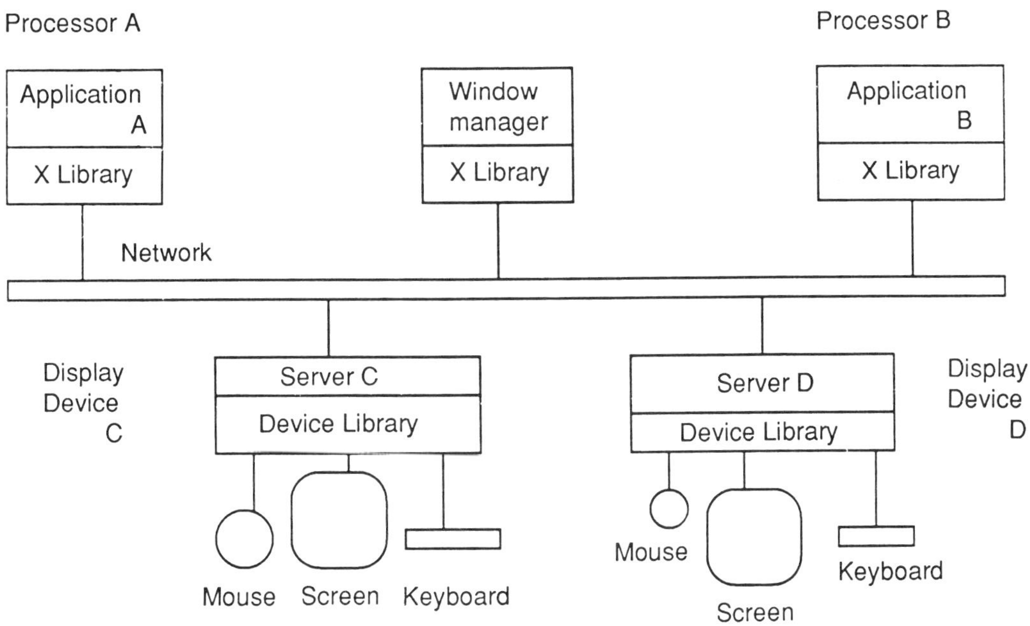


**Figure 4.2.** The X Windows Concept.

is illustrated by two of the more popular systems: SUN's Network File System and Apollo's Network Computing System.

### Network File System (NFS)

SUN Microsystems has made extended support for standards an effective marketing strategy. SUN figured that the more different types of systems it could connect to, the better its equipment would sell. In keeping with this philosophy, SUN developed an NFS for heterogeneous computing environments, and put the source code for the NFS Remote Procedure Call (RPC) and External Data Representation (XDR) protocols in the public domain. NFS provides transparent remote access to file systems across a network of heterogeneous equipment. NFS consists of three pieces: the protocol, the server side, and the client side. The NFS protocol is stateless; it is the client's job to keep sending NFS requests until it has received an answer. NFS does not keep track.

SUN created the Virtual File System (VFS), which defines the generic operations that can be done on any file system. SUN's vnode (virtual node) interface defines the specific operations that must be done within a particular file system. As a result, the operating system can treat all file systems and nodes in the same way without knowing the underlying specifics. AT&T has a Remote Filing System (RFS) that is similar to NFS except that RFS works only with UNIX, while NFS can support a variety of operating systems. Of course, RFS provides a greater depth of support.

### Network Computing System (NCS)

In 1985, Apollo researchers introduced the Network Computing System. They have since made it available in the public domain, hoping to make it an industry standard for implementing distributed computing. They have written code so that it can run in Digital's VAX VMS environment, or in C under UNIX. In fact, the OSF has adopted NCS as part of its standard. The concept behind NCS is that applications requiring more power can steal cycles from other computers on the network. These computers do not have to be similar processors and they can be special-purpose, such as parallel processors, supercomputers, or artificial intelligence engines.

There are four parts to Apollo's proposed NCS standard:

1. A network-independent Remote Procedure Call (RPC) facility
2. The Network Interface Definition Language (NIDL), which lets programmers specify remote computing requirements in a high-level language
3. A compiler for NIDL into C source code that can be compiled on any system
4. A set of software tools that let applications determine at run time which computers can provide the services they require

To take advantage of NCS, an application must be written specifically for it or modified. When writing the application, the programmer needs to think about which subroutines run better on which type of processor. These subroutines are then tagged with NCS RPC's and compiled for all relevant target machines.

## User and Application Interface Standards

The user interface is being standardized toward an icon-based representation of file and system operations activated by a variety of pointing devices—mouse, digitizing tablet, joystick, and touch screen, with simultaneous multiple graphic and text-based programs running in separate virtual screens. This includes what is called the "look and feel" of the system to the user.

Examples of these graphics-oriented user interfaces include: IBM and Microsoft's Presentation Manager; Hewlett-Packard's Motif (which was adopted by OSF); SUN's Open Look (which was adopted by UII); Metaphor Computer System's Metaphor; Macintosh's OS; NEXT, Inc.'s Nextstep; the user interface component of DEC's DECwindows; and Wang's Freestyle. Many of these systems come with a toolkit with a library of templates and images (or widgets) for building and specifying different types of windows, dialogue boxes, menus, and graphic objects that a programmer is free to use or customize for a particular application. Many are integrated with existing window standards and toolkits. For example, OSF's Motif is integrated with the X Window standard and toolkit discussed earlier. More advanced versions, such as the NEXT system's Nextstep, also integrate text and graphics with images and sound (Aseo 1988).

This interface paradigm originated from work at the Xerox Research Center at Palo Alto on the object-oriented language Smalltalk and its use in creating the desktop metaphor. Another early object-oriented language linked to a window system is Actor from Whitewater Group. With object-oriented languages, objects can be created out of generic classes, selectively inheriting their behavior and attributes. Besides their powerful data representations, object-oriented languages have intrinsic control functions such as those in C and PASCAL. Many of these control functions are linked to existing window systems. Actor, for example, emits Microsoft Window calls as output.

This style of user interaction has become the standard in high-powered workstations and has now moved to the less powerful personal computer, first to the Apple and recently, with the introduction of Microsoft Windows, to the IBM PC. More recently, IBM's Presentation Manager has maintained this style of user interaction. Of course each implementation has a slightly different variant of the "look and feel." User interface management systems have been built on top of these window systems, further simplifying user-screen interface building. One such example is Telesoft (Williams 1990). Telesoft is designed to relieve the programmer of having to learn the details of OSF/Motif and its underlying X Windows toolkit. It has four parts. One part helps the developer to design user interface screens in a WYSIWYG, screen painter fashion. Another part lets the developer specify and control the user–computer interaction through a high level language. The third, the user interface builder, integrates the screen layout and user dialog with the run time component and the application code. The fourth maintains and manages a run-time library of all the user interface routines.

Most recently high-powered graphics terminals have been developed that are also capable of supporting this style of interaction. Network Computing Devices was an early pioneer in this area. Currently selling for under $2500, they are a low-cost alternative to the workstation. They have the look and feel of the more powerful workstation. Of course they lack much of the local processing power of a PC or workstation, but they are high-performance graphics terminals and are more robust and easier to set up and control. One file server can drive 16 or more of these terminals. They are often called Xterms because they support the X Windows standard, implementing most of the X Window protocol and function calls in hardware. However as the price of workstations continues to spiral downward, these distinctions and relative advantages and disadvantages begin to blur.

Today, as the boundaries between intelligent graphics terminals, personal computers, and workstations become less distinct, there is a struggle between the currently dominant "look and feel" standards. The major interface systems are IBM's Presentation Manager, DEC's DECwindows, SUN's Open Look, and the Open System Foundation's Motif.

Systems like Hewlett Packard's New Wave, Metaphor, and most recently, Microsoft Windows 3.0, take this interface one step further by integrating all the various services and data represented by icons, and displayed in windows, to the extent that the user can select, cut, paste, pass, and dynamically link data, text, and graphics from one to the other in a manner that is completely transparent to the necessary system calls, communications, and conversions. This interface makes end user programming a reality, for no real programming expertise is required to program in such an environment, at least so long as the programming goals can be realized through the existing linked shells and packages.

## ELECTRONIC FUNDS TRANSFER STANDARDS

The electronic transfer of funds makes it easier for a business to make orders and to pay bills. In fact, it is a natural step for a company to take once it has automated its inventory management system. Its advantages parallel those of the manufacturing industries' JIT (Just In Time) inventory management concept, because it allows the business to manage its accounts receivables more effectively. It makes possible the more timely investment and use of cash flows and permits more precise timing of cash outflows. With the possibility for more precisely controlling the timing of the actual receipt and delivery of funds, it changes the rules of the game, increasing the importance of introducing incentives for early payment (both financial and service-related) and penalties for late payment. It also forms the necessary foundation for a real-time cash management system which reduces and streamlines the overhead associated with billing, ordering, and reordering. Other advantages include:

Reduces lead time and quickens response
Reduces inventory cost levels
Makes better use of warehouse and dock space
Makes possible more accurate inventory projections

Reduces number of expedite situations
Lowers freight costs
Lessens back-order situations
Reduces paperwork and chance of human error
Reduces the need for maintaining a lockbox system for the collection and storage of payments and its associated expense
Provides a service that can be offered to customers
Makes practical the introduction of a third-party clearinghouse service concept
Reduces credit risk
Enables improved auditing and reporting
Reduces bookkeeping and administration overhead
Provides capacity to handle large volumes of transactions

Electronic funds transfer is already widely used in the transportation industry. One example is the RAILINK carrier's Advanced Transportation Control System (ATCS). General Motors is another example. General Motors gave all its suppliers and vendors an ultimatum. They would have to support General Motors electronic funds transfer by 1987 or lose their eligibility to do business with General Motors. American Airlines also has an electronic funds transfer system for its freight management system.

Some of the major suppliers of electronic funds transfer services and software include GE Information Services, IBM Services, Sterling Software, and Control Data Software.

Some of the obstacles facing the spread of electronic funds transfer include:

Resistance to change (why change if the manual method is working?)
Fear of working with computers
Audit finds electronic funds to transfer systems harder to assess
There is less float in paying bills through electronic funds transfer
Users are afraid that by using electronic funds transfer they would lose privacy (Note: encryption and fiber optics can solve this)
There is a high initial cost (the cost to implement, train, and convert has a relatively long-term payback)
There is not yet a commonly acceptable electronic equivalent of the contract signature

Electronic funds transfer systems typically are comprised of the following four main components:

A transaction set, which includes standard formats for documents, e.g., purchase orders, invoices
A data dictionary
Protocols for transmission
Interface software with translate, data, and error checks and acknowledgments

For electronic fund transfer to be practical it must support a variety of different systems. To achieve this goal ANSI has developed standards for Electronic Data

Interchange (EDI), or standards for computer-to-computer transactions involving ordering, shipping, and billing. Specifically there are:

- UCS—Uniform Communication Standard
- WINS—Warehouse Industry Network Standard
- VICS EDI—Volunteer Interindustry Communication Standard

## EDI Standards

Different types of EDI standards have been adopted by companies according to the nature of their business.

Three of the major EDI standards are:

1. Uniform Communication Standard (UCS), used primarily by the grocery industry
2. Voluntary Interindustry Communication Standard (VICS) EDI, used by the general merchandise retailing industry
3. Warehouse Industry Network Standards (WINS), used by public warehouses and their depositor customers

These three major EDI standards are managed and administered by the Uniform Code Council, Inc. (UCC), a non-profit organization that acts as a secretary that organizes and advises various groups who are establishing various standards used by a variety of industries.

## Uniform Communication Standard (UCS)

UCS is the electronic data interchange standard used by the grocery industry and other retail-oriented industry sectors.

UCS was initiated by the grocery industry and is being used by hundreds of companies, manufacturers, retailers, wholesalers, and brokers. It is also being adopted by companies in the foodservice, mass merchandising, wholesale drug, and service merchandising industry.

The Uniform Communication Standard actually consists of two standards—message and communication.

### *Message Standard*

The UCS message standard includes over 20 different transaction sets that replace many of the paper transactions common in retail business today. The most commonly used UCS transaction sets are the purchase order and the invoice. Other transaction sets that have been developed include:

- Purchase Order Change and Adjustment
- Price Change
- Credit/Debit Memo
- Statement
- Shipment and Receiving Advice

- Item Maintenance
- Promotion Announcement and Confirmation
- Remittance Advice

### *Communication Standard*

The UCS communication standard is very straightforward. It states that all UCS users must be able to transmit at a specified speed using certain transmission protocols. The standard also specifies the hours that UCS users must be able to receive transmissions every day.

One of the reasons the founders of UCS developed a communication standard was to ensure that virtually any size company could afford to use UCS.

Therefore the standard is quite simple and uncomplicated. UCS uses the public phone system, with a communication speed of 2400 baud. The modem equipment required is in common use and is relatively inexpensive; the transmission protocol rules are also widely used.

## Warehouse Information Network Standard (WINS)

WINS is the electronic data interchange standard used by warehouses and those industries who wish to communicate with warehouses.

WINS was initiated by the grocery and warehouse industries and is being used by warehouses nationwide. It is also being adopted by companies in the foodservice industry and is applicable to the warehousing activities of other industries, such as mass merchandising and wholesale drug.

WINS also consists of two standards—message and communication.

### *Message Standard*

The WINS message standard contains a number of different transaction sets that replace many of the paper transactions common in the warehousing business today. The most commonly used WINS transaction sets are the shipping order and the shipping advice. Other transaction sets that have been developed are:

- Warehouse Inventory Status Report
- Warehouse Activity Report
- Stock Transfer Shipment Advice
- Stock Transfer Receipt Advice

### *Communication Standard*

The communication standard for WINS users is identical to UCS communication standard.

## Voluntary Interindustry Communication Standard (VICS EDI)

VICS EDI is a subset of ANSI X12 national standards, and is used by the general merchandise retailing industry.

Although VICS EDI is a relatively new standard, it is already being utilized by hundreds of companies—department and specialty retail stores, mass merchandisers, and their suppliers.

A number of VICS EDI transaction sets have been created with several more in the development stage. These sets include:

- Purchase Order
- Invoice
- Ship Notice
- Inventory Advice
- Product Transfer and Resale
- Price Sales Catalog
- Purchase Order Change

### Organization and Structure

The UCS, WINS, and VICS EDI programs are jointly managed by the UCC. In this role a key function of the council is the assignment of a unique communications identifier number for each member.

## CONCLUSION

We see several conflicting trends in today's software systems. On the one hand, there is a growing standardization and commoditization of the basic hardware and software components. For software, this includes not only standardizing on the computer languages (ANSI COBOL, ANSI FORTRAN, C, Common LISP), but the operating systems (UNIX, OS/2), database management systems (SQL data access language), and networking software (OSI standards, Remote Procedure Calls, Network File Transfer System) as well.

Software applications are becoming more integral to daily business operations, services, and strategic planning activities. As this occurs, software becomes an important means for the company to differentiate itself from its competitors; it is no longer just an overhead expense, but a strategic weapon.

These two trends produce two seemingly contradictory needs. The user needs a solution that is both a total solution using commodity products, and yet is a differentiated solution. The following solution for this dilemma seems to be evolving: Standardize on the tools, and help the application builders, be they vendors or end users, who use these tools to integrate and customize on the base of the emerging standards, rather than to build applications completely from scratch. Then, rather than buying arbitrary "applications" with functions determined by a vendor, users will be able to assemble their own sets of cooperating application modules tailored to their own needs. This allows better integration of all parts and modules and individual tasks under a unifying structure.

The nature of the applications is also changing. Traditionally, computers accomplished single-structured tasks that people were already doing or could do given sufficient time. The computer systems performed these tasks in much the same way people would perform them. Examples include payrolls with complex tax calculations, airline reservations, credit card validation, and other kinds of transaction processing. All these applications were aimed at efficiency.

Today's applications are aimed more at improving business effectiveness. They are more flexible, and directed toward less structured tasks. Usually they involve small computers and many small and interrelated tasks such as word processing and model building. Often they require processing or data from the already existing earlier transaction-processing-oriented applications. Thus, these new classes of applications are tending toward vertical integration packages or whole environments, packages that tailor several of these application categories for a given business segment. These applications take advantage of the specialized knowledge of the industry to provide the user with assistance in the more creative aspects of interactive problem-solving and to improve the application's ability to communicate with the user in a more natural domain-specific manner.

# 5

# Future Trends and Projections

Here we will attempt the risky task of forecasting future directions and trends and their implication for the business world and contemporary society. We will debate what the future is likely to hold for this closer marriage of business and technology. Although there are sure to be many changes over the next decade, here we concentrate on two main areas: the likely future evolution of the personal computer, and revolutionary technologies that might replace today's dominant digital electronic semiconductor circuits. Of course these predictions are only what might be, not what will be.

## THE FUTURE PERSONAL COMPUTER

Today computers are everywhere, embedded in television sets, microwaves, automobiles, portable bibles, electronic personal calendars and telephone directories, electronic spelling checkers, electronic dictionaries, language translators (often with voice output), mobile FAX/phone/data terminals, and so forth. It is the age of the information appliance. Already the typical household has more computers than motors. This trend is likely to continue, with still more fantastic computer-based appliances on the way. But nothing is likely to change more dramatically than the personal computer. The PC is expected to be quite different in the year 2000. The following projections are based on many of the ideas coming out of a prediction contest conducted by Apple in the mid-1980s that resulted in a concept known as the electronic notebook (*Personal Computer World,* 1988).

## Physical Description

The future personal computer will look different physically from today's models (See Figure 5.1). It will typically come in three sizes and speeds.

The largest machine will be about 1 1/4 feet by 1 foot by 1 1/2 feet deep. It will fold in half to form a portable package. The next largest will be about half that size, and the smallest is expected to be the size of a pocket diary. It will function as a diary, communications device, and notebook.

The display will quite likely cover the entire face of the computer. It will serve as both an input and an output device for the majority of applications. The screen is flexible, pliant, and touch-sensitive (able to tell which areas of the screen are currently depressed and how much pressure is being used). It produces high-resolution (probably 4098 × 4098 pixels) color images of high brightness, but uses low power. The screen's hardness can be modified electrorheologically by electric current to give the screen the ability to mimic the feel of many substances; e.g., the screen keyboard can mimic the IBM keyboard click.

The display will probably include a feature for time-lapse video overlay to handle video telephone or CCTV (closed circuit television) monitoring features.

Advances in matrix printing and input scanners will allow the coated screen to be used as both a scanner and a printer. You can lay a paper image or photograph on the screen and it will be scanned and captured. If you lay a blank page over the image on the screen, the image can be transferred to the paper.

There is a central processor and two or more standard co-processors (e.g., a 160-bit floating-point processor and an interactive string processor), with slots for optional co-processors. The processor will probably be about 20 MIPS, upgradable at the top end to about 200 MIPS (supercomputers will be in the terraops range in about 15 to 20 years). There is a minimum of 48 megabytes of memory, with room for expansion to 256 or more. The circuits are divided over both sides, which are connected by a flexible ribbon across the hinge, so the computer can be folded in half.

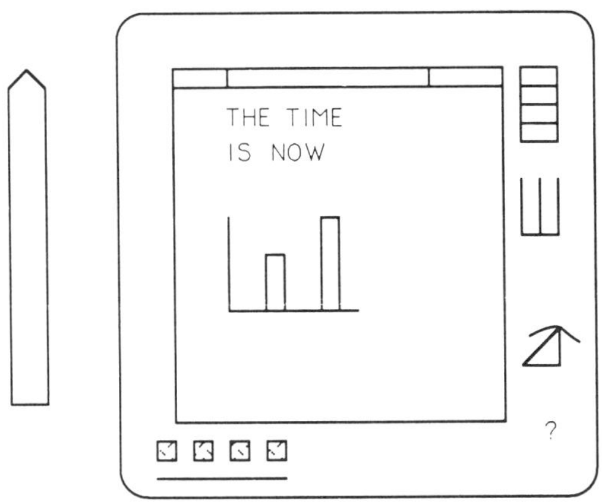


**Figure 5.1.** The Personal Computer of the Future.

Communications ports are standard and most likely optical. They will be capable of handling I/O (input and output). The PC communicates with the outside world to send and receive data, books, faxes, school lessons, and movies loaded into the computer, or processing assistance from remote specialized processors, or to rent and access storage space from third-party vendors, with any associate billing electronically transferred. The fax transmission will employ a fractal-based data compression technique to squash bit-mapped images several thousandfold and allow them to be included as "literals" in a vector description of a picture.

Since the communications ports are optical, there is no need for a physical link to the outside world. It is sufficient to rest the computer on a desk-based cradle for connection. There will also be zone phone points where telecommunications can be established just by standing within a certain distance of a physical marker.

The wide area network port will include a single-chip ISDN (Integrated Services Data Network that includes voice, data, graphics, video, and TV transmission) handler capable of running two channels at prevailing rates (currently 64 Kbps), and one channel operating as fast as 64 to 100 Mbps, perhaps greater (there already exist 32 Mbps optical networks).

The communications port gives access to both a local external device bus and a wide area ISDN network. The local area fiber optic network can run at speeds from 100 Mbits to 1 gigabit. The local port also can connect to peripheral devices such as printers, two 500 megabyte smart cards (they can store data on the card), and a single co-processor bus slot for third-party application-specific processor chips.

The PC will also include a data encryption co-processor for both secure communications and efficient data storage, and a speech analog/digital processor for both speech recognition and speech generation that can be output directly, or via the ISDN for voice messaging.

## User Interface

The future PC is expected to have an intuitive, customizable user interface that includes speech, touch, handwriting recognition, and seamless communication with the external world, both local and wide area, and data, voice, and image. All communication will take place transparently; there are no special commands or procedures for the user to learn. The interface will have a high-level graphic description language for use as a communications protocol for sending messages, data, and faxes over an ISDN line.

The interface will be pictorial and intuitive, with all the services integrated together (METAPHOR, or Hewlett Packard's New Wave). The user will interface with the computer through a graphic-window-based interface. Objects represent tasks, files, applications, background tasks or services and a "soft" keyboard. The interface will include a "natural" integration of all forms of input: keystrokes, mouse-derived pointing, handwriting, and gestures to perform functions. The display changes and adapts to the function being performed. For example, when entering text, a QWERTY keyboard is displayed. When working on a spreadsheet, the display rotates 90 degrees into a landscape mode with a wide spreadsheet displayed, with a numeric keypad that can move around the spreadsheet, and a handwriting note box to allow the entry of smaller amounts of text information. For paint packages, paint pots and stylus brush are provided. For music, there is representation of the musical instrument and a place for writing notes on musical staves on the screen. Each application can have its own unique input and output display.

Because of this application-unique display and input, there will be greater use of application-specific buttons; e.g., for a text editor, there are "save," "load," "font," "style," and application-specific "help" buttons. To retrieve a document, you will only need to point to its symbol or write the new document name on top of a currently accessed document. You can send a document or an application to another user by dragging its icon onto the icon of a telephone.

You will also be able to create your own handwritten shorthand symbols for tasks. To delete a file you may just scribble over it, or select it for removal by drawing a circle around it, or double-click a mouse pointed to it. To merge mail, you hit the form letter, write a plus symbol anywhere on the surface, tap the relevant database symbol, and then draw an arrow toward the required output.

Input and output sound will also likely to be present (the NEXT computer is an example of this). Sound, when used appropriately, can be very effective in helping to reduce the clutter on the display. Sound also provides meaningful clues, such as signaling the arrival of electronic mail. Speech commands are useful to start jobs to run in the background. Assume the screen is occupied with database forms. You start the process to collect your electronic mail, or to look up relevant news stories coming in over the news wires. The computer acknowledges the command with an audible signal and a new active task icon. When the mail is collected, a bell may sound and an icon flash or change color to indicate its arrival.

The ability to customize will be a major feature of the user interface because different people have different styles. Some people like pictorial icons (you will even be able to design your own); others are happier with words. The system will let you place function keys wherever you wish—on top of the keyboard, or to the side. Furthermore, the system will remember your preferences, even if they relate to a remote application.

By putting input and output into the same device, we have for the first time the possibility for truly intuitive interaction with the application. With a spreadsheet, you can slide the numeric keypad anywhere on the screen. You can play chess and move the pieces with your finger.

Although many people use multiple windows on a screen to represent various multitasking activities, most applications and people work best on a full screen. Therefore, the page metaphor is likely to become very popular. With the page metaphor, you change applications like turning pages in a book. There will be simple screen-based buttons to page backward or forward as a standard feature. For cut and paste jobs, or for times when you want to sit back and watch your various computer domains working away on their own, windows, both overlapping and tiled, will be available. When you size a window you will have the option of viewing a portion of the whole application or seeing the full screen scaled down.

## User Scenario

Consider the following scenario: When you turn on your computer, you will see a sheet of electronic paper. You sign your name across it, or speak a command. Your signature or your voiceprint is your password. The system matches your characteristic patterns of pressure, speed, and shape, or sound. Since it is 9 A.M., the time when you normally start work, the system makes the safe bet that it should bring up the document you were revising yesterday when you stopped. The displayed document is a page of printed text covered with handwritten marks and jottings where you have indicated changes. It might even be possible to "grab" the top page of the screen with your fingers and scrunch it into a ball when you want to abandon a badly written document, and then place it on the wastepaper basket.

## Systems Software

The multitasking operating system is resident in 4 megabytes of ROM (read-only memory). Most of the needed functions will be built into the operating system, reducing the applications programming to little more than a sequence of operating systems calls with a user interface. The core of the system modules includes memory management, scheduler, message dispatcher, communications controller, and several service engines, each performing a particular type of generic task. They include a calculating engine for floating-point math, an editing engine, a dialogue engine to support user interface, a typography engine, a drawing engine, a searching engine, a sorting engine, and a filing engine. There could even be a logical (or rule-based) inferencing engine. Flame technology has already announced a Parallel Inference Machine (PIM) that comes as a chip which can be attached to existing computers and workstations. The PIM is capable of 1 million LIPS (logical inferences per second), which is equal to about 1000 instructions/second.

In many cases these engines make use of an underlying hardware co-processor. The functioning of the operating system, however, will not depend on any particular co-processor being available. If a suitable co-processor exists, the operating system will use the module in preference to its own software routines. The operating system will use a software bus to string these engines together in different configurations to solve specific problems. It will be object-oriented; engines will appear as "black boxes" joined by channels along which they exchange encapsulated objects and messages. Application programs will share the same software bus as the operating system, and some will work entirely through operating system's functions. We will be able to treat any application as a new engine for building more applications.

Besides its more conventional functions, the operating system controls the architecture, monitoring the various processors and managing the local power supplied to them in an effort to preserve power. Accordingly, the computer is a "soft" machine. There is an on switch that starts the machine by connecting its local power source (most likely a thin film battery) to the main circuit, but powering down is a software function. There is a secure reset button that can be activated by the machine's own coded stylus. The local power source will be good for at least 12 hours of continuous operation, with the capability to recharge in 10 minutes from any external power source.

## Application Programming

Programming for the user will be by example (or, if preferred, by flowcharts). When programming by example, the user steps through the job sequence in learn mode and then saves the sequence as an intelligent agent which performs the customized task when called upon. The agent may be generalized by asking you to enter data and parameters at run time. It will work like a combination keyboard macro-pipe-batch file-job control program to the 100th power. Because of its seamless communications capability, the computer can use agents on remote computers as well as its own local ones.

The system will contain a full-scale object-oriented database engine whose file structures are designed to facilitate hypertext-style cross-referencing between the contents of different documents. Large amounts of indexing will often be performed on the fly. For example, as you type text, the operating system will examine each word after you press the space bar. It will look it up and consider it a candidate for indexing against already defined categories for cross-reference. And when you load data in batch mode, the operating system will automatically do string functions like searching for categories and spell checking.

## Uses

With such a computer, the possibilities are almost limitless! It could be used as a help in selling. For example, you don't just get a picture of a video recorder on the screen, you get a three-dimensional working image of the recorder. You can touch the buttons and operate the recorder before you buy it. Your working environment will resemble the world around you. Electronic banking will present you with a check to sign that will look like a real check and require a real signature. In database work, you will use forms and charts that more closely resemble the old-fashioned hand-data entry, and sketches rather than the rigorous fields and graphs of the current computer environment. The possibilities seem to be limited only by the individual imagination.

## More Extreme Predictions

There are those who predict a radically different future for the personal computer. They predict that the ultimate personal computer will not look like an electronic notebook at all, but rather will be the size of a golfball. We will communicate with it through speech, and it will respond to us with voice outputs, and where it is useful, with projected holographic images.

Still more strange, the computer might be a set of computer-controlled goggles, headphones, and gloves, or possibly even a body suit (or data suit), that send the user off into an artificial reality where he or she can become part of a scene from a movie, a travelog, or some surreal fantasy world. Such a system would have the potential to transform entertainment, education, engineering, science, medicine, and even pornography (Zachary 1990). Crude artificial reality machines already exist in the university and military laboratories to train pilots in artificial cockpits, and to allow architects to design a building and then to lead a client on a tour of it. There is even a commercial product based on the artificial reality concept. Mattel, Inc., introduced a $90 computer glove that enables users to control some Nintendo games with hand gestures. The glove is partly based on the design of a glove built by VPL Research, Inc., an artificial reality firm.

Of course, artificial reality might become too appealing, like an electronic LSD, and people might seek to ban it. In fact, Timothy Leary, the former Harvard researcher who popularized LSD in the 1960s, claims that artificial reality is "getting closer and closer to the psychedelic experience."

## REVOLUTIONARY TECHNOLOGIES

In recent years, we have seen dramatic increases in performance being achieved with the silicon semiconductor computer. Semiconductors keep halving in linear dimension. The result is a doubling of the speed and a quadrupling of the capacity. Advances with this technology can probably continue only four or five more times before reliability and yields become unacceptably low. Then where will we get the future dramatic improvements from?

Research attention is now being directed toward developing new computer architectures and materials that will further improve speed and performance and mimic human intelligence. Some of the technologies researchers are investigating include parallel processing, including neural networks; superconducting chips and transistors; optics; and biological material. All these projects were included in the newest budget proposals submitted by Japanese government-industry consortiums to MITI, the Ministry of Trade, which is known for funding key research thrusts. There is also the possibility of more exotic breakthroughs like superconductor computers and molecular computers.

### Superconducting

#### *Advantages of Superconducting*

Until the late 1970s, the density of circuits in the state-of-the-art silicon chip had been doubling each year. Since then, the advances have slowed to a doubling every two years. Higher circuit densities also boost the electrical resistance of the chip. Chips with more electrical resistance run hotter, increasing the chances of failure. So as the density of the silicon chips have increased, the need for cooling has increased. Today, some 10 percent of the cost of installing a typical mainframe goes into buying the air conditioning system. In fact, today's supercomputer systems are often dwarfed by their companion cooling systems. If a supercomputer that has no heat energy loss could be built, it could have its circuitry more densely packed, resulting in shorter propagation times and faster processing speeds. Superconducting offers this potential.

## Recent Advances in Superconductivity

Superconductivity was first identified by the Dutch physicist Heike Onnes in 1911. Until a few years ago, the effect was observed only when certain metals were chilled with costly liquid helium to nearly absolute zero, or −459°F. In the early 1980s, two scientists at IBM's Zurich Research Laboratory, K. Alex Muller and J. Georg Bednoz, began looking at ceramic oxides. Ceramic oxides are typically poor conductors, actually insulators, at room temperature. In April 1986, they reported that a ceramic achieved superconductivity at 13°F above the highest temperature achieved for the best metal alloy.

Paul Chu made history in February 1988 when his team of physicists at the University of Houston and the University of Alabama chemically combined four elements to create a compound capable of superconducting at the record −283°F. This is above the boiling point of liquid hydrogen, which is −320°F. Liquid hydrogen is a cheap and easily obtained coolant. The chemical was dubbed 1-2-3 by IBM scientist Grant and his colleagues. The name refers to the atomic ratio of its components: 1 part yttrium, 2 parts barium, 3 parts copper, and a varying amount of oxygen. Soon after rival researchers at the University of California at Berkeley discovered the compound, and since then it has spread like wildfire. Other firms with active research programs in superconductivity include GE, AT&T, IBM, Hewlett Packard, Dupont, Lockheed, Westinghouse, University of Houston, University of Alabama, University of California—Berkeley, Stanford, Cornell, MIT, University of Illinois, Department of Defense, Department of Energy, NEC, NT&T, Toshiba, and Fujitsu. Japan has put together a consortium on superconductivity that is similar to its fifth-generation computer project.

Of course, the stable, high-temperature superconductors discovered to date would require even more expensive cooling systems than the current crop of supercomputers. But a cost-effective supercomputer built using superconductivity could probably be achieved in steps.

### *On-Chip Connections*

Practical problems have been discovered with superconductivity. IBM research indicates that some of the new high-temperature superconductors actually conduct electricity at a slower rate than copper. The current flows through copper at one-fourth the speed of light. Another problem limits the potential of superconductive interconnects when they are used between conventional Integrated Circuits (ICs). As ICs heat up, they could raise the temperature of interconnects enough to lose their superconductivity. On-chip connections could be limited by the same problem. But replacing today's metallic on-chip connections with supercomputers might offer a bigger offsetting gain. They could significantly reduce the chip's power needs, while allowing denser circuit packing. Thin-film fabrication of the

1-2-3 substance was demonstrated at Stanford in March 1987, and at IBM in April 1987.

### *Josephson Junctions*

A more distant prospect for the use of superconductors in computers would be the development of ICs on which even active elements are fabricated from superconductors. One candidate would be Josephson junction devices.

Josephson junctions are superconductor-based switching devices that operate 50 times faster than today's best silicon transistors and 10 times faster than the best semiconductor devices, which are made of gallium arsenide. In addition, they have a very low power consumption and a very low heat dissipation. Problems remain with realizing the practical implementation of superconducting Josephson systems. However, none of the problems appears insurmountable.

### *Superconducting Computers: A Reality?*

An all-superconductive computer is probably at least a decade off. If it comes, it will probably advance in steps. The Nobel Prize-winning physicist and computer scientist Kenneth G. Wilson, currently at Cornell, adds: "Superconductive computers will have to go all the way to mass production before they can be said to have any significant impact on the computing world. As far as I can tell that's a long way away" (Davis 1987). William J. Gallagher, manager of applied cryogenics at IBM's T. J. Watson Research Center in Yorktown Heights, New York, who is overseeing some of IBM's superconductivity research, says: "It's all very much blue sky. But it's somewhat less blue sky than it was last month and an awful lot less than it was a year or so ago " (Davis 1987).

Even if we never do see a superconducting computer, all this focused research is already laying the foundation for another sort of major impact. Materials science has no well-developed modeling; it is still very much in the province of the professional simulation. So the biggest breakthrough of all this activity may not be a computer at all, but a breakthrough in analyzing and modeling materials science.

## Optical Computers

### *Advantages of Optical Computers*

Optical computers hold the potential to reach speeds a thousand times faster than the most powerful conventional machines (Hooper and Schlesinger 1990; Markoff 1990). Light moves faster than electrons through semiconductors; in fact, an optical computer could operate at speeds reaching the physical limit.

Light can transmit a lot more information than electricity. This is what has prompted the use of optical fibers for communications in place of digital electronic transmission. Additionally, an optical computer would be more efficient for routing telephone calls transmitted over fiber optic lines because it would not have to convert back and forth from electricity to light.

Because photons do not interact, light beams can cross each other without interference. Therefore optical computers could be more interconnected than their electronic counterparts. The increased interconnection means we could design computers with shorter paths, and the length of the path determines the speed of the computer.

This property would also make it easier to implement parallel processing on an optical computer, and to solve problems with large amounts of data by accessing lots of data in parallel. Indeed, future optical computers might be a solid 3D block, allowing for still more interconnections.

An optical computer would also be more flexible than an electronic computer, since its circuitry would consist of beams of light that could be reconfigured more easily than wires.

The military is interested in optical computers because they are harder to break into and would not be disabled by the electromagnetic burst resulting from a nuclear blast.

### Recent Advances in Optical Computers

On January 29, 1990, Alan Huang, a researcher at Bell Laboratories, demonstrated an important step toward optical computing: a digital optical processor. The optical computer makes use of an optical switching device called SEED (self-electro-optic effect device), developed at Bell Labs in 1986.

Since light beams do not interact, it is hard to make them turn one another on and off. SEED overcomes this difficulty in the following manner: A voltage is applied to the switch which makes it transparent, permitting a laser beam to shine through. Directing a second beam at the switch material makes it opaque.

Currently the prototype is several cubic feet in size and a little bit slower than today's supercomputer. It is anticipated that the next version could be reduced to several cubic inches and made to process as quickly as today's supercomputer. Of course, this optical computer has the potential to get much smaller and to operate at much greater speeds.

### Forecast for Optical Computers

General-purpose optical computers are expected to be available commercially early in the next century. Bell Laboratories thinks we will see the first application of an optical computer before we are halfway through the decade of the 1990s.

Of course many obstacles must be overcome before optical computers become practical, and there are plenty of skeptics who believe this will never happen. The skeptics admit that it is possible to build an optical computer, but they do not think it is a practical alternative to the electronic computer. IBM did a lot of research on optical computers in the 1960s and concluded that light uses more energy than electronic computers and would not be practical. Bell Labs representatives think optics are good for transmission and connections, but not for much else.

Before optical computers can become practical, they must be miniaturized so they can be mass-produced. We also must learn how to program parallel processes better before we can take full advantage of the optical computer.

## Molecular Computers and Other Advanced Architectures

Of all the advanced, revolutionary technologies, the molecular machine is probably the most exotic, with perhaps the potential for the greatest performance gains, but probably the farthest from reality today. In *Engines of Creation,* K. Eric Drexler (1986) discusses the possibility of using molecular computers. He calls it "nanotechnology" because molecules have the dimensions of nanometers (billionth of a meter). One nanometer is a thousand times smaller than the scale of the present semiconductor chips.

Breakthroughs are expected before the end of the century that will enable us to custom-build single molecules that can store and process information and fabricate other molecules. Molecular machines already exist in nature. Examples include DNA, RNA, and enzymes that assist in the reproduction and repair of biological organisms. Scientists have succeeded in developing simple molecular machines in the laboratory by modification of these natural machines. These early, simple man-made molecular machines are only capable of performing very specific tasks, such as artificial antibiotics and interferon. But in the future there will be new types of these systems capable of performing many functions, only some of which may be biological. These new machines will combine the fields of molecular biology, thin-film chemistry, high-temperature superconductivity, flat-screen technology, X-ray lithography, charge-coupled devices, neural network architecture, and atomic scale microscopy.

### *Types of Molecular Machines*

Molecular machines will probably divide into those that process only information (computers) and those that process materials or energy (robots). Molecular computers would replace semiconductor logic devices with molecular logic devices, although we may see an intermediate technology, such as quantum effect devices, along the way. The molecular logic devices would have linear scales a thousand times less than the present semiconductor devices, and would be three-dimensional rather than two-dimensional. Eventually, they will probably be a thousand times faster and have a billion times greater capacity than present microprocessors and RAM. We can envision a parallel processor of the future being the size of a human brain and having more than a quadrillion nodes. The robotic variety could be capable of programmed movement and manipulation of the environment. They could perform functions on other molecules, such as acquisition, storage, transport, fabrication, or repair. They could mass-produce useful molecules from raw chemicals.

A special case is in the area of I/O and communications. One of the functions of active elements on the outside layers of a lattice design might be to change their response to light so that the entire outer surface of the molecular logic device would function as a holographic interface with the outside world. It could therefore be used as a display or as a high-bandwidth channel for I/O. It might also serve as both a camera and a display so that a pair of such molecular logic devices could be connected over a high-bandwidth channel so that each could display what the other sees in full color and three dimensions.

### *Possible Evolution*

There are many different scenarios for how these molecular engines might evolve. For example, extension of current work in molecular biology might lead to highly modified cells, viruses, or viruslike molecular effectors that could lay down at least the substrate for re-creating other, similar devices. This might then be further structured or permanently "nanocoded" using other such modified bioforms. Another possibility might be to use the tendency for certain polymers, such as some lipoproteins, to form highly regular two-dimensional lattices when stretched into molecular films. Perhaps we could structure such a lattice using X-ray scanning or scanning tunneling microscopy.

## CONCLUSION

As computers continue to permeate society, their impact will grow. Like the automobile and television, they will dramatically and fundamentally alter our way of life. Their impact will affect all facets of our lives.

Recreation and entertainment will become more interactive. They will probably even be delivered, viewed, and billed through computers and computer networks.

We already have electronic translators with voice response output for the future traveler, and electronic pocket dictionaries and spellers for the budding author. Next we will have translating telephones and portable expert advisors.

There will probably be an increase in electronic shopping (shopping through television and electronic computer-based catalogs). Marketing and advertising will integrate with these services and become more directed, focused, and customized.

Education will be more individualized, with greater dependence on electronic tutors and interactive instruction via "smart" television.

Work will be less structured, more creative and thoughtful, with more emphasis on group effort.

Computers may include the ability to transport the user into an artificial reality.

The nature of computer software development will become more one of specifying, analyzing, and integrating pieces of packages. To do this kind of activity well will require greater knowledge of the available packages, their strengths and shortcomings, their availability, reliability, and use, as well as where and how to patch and interconnect.

Even the law will be affected. We will have to consider the rights of consumers and the liabilities of vendors when the computer package gives advice that can affect you or your company's health and economic well-being.

Security and protection against electronic intrusion and fraud will become increasingly critical and sophisticated as dependence upon computers in every facet of life grows.

Computer technology may go through some revolutionary changes. In the future we may all be using computers based on superconducting Josephson junctions, optics, or even molecular computers. The computer's architecture may include large arrays of parallel processors all operating in unison.

Don't throw away your old semiconductor textbooks quite yet. Researchers face a difficult nontechnical challenge in displacing the current computer technology: They are fighting a moving target. While they are doing research, the older revenue-producing technology keeps improving. In fact, it was the anticipation of advances in silicon that led IBM to drop the first Josephson junction research. So it is not certain that superconductors and Josephson junction technology, or optics, or molecular computers, will succeed in playing a major role in the computer of the future.

# Appendix 1

# Key Business Concepts and Theories

Business is concerned with making a profit through the sales of goods and services, or, to quote an old cliché, "the business of business is making money." Furthermore, a business needs financial resources to operate profitably. A business must be able to pay suppliers, to meet payrolls, and to extend credit to customers. "It takes money to make money." Accordingly, we can learn a lot about business by studying its cash flow and financial statements.

## FINANCIAL STATEMENTS

The two most studied financial statements are the balance sheet and the profit and loss statement, alternatively called the income statement. The balance sheet presents a picture of the business's assets, liabilities, and ownership, at a given date, a point in time, whereas the profit and loss statement shows the business income, its net profit or loss, its costs and expenses against sales revenues, over a definite period of time, typically a month or a year.

## THE BALANCE SHEET

Figure A1.1 shows a typical balance sheet. Inspecting this figure, we find that the balance sheet has two main sections. The first section shows the firm's assets. The second section shows the firm's liabilities, or debts, and the owner's equity, or capital. This section represents the claims against the assets. The total of the

Lucky Manufacturing Co. Balance Sheet
Dec. 31, 19xx

| | | ($ in thousands) |
|---|---|---|
| ASSETS | | |
| Current Assets: | | |
| Cash | | $ 50,000 |
| Accounts receivable | 80,000 | |
| Less allowance for doubtful accounts | 25,000 | 55,000 |
| Inventories: | | |
| Finished product | 40,000 | |
| Work in process | 80,000 | |
| Raw materials | 30,000 | |
| Supplies | 15,000 | 305,000 |
| Prepaid expenses | | 5,000 |
| Total current assets | | 415,000 |
| Fixed Assets: | | |
| Furniture and fixtures | 25,000 | |
| Less allowance for depreciation | 8,000 | 17,000 |
| Machinery and equipment | 45,000 | |
| Less allowance for depreciation | 21,000 | 24,000 |
| Buildings | 60,000 | |
| Less allowance for depreciation | 40,000 | 20,000 |
| Land | | 20,000 |
| Total Fixed Assets | | 81,000 |
| Investments | | 35,000 |
| Total Assets | | 531,000 |
| LIABILITIES AND EQUITY | | |
| Current Liabilities: | | |
| Accounts payable | | 55,000 |
| Notes payable | | 100,000 |
| Accrued liabilities: | | |
| Wages and salaries payable | 5,000 | |
| Interest payable | 1,000 | 6,000 |
| Allowance for taxes: | | |
| Income tax | 20,000 | |
| State taxes | 5,000 | 25,000 |
| Total current liabilities | | 186,000 |
| Equity: | | |
| Capital stock | | 335,000 |
| Surplus | | 10,000 |
| Total Equity | | 345,000 |
| Total Liabilities and Equity | | 531,000 |

**Figure A1.1.** A Typical Balance Sheet.

assets always equals the total of the liabilities and the owner's equity, which is why this statement has come to be called a balance sheet.

### Assets

Assets are generally classified into one of three broad categories:

- Current assets—cash and assets expected to be converted into cash, generally within a year; e.g., accounts receivable, marketable securities, inventories, materials and supplies.
- Fixed assets—assets acquired for long-term use; e.g., buildings, machinery, furniture, equipment. They are usually depreciated. This depreciated value does not necessarily reflect the resale value of the asset. *Note:* This is the kind of thing corporate raiders look for when the current return-on-equity (defined in the discussion of financial ratios) is significantly less than the return gained by selling the fixed assets.
- Other assets—these include patents, trade investments, and goodwill, to the extent it has actually been purchased. Other assets, unlike current and fixed assets, are typically intangible (not able to be physically touched, or measured).

### Liabilities

Liabilities can be similarly categorized as:

- Current liabilities—liabilities that are due for payment within a year.
- Long-term (or fixed) liabilities—debts that are *not* due for repayment within a year.

### Equities

The assets of a business minus its liabilities equals its equity. *Equity* represents the owners' investment plus any profits that have been left to accumulate in the business. For example, if the business is incorporated, its books will show a capital stock account equal to the paid-in value of the shares issued to the owners of the business, plus undistributed profits recorded in an earned surplus account.

## PROFIT AND LOSS STATEMENT

Figure A1.2 shows a profit and loss statement for the same fictitious company. This statement conveys the cash-flow characteristics of the company over a given period. It enumerates the various revenues and expenses accumulated over the reporting period, and provides a picture of the health and profitability of the business. The key items on this statement are reviewed below.

Lucky Manufacturing Co.
Profit and Loss Statement
For the year ended Dec. 31, 19xx

| | | | ($ in thousands) |
|---|---|---|---|
| Net Sales | | | $ 890,750 |
| Cost of Goods Sold: | | | |
| Beginning inventory, Jan 1, 19xx | | 145,000 | |
| Merchandise purchases | 560,000 | | |
| Freight and drayage | 70,200 | 630,200 | |
| Cost of goods available for sale | | 775,200 | |
| Less ending inventory, Dec. 31, 19xx | | 280,000 | |
| Cost of goods sold | | 495,200 | |
| Gross margin | | 395,000 | |
| Selling, administrators, and general expenses: | | | |
| Salaries and wages | | 160,000 | |
| Rent | | 110,000 | |
| Light, heat, and power | | 9,000 | |
| Other expenses | | 11,000 | |
| State and local taxes and licenses | | 5,000 | |
| Depreciation and amortization on leased improvements | | 32,000 | |
| Repairs | | 6,000 | |
| Total selling, administrative, and general expenses | | 333,000 | |
| Profit from operations | | 62,550 | |
| Other expense | | 1,800 | 14,200 |
| Net profit before taxes | | 76,750 | |
| Provision for income tax | | 20,000 | |
| Net profit after income tax | | 56,750 | |

**Figure A1.2.** A Typical Profit and Loss Statement.

## Sales

This category represents the net sales revenue obtained, after subtracting sales discounts, returns, and allowances from gross sales.

### *Cost of Goods*

The "cost of goods sold" is the price paid for the products sold during the reporting period, plus transportation costs. Companies compute the cost of goods differently. A common method is to subtract the value of the inventory at the end of the accounting period from the value at the beginning, plus the value of goods purchased during the reporting period.

### *Selling Expenses*

Selling expenses are expenses incurred both directly and indirectly in making sales. They include such items as the salesforce salaries and commissions, advertising, rent, and heat and light.

### General and Administrative Expenses

General and administrative expenses include such items as salaries and wages, supplies, and other operating costs necessary to the administration of the business.

### Other Income

This includes such nonoperating income items as income from interest, dividends, rents, royalties, and gains on the sale of capital assets.

## FINANCIAL RATIOS

These two financial statements, the balance sheet and the profit and loss statement (P&L), are useful in providing a picture of the health of a company, and in providing clues for spotting performance trends. They are useful for management control and planning because they help to identify areas requiring remedial action. They are also useful in comparing a company's performance against other similar businesses. In particular, the financial officer and analyst tend to look at ratios based on these statements. These ratios are used to measure many business conditions, but primarily they address:

1. The company's liquidity, or the health of its financial condition
2. The company's profitability
3. The company's operational effectiveness

The liquidity and profitability measures are used to evaluate and compare a company's performance and future prospects against those of competitors. They help to analyze the monetary condition of a business and to monitor its health. The operating ratios are used in allocating budgets and formulating business plans.

### Liquidity

Two examples of a measure of liquidity are the current ratio and the acid-test (or "quick") ratio. The *current ratio* is the ratio of the company's current assets to current liabilities. It measures the ease with which a company can pay off its debts. What is considered a healthy ratio varies by type of business, current market conditions, and even attitude of company management and creditors, but typically a ratio of less than 2 : 1 is too low. If a company finds its current ratio is too low, it can correct this undesirable situation in a number of ways: by plowing back more profits into current assets, if there are excess profits; by increasing current assets from new equity cash; by paying off some of its debts; or by increasing current assets with loans or borrowings with a maturity greater than one year.

The *acid-test ratio* (also known as the *quick ratio*) is a more stringent test of liquidity because it does not include assets represented by inventories. It is the ratio of a company's cash + government securities + receivables to its current liabilities. This is the same as the current ratio without inventories.

Note that both measures deal exclusively with items from the balance sheet. Typically, a company's liquidity, or financial condition, can be determined solely from its balance sheet.

## Profitability

An example of a company's profitability would be its return on investment (ROI):

ROI = net profit/total assets

Unlike liquidity measures, profitability measures typically require data from both a P&L statement and a balance sheet. In fact, profitability ratios usually relate some profitability item on the P&L to some financial resource on the balance sheet.

## Operational Effectiveness

An example of a company's operational effectiveness would be net profit on net sales. Operational ratios always, directly or indirectly, show the relationship of expense items to net sales.

## Several Popular Ratios

Some of the more popular ratios are listed below, categorized according to whether their primary utility is as a measure of liquidity and financial health, profitability, or operational effectiveness.

*Liquidity and financial health:*

- Current assets to current liabilities (the current ratio)
- Acid-test, or quick, ratio
- Net sales to inventory
- Net fixed assets to tangible net worth
- Total debt to tangible net worth
- Inventory turnover (cost of goods sold/average inventory)
- Current liabilities to tangible net worth

*Profitability:*

- Net sales to tangible net worth
- Net sales to working capital, where working capital is defined as the difference between current assets and current liability
- Net profits to tangible net worth
- Return on investment (ROI) (This is defined as the net profit/total assets)
- Investment turnover, or net sales assets
- Asset earning power, or operating profit/total assets
- Return on owners equity, or net profit/equity
- Tangible net worth (This is the return on owner's equity, except the equity is less the intangible assets.)

*Operational effectiveness:*
Average collection period of receivables
Net profit on net sales

These ratios provide a powerful tool in strategic planning, competitive analysis, and financial operational control.

## Interpreting Financial Ratios

If generated according to accepted principles of accounting, compared with approximately comparable businesses, and interpreted with care, these ratios can help answer many important financial questions. A few words of caution are needed when using these financial tools. Although the balance sheet tries to present a true and fair picture of the financial position of a business at the close of the accounting period, and the profit and loss statement tries to present a true and fair picture of the results of operations during the accounting period, many of the transactions involved are often incomplete at the end of the accounting period, and the figures are determined under conditions of some uncertainty. They depend on the accountant's judgement and choice of accounting techniques. Whether a ratio is within acceptable limits depends on the nature of the business, its cash flow characteristics, the season, the stage of the business cycle, the company's management style, and the external financial climate. Also, the balance sheet reflects cost less depreciation rather than resale or liquidity values. This can often present a false picture of the true liquidity or value of the corporation.

## Other Considerations

Financial reports and ratios are only a measure of past performance and cannot predict the future. To obtain a more complete understanding of a business, we need to explore underlying business concepts from four other viewpoints:

1. The major categories the various types of business can be divided into, and the key attributes associated with each category
2. An understanding and appreciation of the basic macro- and microeconomic principles and how they affect and influence business decisions and operations
3. An understanding of the fundamental concepts, principles, and choices underlying prudent asset and liability management
4. The basic business activities and their unique information needs

# CATEGORIES OF BUSINESSES

All businesses have many common activities, problems, and opportunities. For example, they all have in common the need to market their products, to raise funds, and to invest excess cash. It is these similarities that have allowed many seasoned executives to switch successfully from one type of industry to another by transferring old skills to their new business.

The various businesses also have many unique and special problems that distinguish them and require special knowledge and attention. For example, manufacturing has problems of inventory control, scheduling of parts and subassemblies, tooling lead times, and control over the manufacturing process. Some firms have severe cash flow problems, while others are cash rich and need to look for investment opportunities. Different firms are better, or worse, positioned to take advantage of different vehicles for raising and investing funds. For example, different firms have different credit ratings and cash flow needs, influencing their choice of means for raising cash (use of line-of-credit, venture capital, loans, bonds, selling equity shares) and their choice of investments (investing in funds, capital assets and real estate, stocks, bonds, or making loans). Some industries, such as retail department stores, have seasonal trends. Other firms are cyclic, with dramatic swings in their cash flow situation. Casualty insurance companies have lately experienced these sort of swings, with heavy losses one year and large profits the next. Some firms have a service focus; others are dominated by a concern for low unit cost. These distinctions are particularly important to understand and respond to in the creative decision-making aspects of business. Not only the solution, but the very problems needing solving are strongly influenced by these unique differences.

This suggests that executive-level decision-making and problem-solving is a very knowledge-intensive activity, calling upon a lot of specialized information and experience specific to the business area, including laws and regulations, specialized accounting procedures, industry-specific cost and market trends, competitive outlook, and relevant economic and social demographics. To best understand a company's performance, it is useful to compare it with similar companies of the same industry grouping. That is why stock market investment analysts find it useful to specialize in specific industry categories. For example, to enhance analysis and comparison, Goldman Sachs, an investment bank, divides the companies in the S&P 500 into the major categories and groupings within categories shown in Table A1.1.

If various financial ratios and measures, such as liquidity and past earnings growth, are studied with respect to these business groupings, one can reach conclusions regarding each grouping relative to the general economy and the other groups, such as "Group A's revenue growth is anticipated to exceed the general economic growth," or "Group B's unit volume should be up in 19xx," or "Profitability is at record levels for this group."

The performance of a particular company can then be analyzed by comparing that company's financial measures and ratios with others relative to its grouping and with the overall economy. This analysis should result in a characterization of the company as:

- Investment quality: above-average growth
- Volatile growth: above-average potential
- Emerging investment quality: above-average growth

TABLE A1.1 CATEGORY GROUPINGS

| Category | Grouping |
|---|---|
| Industrial | Aerospace |
| | Aluminum |
| | Automobile |
| | Auto parts |
| | Beverage |
| | Chemicals |
| | Computer services |
| | Conglomerates |
| | Copper |
| | Cosmetics |
| | Drugs |
| | Electrical equipment |
| | Household appliances |
| | Semiconductors |
| | Electronics, defense |
| | Entertainment |
| | Packaged foods |
| | Forest products and paper |
| | Gold mining |
| | Hospital management |
| | Hospital supply |
| | Hotel/motel |
| | Machinery |
| | Newspapers, radio and TV broadcasters |
| | Office equipment |
| | Oils: domestic and international |
| | Oil services |
| | Pollution |
| | Restaurants |
| | Retail, drug chains, and supermarkets |
| | Household products |
| | Steel |
| | Textiles |
| | Tobacco |
| Public Utilities | Independent telephone |
| | Electrics |
| | Natural gas |
| Transportation | Airlines |
| | Railroad |
| | Trucking and air freight |
| Financials | Banks: money centers & regionals |
| | Insurance: property/casualty, multiline, life |
| | Savings and loans |

- Defensive or stable growth
- Cyclical/basic industry
- Cyclical/growth

They should help us understand both the relative security and stability of the firm, as well as its potential for growth. These characterizations can be suitable for taking some relevant action, such as investing in stock or granting a loan.

# Appendix 2

# Principles of Economics

We can gain further insight into the operation of business through a study of basic economic principles. Economics deals with a universal problem. Since goods and resources are relatively scarce, it is necessary to make a choice regarding allocation. If the commodities in question were of unlimited abundance and free of any cost and did not require any scarce resources or labor, there would be no need for a science of economics; we would produce all that was desired. Unfortunately, not all our needs and desires can be fulfilled. In fact, their mutual satisfaction are generally in conflict. Consequently, economics is concerned with problems of organization and allocation using fixed and relatively scarce resources and labor.

## THE CONCERNS OF ECONOMICS

Economics is interested in finding answers to the following sorts of questions:

1. What kinds of quantities of goods and services should we produce?
2. How can we best allocate and use our resources to produce these goods?
3. For whom should these goods be produced, and how should we distribute the income derived from producing these goods?

## CAPITALISM: THE FREE ENTERPRISE SYSTEM

Different societies have addressed these economic issues in different ways: some by custom, some by instinct, and some by fiat and decree. Our society decides these issues through the workings of the free competitive marketplace. We let the marketplace decide what and how much to make, and what to buy. These become important questions for business to answer. If a company overproduces, it will be left with a large unsold inventory. If it underproduces and the demand exceeds the available supply, it can produce more goods, or raise prices, or possibly do both. The idea of letting the marketplace determine the production and allocation of goods, their resulting price, and the distribution of wealth in society is based upon Adam Smith's "invisible hand." It is based on a system of prices:

- Everything has a price.
- What is produced is determined by the consumer's vote.
- How things are produced is determined by competition between different producers.
- What products and services are produced, how many of each and for whom, is determined by supply and demand for them.

These choices may be depicted graphically by plotting the various tradeoffs and choices through the use of production-possibility, or transformation, curves. An example of such a curve is shown in Figure A2.1.

For our society, it is important to study pricing or product valuation. Microeconomics is concerned with how market pricing of a given product is affected by the relative supply and demand, whereas macroeconomics deals with the big picture, the macro aggregates of income, employment, and price levels in the general society. As we shall see, both aspects are important for business to follow and understand.

## PRICING AND VALUATION OF PRODUCTS

Three key principles that relate price to supply and demand are market equilibrium, the law of economy of scale, and the law of diminishing returns.

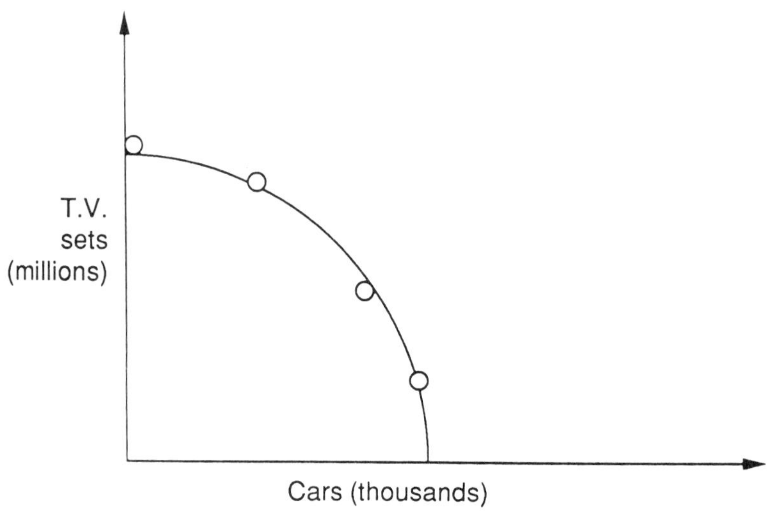


**Figure A2.1.** Production-Possibility Curve.

A product has different values to different people. Some are willing to pay much more for the same product than others. Therefore, in order to sell out a given supply of products (quantity *N*), the product must sell for a price no greater than the *N*th lowest bid price. If this price exceeds the cost of building the product by a large enough margin, then the seller will produce a supply of at least *N* units. If the number of buyers desiring to buy the product, at a cost profitable to the seller, exceeds the available supply, the seller will increase production. If the supply exceeds the number of prospective buyers, the seller will decrease production. The system will reach equilibrium when the available supply exactly equals the number of people/organizations wanting to buy the product at a price yielding an acceptable profit to the seller. Thus market price is determined by the relative levels of supply and demand.

This balancing of the price and supply to the resulting demand results in a market equilibrium. In a free market, without external disturbances, all product prices will eventually reach their market equilibrium. This equilibrium can change with fluctuations in overall consumer income, and as new products enter the market to compete for the consumer's money. It can also be upset by market imperfections that arise when someone buys or sells in large enough quantities to affect price, at least temporarily.

## HOW AND HOW MUCH TO PRODUCE

The amount of money spent in manufacturing a product is another important variable. An initial minimum outlay of funds is usually required before the seller can begin any serious production output. Often the number, quality, and unit cost of products outputted will continue to improve and grow with an increased outlay of funds. This decrease in the cost of producing a product as the quantity produced is increased is known as "economy of scale." Full savings in the production cost do not come into play until a sufficiently large number of products can offset initial setup costs. For some products, however, this infusion of capital and labor eventually reaches a point of diminishing returns, where further outlays cause little gain in unit cost, production quantity, or quality.

An example of this is farming on a fixed parcel of land. A minimum outlay for basic farm machinery, pest control, and fertilizer is required before a harvest of any size can be reaped. Initially, increasing the amount one plants on the land increases the yield, or output, for little or no more increase in cost (not considering government farm subsidies). Eventually, however, if we overplant, the land will become poor in nutrients, and the planting too overcrowded. At this point of diminishing returns, the unit cost will begin to increase again, and the usable output may even decrease.

## NEED FOR GOVERNMENT INTERVENTION

The free market system is not designed to be fair or equitable. People and businesses will act in their own best interests under a free enterprise system, and what is good for the individual, or business, is not always good for the society. This effect is known as the "fallacy of composition." So the government often imposes taxes, rules, and regulations in an attempt to ensure more equity in the system and no major abuses. Government intervention, or the potential for government intervention, is an important factor to consider in business planning.

## THE GENERAL ECONOMY

It is important to understand the dynamics of the larger economy and how it can affect the product demand, expenses, and fair market price of a particular business. The health of the overall economy affects available consumer wealth. Greater per capita income increases available consumer dollars; population growth increases the demand and decreases the resources available per capita; advances in technology and the economics of mass production influence the availability and cost of a product. The emergence of new products can result in increased competition for the resources and consumer wealth of more established products, and increased specialization and division of labor raises productivity but increases the mutual interdependence between companies and even between countries.

## BUSINESS CYCLES AND SEASONAL TRENDS

These complex economic interdependencies can pull a business in opposing directions, causing cyclic swings in its fortunes, just as the opposing forces of gravity and the tension on the string holding a pendulum causes it to swing back and forth about its pivot point. Certain types of businesses can also experience seasonal swings. These cycles and seasons often form detectable and to an extent predictable patterns, but these patterns can be obscured by unexpected, random, and short-lived fluctuations in supply, demand, and price equilibrium conditions.

Insurance companies can be observed to go through predictable cycles of profit. These lead to increased competition and price cutting to increase market share. This leads in turn to lower profit margins and eventually, in some instances, to losses, which result in industry wide price increases, which lead to increased profit margins, which lead to price cutting to gain market share, and so forth. The cycle seems almost preordained, but the exact period can vary and is not known. Moreover, a sudden unexpected surge in accidents could temporarily depress a company's earnings despite high rates. The retail trade provides an example of the seasonal effect. Sales tend to peak in December and to decrease to lows in January. External events could cause short, temporary fluctuations, but the seasonal trend is generally unmistakable.

Effectively running and planning a business requires understanding, measuring, and forecasting the business cycles and seasonal effects, using statistical methods to correct for them and to detect fundamental trends, or shifts, in an industry.

## THE BARTER SYSTEM

Different societies have adopted different mechanisms for buying and selling goods in the marketplace. In the most primitive societies, people simply exchange goods, or *barter*. For example, the shoemaker might pay the restaurant owner for his lunch with a pair of shoes. This method is still used on a limited basis in certain circumstances; e.g., a gardener agrees to pay dental bills by landscaping the dentist's front lawn. The barter method is cumbersome, for the following reasons:

1. It may be difficult to find someone who has a product you want and who simultaneously wants a product you have. It may be necessary to find an intermediary who wants your product and who owns a product that the other party needs. Then a two-way swap can be arranged. Sometimes it may be necessary to arrange a three-way swap, or an even more convoluted swap, before you can purchase what you want. Arranging these swaps is difficult and time-consuming.
2. By allowing anyone to swap anything for anything else, it is necessary to be able to value the products for sale in terms of a potentially unlimited number of different commodity units.
3. It may be difficult to break the products to be exchanged into small enough units to allow for a fair and equitable swap.

Many over-the-counter financial products have these characteristics, but buyers and sellers use computer and communications technology to ease the search for a counterparty and the valuation processes.

## COMMODITY MONEY

Another, more practical method is to declare a particular commodity, such as gold, as the standard medium of exchange, or *money*. This overcomes the first two problems associated with the barter system. If gold is the common medium of exchange, as long as you have gold, you can buy whatever you wish and you can get gold by selling your products. You do not have to match buyers and sellers. The total transaction never gets more complicated than two exchanges. Party A sells goods to party B for gold, and then uses that gold to purchase a product from party C. Furthermore, gold can be divided into arbitrarily small sizes.

The disadvantages associated with commodity money are that it may become difficult to carry or store, because of its bulk, and that an unexpected supply or loss of this commodity can result in an undesired creation or loss of wealth.

## PAPER OR BANK MONEY

A third medium of exchange is paper money, or bank money. Like commodity money, it represents a unit of account, a common standard of value. In addition, it is easy to handle and store. It is also easy to control the available quantity in circulation, and facilitates entering into a contract with either standard or deferred payment. Even with paper money, however, the money's future worth, or "store of value," will depend on the future trend of prices. Inflation can destroy the purchasing power of such money.

## ELECTRONIC MONEY

Even with paper money there is a transactional cost of handling. In a totally computerized society, a transaction involving the transfer of wealth (a purchase) reduces to an electronic information transfer. The transaction can be captured, transmitted, and recorded electronically, with negligible use of manpower and physical energy. This is inherently the most efficient and flexible mechanism for the transfer of wealth and can be expected to grow in usage. At this stage, most of the functions of the financial intermediary (e.g., banks) reduces to the management of a large electronic communications utility directly connecting and matching financial transactors.

# Appendix 3

## Basic Business Activities

All business activities can be divided into the following eight basic categories:

1. Sales and marketing
2. Manufacturing and product development
3. Customer service
4. Distribution
5. Operations and administrative support
6. Accounting and financial control
7. Personnel
8. Management

Each has its own peculiar concerns and information needs.

### SALES AND MARKETING

Sales and marketing are concerned with obtaining customer orders for products and services. The sales function is tactical; it is focused on obtaining specific orders for existing products. Marketing is more strategic; it is aimed at generating long-term plans for maintaining and broadening the existing customer base, and for setting the general direction and future sales focus. It is also concerned with the introduction of new products and product enhancements. To do their job effectively, sales and marketing need access to the following information:

- Customers' current and projected needs and requirements
- Present and future competitive offerings

- Measurements of effectiveness (both volume of sales and profitability)
- Strategic goals and objectives

## MANUFACTURING AND PRODUCTION

Manufacturing and production are concerned with ensuring that products are produced on schedule, with minimum waste and defects. They need to keep the cost of labor and materials down and productivity high. They want parts to arrive on time, when needed, but not too early, which requires costly storage. They need sales projections so that they can adjust production output accordingly. The goal is to have a ready supply of goods so that customer orders can be fulfilled with little or no wait time. This should be achieved while maintaining little or no inventory (having to store inventory costs money). This requires good sales projections and quick turnaround times. So manufacturing and production are concerned with continuously monitoring inventory levels, goods in the process of manufacture, and outstanding and forecast orders.

Manufacturing and production are also concerned with producing high-quality products with minimum waste of material and time. Therefore, they are concerned with early detection of errors and defects for prompt correction or rejection. Ideally, they would like to continuously monitor and control the manufacturing process in real-time to minimize or eliminate errors and defects altogether. They want to maximize the efficient scheduling and utilization of expensive capital equipment and human resources. They want to allow for more flexible manufacturing operations. This would enable more rapid retooling and adjustment to manufacturing advances and changes. It would help minimize the time required to move from design of a new product to full production. A truly effective manufacturing operation allows for individual customization of products. The ultimate manufacturing process would be a completely automated factory with sufficient flexibility that each product can be individually built to custom specifications.

The information needs of manufacturing and production include:

- Observables from the manufacturing process that can measure product quality and elapsed time at various points and stages in the process
- Productivity measures
- Projections of future sales

## CUSTOMER SERVICE

Customer service is concerned with customer satisfaction. Polls, questionnaires, surveys, and spot checks are the main sources of data for determining how well the job is being performed. These sources are internally generated, and can also be obtained from external independent agencies that perform comparative analyses and customer ratings and surveys. External sources are quite valuable because of their objectivity and as a source of competitive information. To be effective in customer service, one must be knowledgeable, prompt, sensitive, tactful, and pleasant under pressure. Obviously, people working in customer service areas need a lot of training and near-instantaneous access to a broad area of specialized knowledge.

## DISTRIBUTION

Distribution is concerned with the transportation and delivery of raw materials to plants, and of goods from plants to stores and storage facilities, and from these to the customer. Generally there are many different plants, stores, storage facilities, and customer locations whose outputs and needs rise and ebb over time in ways that are not always predictable. Together, they constitute a complex network of random fluctuations in supply and demand. Success in distribution requires advanced knowledge regarding these fluctuations. It also requires computational power to run highly sophisticated allocation and assignment algorithms, often utilizing sophisticated linear and quadratic mathematical programming techniques.

## OPERATIONS AND ADMINISTRATIVE SUPPORT

Operations is the support arm of the organization. This group is concerned with supporting the actions required to complete the decisions and actions of the other parts of the business. Duties include paying the bills; managing the facilities; overseeing the receipt and delivery of products and customer payments; preparing reports, mailings, and memos; keeping records; and ensuring and reporting on legal and audit compliance with governmental regulations.

These functions do not always have a unique identity. They are not always concentrated in a single organizational area, but are sometimes distributed among various entities. The existence of a separate operational element is dependent upon the nature of the business, the size and complexity of the operational function, and the management style. The operational and administrative support functions have been one of the heaviest users of computers. In fact, this is one of the most popular organizational components within which to place the functions of computer and communications operation and maintenance. Operations uses computers to speed response time, to increase capacity, and to minimize the clerical costs associated with recordkeeping and report preparation and distribution. These have been the traditional uses of the computer.

## ACCOUNTING AND FINANCIAL CONTROL

Accounting and financial control are concerned with maintaining the financial records and general ledger of the organization, and reporting on the financial health of the company to management, investors, and the general public. They develop and enforce the accounting and financial reporting procedures used throughout the organization. This includes methods of billing customers and paying vendors, allocating expenses and revenues, depreciation guidelines, and credit authorization. They are concerned with the investment of excess funds (asset management) and raising funds to meet payroll and bills (liability management). Because of the large number of records and computations associated with these functions, accounting and financial control, like operations, has been a heavy user of computers almost since their inception, and is often the organization component in which management of computer operations has been placed.

## PERSONNEL

Personnel is concerned with the employees of the company. Its duties include hiring and firing; promotions, demotions, and transfers; providing for employee training and career development; maintaining employee records; assessing and evaluating employee performance, administering guidelines for salary and bonus reviews. To do this job well, extensive files on employee skills, training, performance, and employment history need to be maintained. Personnel files are usually personal and confidential. When maintained in computers, this information must be assured security and privacy.

## MANAGEMENT

Management is charged with setting the general direction of the company through establishing the goals, plans, and objectives of the organization; determining the organizational structure; and selecting the people and providing them with the proper motivation. Management must take a view and set a tone and strategic direction for the entire company. To help shape this view, management needs feedback on the effectiveness of decisions, including others' responses and reactions to them. They need measures of the company's performance relative to the economy, to market conditions, and to the competition. The balance sheet, P&L statement, and associated financial ratios are important tools for the manager. So are employee and customer surveys. Management also needs to gain a sense of trends and how they are likely to affect the business in the future. This helps to identify areas of future opportunity and new initiatives. This activity requires a lot of external data.

Management achieves its objectives by making adjustments to current plans, goals, organizational structure, and product lines. This requires maintaining and interpreting voluminous, diverse, and complex interrelated data. These analyses must include techniques for forecasting, and for anticipating and managing against future trends, events, and likely scenarios. Much of this interpretation, prediction, and decision-making under uncertainty is highly judgmental and inexact, involving a good deal of hard-to-define experience and intuition.

# Appendix 4

# Principles of Investment

## ASSET AND LIABILITY MANAGEMENT

Because a business's cash flows are uneven and not exactly matched (or gapped), even a healthy business may at certain points in time experience a cash surplus, an excess influx of funds; at other times the business may be short of cash when more money is paid out than is received. For example, every month a business may have to meet a payroll and settle its outstanding bills, while it may not receive any sales payments until fifteen days later. And the gaps can be much greater; e.g., annual tax bills, principle due on a 20-year bond, a one-time sale of a piece of property, or a one-time outlay for the purchase or repair of some needed capital equipment. This last example illustrates that these cash flow fluctuations cannot always be predicted in advance. Added to this complexity, in our increasingly globalized economy the flow of funds will often involve future exchanges of different country currencies.

## GAP MANAGEMENT

A business is concerned with minimizing the costs of borrowing needed to cover temporary shortages, and with maximizing the profit obtained by putting temporary surpluses to work. Thus a business is concerned with efficient liability (debts, borrowings) and asset (investments, loans, stocks, bonds) management. The business is likely to try to keep its borrowings short and its investments long because interest rates are typically (but not always) lower, the shorter the holding period of the loan/bond. Interest costs and earnings are a direct function of both rate and time held. Of course if the borrowings need to be renewed at different times in the future, the total cost of borrowing will be unknown because the future interest cost fluctuates unpredictably.

Often, the management is split between two different persons or offices, one managing the liabilities and the other managing the assets, each with some overall constraints to ensure some level of coordination. For example, the liability manager needs to know how long the shortage is likely to persist, whereas the asset manager needs to know when cash will be needed next and an investment needs to be liquidated. Lately, there has been a growing trend to manage both liabilities and assets from a more common, integrated viewpoint, often under the same manager, to take advantage of various synergies and tax nuances.

## AVAILABLE CHOICES

The tasks of liability and asset management are made more difficult because the business cannot always adequately predict exactly when a surplus or shortage will occur, or for how long this condition will persist. They are further complicated by the multitude of ways available to raise and invest funds. For example, to raise funds, the business could:

- Borrow from a bank or group of individuals
- Issue stock, common or preferred, with or without warrants
- Sell bonds, with or without call features, with or without warrants, with fixed or variable rates, with or without put options, with or without payments or principal in foreign or mixed denominations
- Sell or lease capital equipment or real estate

To invest its surplus, the business could:

- Buy stocks, bonds, futures, and options
- Make loans
- Provide venture capital for startups
- Buy real estate
- Buy capital equipment
- Plow the money back into research, advertising, or some other aspect of the business
- Keep the funds in a liquid bank account

Many of these choices involve complex and often uncertain cash flows of their own. Many involve payments at points in the future.

## THE DISCOUNT FUNCTION

In order to compare our choices meaningfully, we must be able to relate and value them with respect to each other. For example, we need to know if $2000 received two months from now is better or worse than receiving $1000 a month from now. To see how to attack these problems, we need to learn a little about finance theory.

In order to compare dissimilar cash flows, we need to know the current time value of money. By *time value of money* we mean that a dollar received sometime in the future is worth less than a dollar today; it is discounted. If we agree to receive a dollar at some time in the future we lose the opportunity to put that dollar to work—for example, to invest it. This lost opportunity is worth money; hence the discount. The discount is, of course, a function of time. Furthermore, this discount function can change. That is why we used the adjective "current" time value.

So how do we know what to use for the current discount function? One approach could be to use a series of U.S. Treasury bonds. They are relatively riskless. We can assume no premium for credit (default) risk. They are actively traded, they are liquid, and consequently there is generally a valid fair market price quote available; and, they are issued in reasonably regular intervals, making it practical to extrapolate a discount function from a series of these bonds. A brief example of how this is done is provided below.

Consider the following series of Treasuries (note these are conversions from the actual bill quotes; U.S. T-bills are quoted as the percent discounted):

| Name of treasury | Market price ($/100) |
|---|---|
| 3-month bill | 99.000 |
| 6-month bill | 98.500 |
| 9-month bill | 97.800 |
| 12-month note with 10% coupon | 97.000 |

The Treasury bills make only a single payment, at maturity, whereas the Treasury note pays the principal at maturity, but in addition makes semi-annual interest payments. The 10% coupon refers to the annual interest paid. In actuality 5 percent is paid every six months. The price shown is the price paid today for every $100 paid out at maturity. From the table above, it is possible to compute the discount function at 3-month intervals, out to 12 months. Other values of the discount function can be interpolated using geometric ratios.

The discount function at time = 0 into the future is clearly 1.00, since a dollar spent today is currently worth a dollar. Since the bills represent only a single payment at some point in the future, they represent the discount function at a time in the future equal to when they mature. Therefore, from the information above, it is straightforward to conclude that the discount for a payment three months from now is .990, six months from now, .985, and 9 months from now, .978. The bond's price of 97 must equal its discounted cash flow. Its cash flow is 5 percent of $100, or $5, six months from now, and $100 plus 5 percent of $100, or $105, twelve months from now. We know that the discount six months from now is 98.500, so we can solve for the discount twelve months from now, equating

$$97 = 5(.985) + 105x \qquad \text{(A4-1)}$$

where $x$ represents the unknown discount twelve months from now. From equation A4-1, we can derive that $x = .877$.

## CREDIT PREMIUM

To make informed decisions and valuations, we also need to be able to equate the value of cash streams, such as loans and bonds, guaranteed from different counterparties. We need to be able to compute how much more an obligation from General Motors to pay back a loan of $1 million at 8 percent interest is worth than an obligation with similar terms, from the owner of the corner newsstand. We probably would demand some premium on the interest charge paid by our newsstand owner over General Motors because of the greater likelihood that the newsstand owner will default. But how much of a premium should we charge?

This discount function can be used to compute the premium price paid for a less creditworthy bond by comparing that bond's market price with its theoretical price, computed by using the discount function. The difference can be attributed to the premium paid for its poorer credit quality. Bond ratings are provided by rating agencies such as Moody's and S&P. They study the financial stability of the company backing a bond and determine its likelihood of defaulting on obligated bond payments. They indicate their assessment of the credit risk of a bond issue by assigning a letter rating such as AAA, AA, A, BBB, where AAA is the highest, most creditworthy rating. Bonds can be valued using these ratings by computing the bond's price using the current discount function and then adding the appropriate premium for the rating. Similarly rated bonds should pay a comparable premium. It should be noted that these premiums, like the discount function, change over time and must be continuously updated.

## DEDICATION

One way to manage cash flow surpluses and deficits is to attempt to choose investments whose payoff, or cash influxes, will always precisely match cash outflows, with the possible exception of some minimal need for short-term (few days) borrowings as a bridge. Achieving this objective requires complex cash flow matching searches among a large list of investments to find an optimum match. Computers are generally used in this analysis, using algorithms called dedication routines. These algorithms are complex and highly computation-intensive. Of course, every time the cash flow constraints change, the anticipated liabilities or investment cash flow will not match expectations. The optimization analysis must then be rerun, and old investments liquidated and new ones bought. Even when the cash flow constraints have not changed, an unusually favorable investment or borrowing climate (unusually high or low rates) may prompt the manager to readjust the portfolio.

Increased gains can usually be achieved if the portfolio manager is willing to make investments with greater risk. For example, the manager could buy a security of a higher yield but greater risk. This risk could be due to a number of things. The security could have a history of unstable, volatile market price swings. It could represent an uncertain term; it could be susceptible to being called or repaid early. The issuer could represent a greater credit risk, a greater likelihood of default.

## IMMUNIZATION

Another approach to portfolio management is to attempt to lock in a guaranteed rate for a fixed investment horizon by matching composite portfolio parameters, rather than attempting to match each particular component's cash stream. For example, a portfolio of bonds is often engineered to remain invariant under market price fluctuations. If a bond makes only a single payment, at maturity, then one way to protect a portfolio against price fluctuations is to invest solely in bonds that provide a single payment which perfectly matches the desired investment horizon. Such bonds are often called *zero coupon bonds* because they pay no coupons (interest) until maturity. Such a portfolio is said to be "immunized."

Of course, we cannot always find zero coupon bonds with the exact desired maturity, and when we do, the resulting yield might be much lower than desired. We can buy bonds with periodic interest payments for our portfolio, but then the realized rate of return will vary, depending upon the future rate at which we will be able to reinvest the interest payments. Because this is uncertain, we are exposed to reinvestment rate risk. In this case, we can immunize our portfolio of bonds against small movements in the yield so long as the portfolio's composite duration matches the desired investment horizon. *Duration* is defined as the point in time at which half the bond's payments are received.

It can also be shown to be proportional to the slope of the tangent of the price–yield curve at the current yield, divided by the current price. The slope, or first derivative, represents the change in price experienced for small changes in yield. When a bond is held for a time equal to its duration, any moneys lost (or gained) by a change in the reinvestment rate will be exactly matched by the corresponding gain (or loss) in the price of the bond, for small changes in yield. At larger shifts in yield, the corresponding change in price is no longer linear, and we will have to match higher-order derivatives of the composite bond portfolio against the liability cash stream in order for the portfolio to remain immunized over its investment horizon. This is particularly important when the price–yield curve has a lot of curvature, as it does for mortgage-backed bonds and bonds with embedded call options. In this case, even relatively small changes in yield can produce large nonlinear changes in price.

The second-order derivative, convexity, is usually sufficient to provide immunity for most bonds against the yield shifts experienced in practice. An advantage of matching overall portfolio duration and convexity, rather than specific cash flows, is that the liability cash stream does not have to be exactly balanced, only its composite duration and convexity. This relaxation of the criteria for suitable investment candidates permits the manager to choose from among a much larger universe, and therefore increases the likelihood of finding a set of bonds that will produce a higher rate of return.

Of course, if we immunize a portfolio, we will not only be protecting the portfolio from undesirable price declines or losses, we will also be denying the portfolio the chance of realizing gains if prices move up. When the bond's prices change over time, the portfolio will have to be rebalanced, because with the exception of zero coupon bonds, durations and convexities will change as the price (and yield) of the bond changes, moving up and down the price–yield curve. In order to keep a portfolio immunized against movements in price/yield, the portfolio's composition will have to be adjusted periodically. These adjustments are minor in comparison to the losses that could be experienced at the end of the investment horizon if the portfolio is not kept immunized.

## HEDGING

One can also protect a portfolio against price declines by judicious investment in futures and options.

### Futures

A *future* is a contract to buy a security, such as a stock or bond, at a fixed price sometime in the future, typically, 3, 6, or 9 months. If the future contract is for purchasing a bond in the manager's portfolio, changes in the bond's price and in the future's contract price should be strongly correlated, because at contract expiration the future price and the bond price must be equal. This is because if the bond increases in price, the futures contract on the bond will also increase proportionately in value. Of course the two markets are not perfectly linked, and the difference between the two prices, often called the *basis,* will not remain completely fixed throughout the contract period, but will experience random fluctuations. Nevertheless, one can protect a portfolio against potential price losses by *shorting,* selling an appropriate number of closely correlated futures contracts. In this case, the gain realized by selling the futures contracts high and repurchasing them at a lower price should approximately balance the portfolio loss experienced by the decline in bond prices.

### Options

*Options* represent the right, but not the obligation, to purchase or sell an underlying security, such as a bond, bond future, stock, or stock future, for a fixed price at some time in the future. Thus, for the price of the option, the portfolio manager can protect against unexpected future declines and increases in the values of stocks and bonds. For example, the portfolio manager can protect against a decline in value of an individual bond or stock by buying a *put.* A *put* is a right but not an obligation to sell for a fixed price, called the *strike price.* If the price of the underlying stock or bond increases, the manager lets the option expire, and merely loses the cost of the put. If the value of the underlying stock or bond decreases, the manager can exercise the put to sell the stock or bond at a profit established by the agreed-upon strike price. Similarly, the portfolio manager could have sold (written) a *call.* A *call* is a right but not an obligation to buy at a fixed price. In this case the manager is selling the right. If the underlying bond or stock declines in value, the holder of the call will let the option expire unexercised because he could purchase the stock or bond in the open market at a lower price than the call strike price, and the manager earns a call premium. If, on the other hand, the underlying bond or stock were to increase in value, the call would be exercised, and the manager would be required to sell at the agreed-upon strike price and would not realize the full profit that would have been possible if the stock or bond could be sold on the current open market.

# Appendix 5

## Business Decision-Making

It is helpful to understand the decision-making process itself in order to design effective decision support systems. The basic structure and elements of decision-making have been studied and analyzed extensively. Fundamental to virtually all business decisions are the elements of risk and uncertainty. Making profits is closely linked with taking risks under uncertainty. Whenever we make a management decision, be it increasing output, investing in R&D, launching a new sales campaign or a new marketing strategy, introducing a new product, or making an investment in stocks and bonds, we are taking this action in anticipation of financial reward. But we are committing resources (money, material, people) which we are putting at risk should our hopes, plans, and assumptions about future outcomes and responses to events not hold true. Worse still, in some cases we might even lose more than the original investment.

Certainly the most challenging aspect of decision-making is that it usually must be performed under uncertainty. It is the uncertainty associated with both the input information used in the decision process and the likely results obtained from taking various contemplated actions that makes the process so challenging and stimulating, prevents it from ever becoming purely rote and routine, and helps to distinguish the typical business problem and its associated decisions from more academic problems. Business decision-making is like playing chess; no matter how many games one has played, each new game presents a fresh challenge. The player's experience and knowledge may help to make better moves, but no matter how many times the game is played, decisions cannot be reduced to routine.

Various structured approaches to decision-making exist. They include statistical techniques such as Baye's rule and regression analysis. Commonly employed human heuristics are also used, attempting to capture some or all of the approximate reasoning processes. The role of experience and the process of learning are used to improve the effectiveness of problem-solving and decision-making.

## DECISION ANALYSIS

Common to all decision-making structures is the idea of making a choice among various alternative courses of action in response to an objective(s). Decision-making under uncertainty adds the dimension that the problems addressed have an element of uncertainty with respect to the consequences of taking any of these actions. Various structured methodologies have been developed to address providing a structured, unbiased, and consistent approach to decision-making. These approaches have often involved the use of computers to assist the user in their application. They generally make certain simplifying assumptions, such as:

- The decision-maker is a single individual.
- The choices are manageable.
- The goals are clear, unambiguous, and constant.
- The courses of action produce directly measurable results.

### Measuring and Comparing Outcomes

When we say that the results are measurable, we mean that their outcomes can be quantified and compared. This suggests a decision-making structure where the choices are explicitly enumerated and the values of outputs determined. It is often the case that an output has many different aspects. In this case, each aspect has to be quantified, and ranked and weighted in importance. An overall measure of the value of the outcome can now be determined by taking a weighted sum of all the aspect values for that outcome. A choice can then be made by comparing the relative values associated with each outcome. This technique is known as *decision analysis*.

To illustrate this approach, consider the example of deciding which of two different brands of computer to buy for your office. You have decided that the criteria for this selection are: cost, performance (measured in terms of the number of instructions/second), and availability, which is equal to:

Mean time between failures/(mean time to repair + mean time between failures)

To keep these terms comparable, we normalize them by dividing each candidate's values by the equivalent value for a notational computer that costs $3000, has a performance of 1 MIPS, and is available 99.5 percent of the time. Since the decision-maker finds cost as important as performance and availability combined, a weight of 5 out of a possible 10 is assigned to each computer's normalized cost, while a weight of 2.5 is assigned to normalized performance, and a weight of 2.5 to normalized system availability. The decision of which computer to buy is made by comparing the weighted sum of these three normalized parameters for each computer under consideration and choosing the one with the largest value.

### Decomposing the Decision

If the decision is too complex, contains too many choices, the problem is generally broken up into a series of smaller, sequential steps, where each step is conditional upon the results of the previous one. The decision structure is reduced to a *decision tree* made up of a series of smaller decisions. The process for making these smaller subdecisions follows the sequence outlined above.

### Handling Uncertainty

Decision analysis can be extended to handle decision-making under uncertainty. The most straightforward approach is to employ *probability theory,* with a probability of occurrence assigned to each possible outcome. In this case, each of the previously weighted normalized outcomes is multiplied by probability of occurrence, given that a particular action is taken. The new sum constitutes a statistical average (or expected value). This is the same procedure as described earlier, with the probability of occurrence of an outcome introduced as an additional weighting parameter.

## BAYE'S RULE

In many cases the resultant outcome cannot be measured directly, but can only be indirectly derived from related variables. Often the outcome can only be predicted or forecast. Suppose we wish to make a decision concerning whether or not to manufacture a new product. The decision is based on consumer demand, but consumer demand cannot be measured directly until the product is produced and offered for sale. Until then we can only measure variables that have an indirect bearing on consumer demand, such as responses on a questionnaire, or demand for similar products now on the market which this new product hopes to supplant. Based on these observables, the responses to the questionnaire and/or the current demand for competing products, which we denote by the letter $D$, for data, we hope to determine whether the hypothesis, $H_1$, that there will be a strong demand for the new product is true, or whether it is false, which we denote by the alternate hypothesis, $H_0$. To help decide, we measure the ratio between the conditional probability that hypothesis $H_1$ is true given data, $D$, and the conditional probability that hypothesis $H_0$ is true given data, $D$, or, $P(H_1/D)/P(H_0/D)$. If the ratio is greater than a given threshold, we can conclude, from the observed data, that the hypothesis is true with a given confidence of being correct. The higher the threshold, the lower the probability of error.

If we cannot directly compute the conditional probabilities, $P(H_1/D)$ and $P(H_0/D)$, which is generally the case, we can use Baye's rule to compute the desired ratio in terms of the posterior probabilities, $P(D/H_1)$ and $P(D/H_0)$, and the prior probabilities, $P(H_1)$ and $P(H_0)$. The posterior probabilities are the conditional probabilities that the data is $D$, given the hypothesis $H_1$ and $H_0$, respectively. The prior probability is the probability that a hypothesis is true before the new data $D$ is observed. Specifically, Baye's rule is given as:

$$P(H_1/D)/P(H_0/D) = P(D/H_1)/P(D/H_0) \quad P(H_1)/P(H_0). \qquad \text{(A5-1)}$$

For more details on Bayes rule, see Helstrom (1960, p. 188).

## REGRESSION ANALYSIS

The outcome of a decision process is not only a function of the actions taken, it is also influenced by uncertain external events outside the decision-maker's control. Determining the proper decision to make under these circumstances requires predicting or forecasting the likely outcome for each of the candidate actions under consideration. Often a meaningful forecast can be obtained through a mathematical model whose output is an estimate, or predictor, of the likely outcome resulting from a number of inputs. The predictor generally includes a measure of the "goodness" of the estimate; e.g., the mean square error between the predictor and the actual observed outcome. When the likely outcome of each alternative can be estimated to an accuracy that is sufficient to distinguish between the possible alternatives, we can make a selection based on the preferred estimated outcome. *Regression analysis* refers to the process of determining the optimum combination of a set of predictor variables that maximizes the correlation between the composite predictor and the actual outcome.

### Proper Linear Models

A composite predictor can be formed by a linear weighted sum of the predictor variables. The predictor is called a "proper linear model" when the weights are chosen to minimize the mean square error between the predictor and the actual outcome. Proper linear models have been used successfully in a number of business applications, including credit and loan approval. In fact, there are many documented cases where it has been shown that the predictor based on a proper linear model did a better job of predicting than people presumably skilled in such predictions (Kahneman, p. 391). The performance of proper linear models of a predictor is, however, dependent upon selecting good predictor variables that have a conditionally monotone relationship to the criterion.

### Improper Linear Models

"Improper linear models" are predictor models where the predictor variable weights are chosen by some nonoptimal method. Improper linear models are important and frequently used, even though they are not optimum. One reason improper linear models are used is inadequate sample size. Typically, at least 15 to 20 samples are needed for each predictor variable in order to optimize. Another reason for using improper linear models is that the criterion is not measurable. For example, when a university decides on which students to admit, the criteria it uses to select students is who will demonstrate future professional success. This is a quality that is easy to enunciate but difficult to measure (Kahneman, p. 395). But it is a prerequisite for optimization.

Improper linear models have also been shown to perform better than experts (Kahneman, p. 392). In fact, even in experiments where the weights for the improper linear models have been derived from human experts via a technique called "bootstrapping," these *paramorphic* representations (models that do not mimic psychological processes, but simulate them by appropriately weighting the inputs) have been found to do better on the average than the experts from which they were derived when the measure of goodness is correlation between predicted and actual events and the predictors have a conditional monotonic relationship to the criterion (Kahneman, pp. 395–396).

In fact, even when random linear models (models where the weights are randomly selected) were used, they generally performed as well as the paramorphic models (Kahneman, p. 400). Assigning equal weightings did even better than random weightings. This is to be expected. Since each of the random predictor variables is positively correlated with the criterion, the correlation of the average of these random variables, which is the unit weighted model, is higher than the sum of the individual correlations of each predictor variable with the criterion (Kahneman, p. 400). These results imply that the proper linear model has a flat maximum; in other words, the linear model's performance is robust over deviations from the optimal weightings.

Why do linear models seem to do so much better than the experts? Although people are much better at selecting, coding, and integrating information, they are poor at integrating information from diverse and incomparable sources in a consistent fashion (Kahneman, p. 395). But people have an important role. The trick in building a good linear model is to know what predictor variables to look for and how to add them such that we have positive, not negative, correlations between the predictor variables and the criterion. People are required to choose the model's predictor variables and to know the directional relationship between the predictor variables and the criterion of interest. For example, in chess, the ability to code the board in an appropriate way to "see" the proper moves is what distinguishes the expert from the novice.

## Advantages of Linear Models

Linear models have been shown to produce optimum decisions over a wide range of problems. Consider the following two examples:

One study showed a linear regression model to be superior to a group of expert doctors in predicting the survival time of patients with Hodgkin's disease (Einhorn 1972). In Einhorn's study, expert doctors coded the biopsies of 193 patients, all of whom died with Hodgkin's disease. They each made an overall rating of the severity of the disease. They did not do a good job of predicting the survival time of the 193 patients. The correlation between the expert's severity ranking and the patient's survival time was effectively zero, with some actually in the wrong direction. However, the variables the doctors coded, when used in a multiple-variable linear regression model, did a good job of predicting survival time.

More closely related to business, Libby did a study comparing the performance of loan officers with improper linear models in assessing the financial health of corporations (Libby 1976). In Libby's study, 43 loan officers used five financial ratios to predict which 30 of 60 firms would go bankrupt within three years after their financial statements were issued. In this study, the loan officers, on the average, correctly categorized 44.4 businesses (74%), whereas 43 linear models, each modeled after one of the loan officers, could correctly classify only 43.3 (72%) on the average. Based on these results, it would appear that the experts outperformed the linear model for this business application. This was not the case, however, as L. R. Goldberg showed (Goldberg 1976). Goldberg noted that many of these ratios had highly skewed distributions. He normalized the ratios before building his models. Goldberg's new model predictions proved superior to 72 percent of the experts.

But this is an average statistic. Is it possible that a few experts do much better than average, and that we are really obscuring the performance of some outstanding experts by averaging their performance? Well, the data indicate otherwise. Even before Goldberg's normalization, Libby found only 9 out of the 43 experts to be better at predicting bankruptcies than a simple linear predictor using the ratio of assets-to-liabilities. Only 3 did as well. In another study, Goldberg found that only 5 out of 29 trained clinicians were better than a unit weighted model, and none did better than a proper linear model (Goldberg 1970). Wiggins and Kohen found that no judges did better than a unit weighted model (Wiggins and Kohen 1971).

## Nonlinear Models

Other structured methodologies include nonlinear models and discriminant functions. Nonlinear models represent the outcome by a nonlinear combination of predictor variables:

$$Y = a\,X_1{}^2 + b\,X_1\,X_2 + c\,X_2{}^2 \qquad \text{(A5-2)}$$

is an example of a nonlinear model.

Discriminant functions assign weights to predictor variables in a way that maximizes the discrepancy between different hypotheses or groupings. This allows us to distinguish more easily between two or more groups, or hypotheses, by first transforming the input variables with a discriminant function that maximizes the differences in the result of the discriminant function between the different hypotheses.

## REJECTION OF STRUCTURED DECISION MODELS

Given the success of these structured decision models, we would expect that they would be used rather routinely. Although structured approaches to decision-making are widely published and taught, and have been shown to produce optimum decisions over a wide class of problems, psychological studies show that managers and experts often reject this approach and instead rely on a limited number of heuristics, approximate rules, to reduce the complex tasks of assessing probabilities and predicting values. Why is this so? A total reliance on a structured methodology both lacks intuitive appeal and is limited in its applicability to real-world problems.

### Lacks Intuitive Appeal

These techniques fly in the face of our own intuition. For example, people want to believe in predictability. People think, "I want it to be predictable, especially when . . . [what] . . . I want to predict is important to me" (Kahneman, p. 406). So people will, quite irrationally, reject linear models when these models are found to have low predictability power (which is often the case for highly random phenomena) because they believe things are highly predictable and that there must be another method that is better.

People do have a remarkable ability to find some pattern, order, or meaning in data. But they look for order even where there is none, such as in randomly produced data (Kahneman, p. 344). Even though Fama argued quite convincingly that fluctuations in stock market prices are best understood as reflecting a random walk process (Fama 1965), we find market analysts unable intuitively to accept the notion of random price changes and always have an explanation for every change in price, whether purposeful or not. Denying the possibility of any random component, when all other explanations fail they call it a technical adjustment. Technical chartists, who believe they can find price movement patterns they can reliably trade against, abound in the world of trading. Of course, if there are enough believers who are willing to act on these imaginary trading signals, their actions could become a self-fulfilling prophesy.

The illusion of the superiority of good expert judgment over structured models is reinforced by the "availability" heuristic discussed in Chapter 2. Known exceptions and successes to predictions stand out and have a greater impact on our judgment than statistics. Often, an expert's decision can be a self-fulfilling prophesy, creating a false sense of the expert's success at prediction. For example, a selective university such as Harvard will accept students based on an assessment of the student's chances for success in school and later life. However, the mere effect of selection or rejection will affect the student's attitude and chances for success. There are, of course, many important, more legitimate reasons for rejecting the "pure" structured approach.

## Time Constraints and Other Real-World Considerations

Tight time constraints often make structured analysis techniques impractical. A proper structured analysis can just take too long to produce a result. Consider a trader who must make a bid on a security to a customer while still on the telephone. Other real-world considerations may make the assumptions used in structured analyses unsuitable as the sole input to a decision-making process. For example, reliance on analytics that make assumptions concerning market efficiencies and liquidity (the ease of finding a willing buyer or seller in a reasonable time frame) in trading can lead to disastrous results in an event-driven illiquid market. Models cannot represent the realist's more complete description of the problem. The realist classifies industries and agencies in terms of the kinds of decisions each makes and notes all the unique realistic constraints. Instead of saying: "Given the problem to determine the demand, this is the model that will work," the realist says: "If this organization is of such and such a type, these are the objectives, these are the constraints, these are the demands, and so on."

## Satisfier versus Optimizer

The user is often willing to accept "satisfactory" results in lieu of "the optimum," often realizing an optimum return introduces unacceptable risks. Consider the case of the waiter who is too busy to give good service to all his customers. To maximize his income, the waiter tries to predict the good tippers and works accordingly. Since a poorly served customer is less likely to give a good tip than a well-served customer, this action reinforces and confirms the waiter's predictions. This is called "treatment effect."

The waiter can disentangle the treatment effects by creating a control group. He can give poor service to some judged good tippers and good service to some judged bad tippers. With these data, he can evaluate his predictive powers without the impact of the treatment effect. But to follow this procedure, the waiter must be willing to risk possible loss of income if his judgment is accurate. If the waiter followed this procedure, it would help him to make better predictions. But will the waiter find it worth doing? Is he willing? The waiter's current rules and predictions might not be optimal, but they could still be "good" relative to other waiters' experiences. Relative to his peers, the waiter might enjoy a very satisfactory income, even if it is not a theoretical maximum.

Often developing an optimal plan requires measurable results that are not obtainable in advance. For example, the demand for a new product cannot be measured directly until the product is offered in the marketplace. Sometimes an optimal result is not even identifiable. It is for these reasons that Simon claims "satisfying" may more aptly describe a decision-maker's goal than "optimizing," and that decision-making is often just a planned series of suboptimizations (Hitch 1953).

## The Decision-Maker as a Learner

In the study of decision processes, it is often unrealistic and economically bad research to consider decision-makers as people trying to select an optimal alternative from a known action set. Instead, we should be concerned with the decision-maker as a learner who attempts to improve choices (Russell 1966, p. 44). For example, Simon (1957) and others have stressed the importance of learning and search in decision-making.

## Multiple Conflicting Goals and Viewpoints

For many organizations, decision-making more properly includes the decentralization and sharing of responsibility and authority among various members of the organization. This involves a combination of different viewpoints and goals, and entails some give and take. After all, even if we feel competent to make a decision on our own, we may want to involve others if they are needed to execute the decision. In a business organization we are concerned not just with making a good decision, but with execution, with getting the whole organization to move along some preconceived path.

Often there is more than one goal, and goals can conflict. Moreover, goals do not necessarily remain constant. For example, it is not clear that decision-makers attempt to maximize just the expected profit, or to minimize just the expected costs in risk-taking situations. Subjects do not behave in accordance with a simple preference of one goal over the other (e.g., maximum net profit, cash, probability of winning). Since people do not prefer one goal over the other on a "pure" basis, the context and current circumstances, as well as a certain amount of chance, partly account for an individual's behavior.

## Irrational Behavior

Subjects do not follow so-called rational rules in making choices when outcomes are predictable within probability limits (Preston and Berrata 1948). Some subjects have been found to "favor" certain probabilities independent of their expected value (Edwards 1956). For example, some people are so risk-averse that they will choose the more certain outcome, even if its value is less than the average value achievable by choosing a riskier but more profitable alternative, like gaining a sure dollar versus taking a 50 percent chance on winning $10 and a 50 percent chance on winning nothing.

Evidence of irrationality in decision-making can also be observed in competitive games. The "minimax rule" is an attempt to provide a rational rule of choice for each player in a zero-sum game. It states that a player should attempt to maximize the objective function, while assuming that the opponent will be trying to minimize it. In a non-zero-sum game, however, it is possible for both sides to maximize their returns.

An example of irrational behavior in non-zero-sum games is the "prisoner's dilemma." This is a non-zero-sum game where each player has two choices, A and B. If both choose A, then both are rewarded alike, and rather well. If one chooses A and the other B, then the one who chooses A does badly, while the one who chooses B does very well. If both choose B, then both will be rewarded, but rather poorly. If the two players were "one" person, then A-A would be the optimal choice. Experiments were run in which subjects were given the opportunity to communicate and cooperate, and where the rewards for A-A were extraordinarily better than those for B-B. Even though they were allowed to cooperate, the subjects all showed a strong reluctance to converge on A-A (Scodel 1959). Hoggatt investigated similar situations in competitive business games with much the same results (Hoggatt 1959).

## Limitations of Probability Theory

Probability evolved from a study of nature. It is a theory of random mass phenomena. Random mass phenomena is unpredictable in certain details, but predictable in terms of attaining a certain numerical proportion of the whole for a large enough number of experiments. Although the language of probability can be used to express any form of uncertainty, the laws of probability do not apply to all variants of uncertainty with equal force (Kahneman, pp. 516–519). It works best when the uncertainty is external (events the subject cannot control), and tends to break down when the uncertainties are internal (events the subject can control, such as feelings and uncertainties attributable to doubt and ignorance rather than randomness).

External uncertainty can be assessed in a distributional mode (classes for which relative frequencies of outcomes are known or can be estimated), or a singular mode (where probabilities are assessed by examining the particular case at hand). To evaluate using the singular mode, people construct plans and scenarios with some allowance for safety margins for unforeseen contingencies. People generally prefer the singular mode to the distributional mode because it seems more causal, although it is usually less accurate (Kahneman, p. 518). The rules that govern perceptual expectancies, doubt and ignorance, differ from the rules of probability.

### *Plausible Reasoning*

Plausible reasoning attempts to deal with ignorance and not randomness. Plausible reasoning attempts to deal with this class of uncertainty by linking probability to logic and induction. For example, deductive, or demonstrative logic, says that if $A$ implies $B$, and $B$ is false, then we can conclude that $A$ is false, whereas plausible reasoning (Polya 1968, p. 113) says that if $A$ implies $B$, and $B$ is true, then $A$ is more credible. Attempts to link induction with probability date back to Laplace (Polya 1968, p. 133).

### *Ignorance versus Randomness*

Plausible reasoning has proved difficult and misleading to apply quantitatively; it has proved useful only as a qualitative tool. For example, the following rules can be derived through application of Baye's rule (Polya 1968, p. 134).

- *General Rule of Succession:* Given that m trials have proven successful, the probability that the subsequent m′ trials will prove successful is prob($m'$ subsequent) $= (m + 1)/(m + m' + 1)$.

- *Special Rule of Succession:* Given that $m$ trials have proved successful, the probability that the next trial will be a success is $1 - 1/(m + 2)$.

This application of Baye's rule to beliefs and ignorance, rather than physically random phenomena, can lead to serious errors. Consider the following examples.

*Example 1:* Suppose we form the hypothesis that all the terms in the following series of even numbers: {6,8,10,12,14,16,18,20,22,24, . . .} can be represented as the sum of two odd prime numbers. We test the first ten terms in the series and find the hypothesis to be verified. Then, by applying the special rule of succession, we erroneously conclude with a probability of 11/12, that 26 can be represented by the sum of two odd prime numbers (Polya 1968, p. 136).

*Example 2:* Another example of the misapplication of the special rule of succession is using it to predict life expectancy based upon age. If a boy has already lived 10 years, we could interpret this fact as his having survived 10 years in a row. We are ignorant about the boy's chances of surviving to age 11, but we know that he has lived for 10 years already. We could apply the special rule of succession and determine that the boy has a probability of 11/12 of living for another year. Following a similar line of reasoning, we can conclude that the boy's 70-year-old grandfather has a probability of 71/72 of living one more year, clearly an erroneous conclusion (Polya 1968, p. 136).

We got in trouble in these two cases because they were misuses of probability theory. We know that eventually the boy and the grandfather will die, we just don't know when. Our uncertainty is due to ignorance, not to statistical randomness. These events are not from a series of statistically identical but independent events, as in the case of a series of unbiased coin tosses, and evidence that the boy has already lived for 10 years and the grandfather has lived for 70 years does not help in our prediction.

### Complementary Beliefs

The sum of probability measures of complementary events must add to one. For example, when one tosses a coin, it must come up either heads or tails, so the probability that heads is shown plus the probability that tails shows must equal one. This is not the case with beliefs, as they are not constrained by physical limitations. For example, I do not know whether New York City is south of Rome or north of Rome. These beliefs and their corresponding uncertainties do not necessarily have to sum to one (they could be less or greater than one), though New York can only be north or south of Rome, not both. In other words, there exist situations in which two mutually exclusive exhaustive hypotheses both have substantial support and other situations where neither has substantial support (Kahneman, p. 520).

### Evidence Cannot Be Compared

If you discover a burial place on Labrador with Viking shields and swords, how much is this evidence worth with respect to reaching a conclusion that Norseman landed on America? (Polya 1968, p. 136). If you know that all even numbers up to

1000 can be expressed as the sum of two odd primes, how useful is this fact as a verification of the hypothesis that all even numbers can be expressed as the sum of two primes? And how does this relate to the knowledge that all even numbers up to 2000 can be expressed as the sum of two odd primes? Is this information any more valuable for predicting whether all even numbers can be expressed as the sum of two primes? How does one compare the relative strength and importance, quantitatively, of the Norsemen's burial place to the fact that all even numbers up to 2000 can be expressed as the sum of two odd primes? (Polya 1968, p. 138). The evidence is not comparable and/or quantitative. It cannot be assessed with respect to relative strength and importance.

### Evidential Reasoning and Fuzzy Sets

To get around these various deficiencies, extensions to probability theory, such as Shafer and Dempster's theory of evidential reasoning, and Zadeh's fuzzy set theory, have been proposed. Shafer and Dempster have promoted their theory as a generalization of probability theory to accommodate beliefs and ignorances. In the theory of evidential reasoning, rather than a single number, the probability measure, a range is maintained. The lower number is the degree to which we believe we have evidence which supports, or does not refute, a hypothesis. At the upper level, we carry a number which conveys the degree to which we have evidence that makes us believe in the hypothesis. In many respects, this approach is somewhat modeled after the judge and jury paradigm.

The judge and jury paradigm is a useful analogy to apply to a more qualitative, but correct, method of plausible reasoning about uncertainties, beliefs, and ignorances. In the trial situation, the judge provides a logical set of rules to determine the admissibility of evidence, whether the evidence is valid to consider as an appropriate support or refutation of a given hypothesis, but the task of determining the credibility of the evidence, the weight of the collective evidence, both for and against the hypothesis, is given to the jury to decide. The jury uses their collective personal discernment to determine what weight to give each piece of evidence (Polya 1968, p. 1401).

Fuzzy set theory introduces the idea that an object can belong, with a graded membership, to more than one mutually exclusive set at the same time. For example, a tall man can belong to both the set of heights, greater than 5 feet and less than 6 feet, as well as to the set of heights greater than 6 feet, each with a different strength of belonging, or membership.

## HEURISTIC PRINCIPLES

Considering the important contribution of intuition and heuristics to the decision-making process, it is useful to understand and to study their strengths and limitations. People rely upon heuristic principles to reduce complex tasks. For example, we can rely on clarity of an image as an indication of distance. This usually leads to a correct judgment concerning the distance of an object, but sometimes, like on an unusually clear day, it can lead to errors. Likewise, people use heuristics for simplifying the judgmental operations associated with assessing probabilities and predicting values. These heuristics are generally useful, but sometimes they can lead to severe and systematic errors. That is why the current status of decision theory can be described as an attempt to find a suitable ground between extreme realism and extreme idealism. To better understand how people reason under uncertainty, it is helpful to review some of these principles.

## Representativeness

People rely on the representativeness heuristic. We expect that a sequence, no matter how small, will be representative of the larger pool from which it came. This can lead to powerful reasoning processes such as reasoning through stereotypes, a popular artificial intelligence technique. For example, we recognize certain key features of a bird, such as that it flies, it has wings and feathers. So if we see a creature that flies and has wings and feathers, we classify it as a bird. Occasionally we may make mistakes by relying upon this form of reasoning, such as in the case of the ostrich, a bird that does not fly. This heuristic can be particularly troublesome when applied to random phenomena. We expect a small sequence to look random. This leads to our taking samples of inadequate size and overinterpreting the results. It causes us to be insensitive to the prior probability of outcomes.

## Availability

Availability of examples is a useful cue for assessing the frequency or probability of occurrence because instances of large classes are usually reached more often than less frequent classes (Kahneman, p. 11). However, availability is often affected by factors other than frequency and probability. For example, the ease or difficulty of retrieval of a past instance is often influenced by familiarity with the subject. If people predict solely on the basis of their familiarity with the description, they will be insensitive to the reliability of the evidence and to the expected accuracy of the prediction. Failure to appreciate the limits of available data may lull people into complacency (Kahneman, p. 470).

## Consistency

The internal consistency of a pattern of inputs is a major determinant of confidence in predictions. However, highly consistent patterns are most often observed when the input variables are highly redundant or correlated. But redundancy among inputs decreases the accuracy of the predictions. Thus redundancy increases confidence even as it decreases the accuracy of prediction (Kahneman, p. 9).

## Ignore Contradictory Evidence

People are resistant to change in their ideas and viewpoints. They look for confirming evidence, and they ignore contradictory evidence and show extraordinary persistence in the face of such evidence (Kahneman, p. 478). There is a contrast between people's expectations and evidence. Reported covariations are taken more seriously when they are based upon theory-based preconceived ideas about relationships that ought to exist. People typically have overconfidence in their judgments based on such heuristics (Kahneman, p. 472). This includes trained experts. Once experts are forced to go beyond their limited domain of expertise and rely on personal judgment, they usually prove to be as overconfident as ordinary people (Kahneman, p. 475).

## Selectivity

Making a decision can be self-fulfilling. One example is the Harvard selection process discussed above. This is called the "treatment effect." The outcome is influenced by the decision or the measurement process. Selectivity can end up reinforcing rules for the wrong reason. Treatment effects can be overcome by use of a $2 \times 2$ factorial test. For each judgment, we take one action on half the examples, and another action on the remaining half. Sometimes, however, this requires taking unacceptable actions.

## Hyperprecision

People think they can estimate uncertain quantities with greater precision than is actually the case (Kahneman pp. 475, 480). Furthermore, people look for patterns even in pure randomness. Of course, if one looks hard enough, one can find patterns in anything. But these patterns may not be sustained over the long term. Consider an analogy from regression analysis. Given a set of events and a sufficiently large set of possible explanatory factors, one can always obtain a tight (highly correlated) fit for a finite interval of time by expanding the set of independent variables. The penalty we pay is "shrinkage," a failure of the derived model to work on a new sample of cases. So when market analysts look too hard for patterns in the fluctuations of market prices, the penalty they pay for overfitting is long-term failure to predict any better than market averages.

## Pseudocertainty

Actions that produce outcomes that are merely probable are underweighted in comparison with certain outcomes. For example, if we take an action that reduces the probability of an outcome from .01 to 0, then it is valued more highly than one that reduces the probability of an outcome from .02 to .01.

## Anchoring and Context-Dependent Reasoning

There is a tendency for our judgments to be anchored in the initial values presented to us (Kahneman p. 74). The way a problem is worded or displayed affects our response. Thus presentation is important, for it can have a major impact on our perceptions and behavior. When the starting conditions vary, the same problem does not always yield the same outcome.

It is most natural for us to organize our action/outcome knowledge by subject matter, as encountered by our experiences, rather than by task structure. Our sense of recall and reconstruction resembles the running of a simulation model. Learning from experience is basically inductive. We experience specific instances, or cases, and we use heuristics to provide a general way to deal with them. We call this "case-based" reasoning, and it is another paradigm used in artificial intelligence. These heuristic rules are extremely context-dependent. The same problem framed in a different background environment can evoke a different response. And, without knowledge of the task structure, outcome feedback can be irrelevant or even harmful for correcting poor heuristics (Kahneman p. 282).

It takes training to transform our context-specific rules into abstract task-structured rules. Much of professional training is just this, learning to organize experience by task structure. With a more task-oriented, or model-based structure, solutions can be arrived at more rapidly and more consistently than with a pure case-based approach, but it requires a well-developed field with a thoughtful structuring of the subject matter. In this case, we recognize a problem as belonging to a class of problems having the same structure and a known solution (Kahneman p. 273). Of course, there is a danger here. Professionals view problems within the structure that they have been trained to see even when it is a forced fit, an inappropriate structure.

## Illusionary Correlation

There is a tendency for people to believe that all actions and outcomes are linked to a cause. It is the way we learn, by searching for and finding causal relationships; we use "if . . . then" rules. Therefore, when two events co-occur, it is immediately assumed that they are related. They provide the illusion of being correlated even when they are not correlated at all.

Additionally, people tend to overestimate the probability of conjunctive events (Kahneman p. 9). For example, when tested, subjects generally preferred a situation where they would receive a prize if seven highly likely (each with a probability .9) independent events were to occur, over a situation in which they would get the same prize if a fair coin fell on "heads." This is in spite of the fact that the probability of the seven compound events occurring is actually less than 0.5, whereas the probability of receiving a "heads" on a fair coin toss is 0.5. People have trouble intuitively accepting the conjunction rule $p(AB) <= p(A)$, and $p(AB) <= p(B)$. The joint probability of two events, $A$ and $B$, occurring is less than the probability of either event occurring.

## Regression Toward the Mean

People tend to misinterpret the phenomenon called "regression toward the mean." In cases of repeated examination of outputs from a random experiment, an improvement will usually follow a poor performance, and vice versa. People tend to attribute cause to all such changes (Kahneman p. 10). Thus it often leads one to overestimate the effectiveness of corrective actions, such as punishment, and to underestimate the effectiveness of reinforcing actions, such as reward. We imagine the subsequent improvement and degradation in performance are due to the punishment and rewards, even though it is often due just to regression toward the mean (Kahneman p. 10).

### Multistage Inferences

People are found to be more conservative than Baye's rule in accepting a hypothesis based upon given evidence; they tend to underestimate the likelihood of the hypothesis being true (Kahneman pp. 362–64). However, in a multistage inference people are more optimistic (they tend to overestimate, to be more certain) than a properly structured Baye's theorem modified to handle a series of sequential decisions (Kahneman p. 370). In multistage inferences we make a series of dependent estimates, and the output of one inference serves as an input to another. Each preceding estimate, once selected, is taken as a certain fact when input into the next stage. The net result is that we predict with more certainty than the process warrants.

### Risk Perception

People have a predilection to view themselves as immune to hazards (Kahneman, p. 468). We find it hard to imagine something bad happening to us, our becoming a statistic. Consequently, most people do not fully appreciate, or account for, the risks that they take in an uncertain environment.

## CONCLUSION

Decision-making under uncertainty is an inevitable aspect of running and managing a business. Various structured approaches have been applied with some degree of success, but they have limitations and shortcomings. Many of these shortcomings can be overcome by applying human judgment and intuition. But humans are "satisfiers." In order to accommodate real-world time constraints and other complicating factors, people make assumptions and take shortcuts. They apply their insights and judgments based upon simplifying heuristics and rules of thumb. These heuristics usually work under normal conditions, but they can lead to errors of judgment and misconceptions. The general conclusion is that the preferred decision is one where the decision-maker has succeeded in effectively combining structured, analytical techniques with good, but qualified, human judgment and intuition.

# Appendix 6

## Introduction to Computers

Over the last three decades, digital computer technology has experienced dramatic advances in performance accompanied by reductions in both cost and size. This has served to add to the list of applications for which it is cost-effective to automate. But cost savings and efficiency are not the only reasons why we should consider using computers in place of people. Computers differ from the human brain, and these differences can be used to augment the problem-solving process. They enable business to perform services previously impractical, and qualitatively to improve the current level of service and the decision-making. For example, today's computers process at faster sequential speeds than the human brain, whereas the brain does more in parallel.

In addition to raw speed, some of the characteristics of the computer that make it an attractive assistant include the following:

- Computers do not experience fatigue or boredom.
- Computers can work around the clock.
- Computers communicate in unambiguous commands; they are less likely to misinterpret.
- The computer's performance is consistent; the same input always produces the same results.
- Computers have no private agendas or objectives.

The computer also has many disadvantages as an assistant, including the following. The computer:

- Has no sense of humor
- Offers no friendship

- Can't "network," in the sense of relationship building
- Is a poor communicator
- Lacks creativity, resourcefulness, and "common sense"
- Is weak in independent problem-solving
- Is less capable in providing physical assistance in such activities as lifting, carrying, coffee-making, phone answering

Let's review and compare the characteristics of the digital computer system to the human cognitive processor from the point of view of what makes the computer a suitable supplemental aid to humans in support of business.

## BASIC CHARACTERISTICS OF COMPUTER SYSTEMS

A computer's architecture is determined by its basic components, or elements, and the manner in which these components and the communications paths among them are organized. The architectural components of a computer have not changed much since its introduction in the 1940s. A computer system is comprised of the following major components:

- A central processing and control unit
- Specialized processors
- Memory
- Input and output units
- Communications
- Software

Because of the rapid advances in technology, the physical characteristics of these components keep changing and their performance continues to improve dramatically. Most likely the speed and capacities given in this book will be obsolete by the time it is published.

### The Central Processing Unit

The central processing unit (CPU) performs the arithmetic, logical, and control functions and interacts with all the other hardware components. Current CPUs range from less than 1 MIPS (million instructions per second) to several hundred MIPS, and even more for some supercomputers (the Cray Y MP, an eight-processor upgrade to the Cray 2X MP delivered to NASA's Ames Research Center, topped 1 Giga FLOPS, and the announced Cray 3, made from gallium arsenide technology, is expected to run at least three to four times as fast as the Cray 2 series). A computer can have more than one central processing unit. It is then called a multiprocessor. We construct multiprocessors to increase processing speed and to improve system reliability. We improve system performance (processing speed) by using multiple CPUs to perform several operations in parallel. We improve system reliability through the added redundancy.

## Specialized Processors

Specialized processors are often used to achieve desired performance improvements. Many types of specialized processors exist. They include: math coprocessors, vector processors, digital signal processors (DSP) for voice and image signal processing, and superperformance compute engines.

## Memory

Memory is where the data and programs (computer instructions, or software) are stored and retrieved from. There are many different types of computer memory. These different types tend to fall into one of two categories: primary memory and secondary memory. Most computer systems will have at least one primary memory component and one secondary memory component. The primary memory components are faster, but more expensive and therefore generally have smaller capacity. Because of its higher processing speed, the CPU usually retrieves and stores data only through the primary memory.

The selection of an appropriate hierarchy of memory components can often make or break the function and performance of a computer system. Too little memory often will result in a system with too little function. Inadequate memory results in poor performance, due to the need for excessive swapping in and out of programs and data from secondary storage to primary. Software is more difficult and expensive to design when only tight memory resources are available.

### *Random Access Memory*

The most common form of primary memory is random access memory (RAM). This memory is typically comprised of very large scale integrated (VLSI) semiconductors. It has the property that its contents are nonpermanent; they are erased when the computer is turned off. Random access memory can store hundreds of millions of bytes of data. Supercomputers and large mainframes typically have RAM main memories with capacities of 10 to 100 million bytes. Whereas the first personal computers had less than 64,000 bytes, now even personal computers can store millions of bytes in primary memory. Data in a computer are normally stored as bits (1s and 0s, usually represented by two bistable states of an electronic device). A *byte* is an 8-bit alphanumeric character of information (for example, the number four can be represented by the three bits, 100, or $2 \times 10^2 + 0 \times 10^1 + 0 \times 10^0$).

### *Read Only Memory*

Read only memory (ROM), often called firmware, is another form of primary memory. It is also generally a semiconductor. It is used to store small programs permanently. It comes manufactured with instructions and/or data permanently (and unalterably) inscribed inside it. It maintains this information in the absence of electrical power. Many personal computers use a ROM to store a bootstrap program that, activated when the computer is first turned on, is used to read the operating system into primary memory.

Other forms of primary memory include programmable read only memory (PROM), and erasable programmable read only memory (EPROM). PROM can be programmed using a relatively low-cost microprocessor development system, but once programmed, is not alterable. EPROM can be programmed by the user and can also be erased and reprogrammed, but this process is time-consuming and not easy.

### *Magnetic Disk*

Magnetic disk is the most popular form of secondary storage in use today. Data are stored on the disk by altering small magnetic locations arranged in tracks on the disk. The data can be read by sensing arms that move over the disk, across the tracks. Since the disk rotates and the arms move, data anywhere on the disk can be accessed relatively rapidly, independent of its location. One can generally access data from a magnetic disk in milliseconds, as contrasted with primary memory access times that range from several nanoseconds to a microsecond. Data stored on magnetic disk are retained when the computer power is turned off. The capacity of a magnetic disk, the amount of data it can store, can vary from as low as 400,000 bytes for a low-density floppy disk to over 1 billion bytes for disks on large-capacity mainframes. Capacity keeps increasing and the cost/bit keeps dropping.

Some of the more common magnetic disks found in personal computers and workstations include:

- The 5 1/4″ floppy disk. This disk is removable. When it first came out, this disk held 360,000 bytes. More current versions can hold up to 1.2 million bytes.
- The 3 1/2″ micro floppy disk. This disk, like the 5 1/4″ floppy, is removable. The first version stored 400,000 bytes, but today its capacity has increased to 800,000 bytes.
- The 5 1/4″ Winchester fixed disk drive originally stored 5 to 10 million bytes. It can now handle 20 to 40 million bytes. The most advanced can address 760 million bytes.
- The 3 1/4″ Winchester fixed disk was recently introduced for laptops. It can currently store up to 40 megabytes. More advanced drives are being developed that can store over 700 megabytes.

### *Magnetic Tape*

Magnetic tape is relatively slow compared to magnetic disks, but inexpensive. Magnetic tape, like magnetic disks, retains data in the absence of electrical power. In order to read a piece of data on a tape, we must wait until the tape unwinds sufficiently to allow the desired location to pass under the tape reader. If the desired information is at the end of the tape, we must read the entire tape until we get to the piece of data we desire. Therefore we generally read and write from magnetic tape in sorted serial batches. Because of these constraints, magnetic tape storage is used today primarily to archive and backup data, not to support processing.

### *Optical Disks*

Optical disks are a relatively new technology that has the potential for larger capacity and faster access time than magnetic disk. There are two basic types. The older and more mature is read-only, while the newer optical disk technology supports erasable disks. The compact disk, CD-ROM, is similar to the CD audio disk player, and is representative of the class of read-only optical disks. The data are retrieved by laser beam that scans the tracks of microscopic holes in a rotating disk. It is capable of storing 550 megabytes. The data are typically burned on the disk using a special device that is not usually provided with the CD-ROM reader. It is known as a W.O.R.M. (write once, read many) because once written, the optical disks cannot be rewritten.

In the fall of 1988, a 5 1/4″ erasable magnetic-optical disk was announced for sale by several manufacturers. Sony, Canon, and Olympus announced magneto-optical disks for sale (Markoff 1988e). These removable optical disks' access times currently average 30 milliseconds, but have the potential for eventually achieving access times as low as 4 milliseconds. Unlike the W.O.R.M., which stores information at the time of manufacture, magneto-optical drive memory can be altered repeatedly at will, in the same manner as the floppy and hard magnetic disks.

It both reads and writes with a laser beam on the disk. The write time takes longer than the read time. This optical disk is capable of storing 12 to 15 times the amount of information currently packed on the magnetic hard disk drive known as the Winchester drive. Up to 250 million to 1 billion bytes can be stored on the optical disk. In January 1989, the first manufacturers announced computer workstations using optical disk drives. This included Steven Jobs' new company Next, Inc. (Steven Jobs was one of the founders of Apple Computer), Sony, and Tandy. Tandy's erasable disk drive, however, was initially designed for audio data storage applications; it is based on a different technology than the others.

## Input/Output

For a computer to be useful, it must be able to receive external data and instructions (input), and to present results (produce output). For most applications, this implies human input and output. An exception is embedded computers in a manufacturing plant that receive sensor inputs and output commands to robots and milling machines. Some of the more common input devices for communication with humans are:

- Alphanumeric keyboard
- Keypad
- Function keys

- Mouse
- Joystick
- Light pen
- Touch screen
- Tracker ball
- Digitizers
- Optical scanners (includes optical character readers and optical mark sensing devices)
- Analog-to-digital converters
- Voice input

Most recently more exotic inputs have appeared such as eye trackers (they detect and respond to movement of the eyes) and special gloves. Some output devices include

- Printer
- Plotter
- Touch screen
- CRT (cathode ray tube)
- Plasma display
- LCD (liquid crystal) display
- Voice synthesizer and other audible sounds

More exotic output devices recently announced include a device that mounts over the eye and projects holographic three-dimensional images.

Often input and output devices are combined into a user terminal. These combined input and output devices can be designed to support a variety of human-machine interactions, including menu selection, command sequences, pointing and selecting icons, and voice commands. The type of interface selected should vary with the skill level and expertise of the user. Most recently, the actual input/output terminal is equipped with a small processor capable of supporting more sophisticated interactions and offloading the main processor through the use of local editing and storage functions. Some systems are actually sophisticated enough to observe the speed and nature of the user's responses and adapt their response to match the observed characteristics.

## Communications

Communications devices interface the computer components to physical communications media. They translate and buffer signals back and forth from the forms and speeds best suited for communications (modulated, continuous analog) with the speeds and forms best suited for processing in a digital computer (binary, discrete digital). They generally include built-in error detection and data synchronization features, as these are more of a concern over communications media than within the digital computer. Some connect various computer components (terminals, printers, CPU); others connect different computer systems. The connected components and systems can be local, in the same room or building complex, or they can be separated by thousands of miles. Computers are capable of interfacing to a variety of physical communication media, such as common carrier networks (both public and private leased lines), wires, microwave, radio, satellite, optical fiber.

### Buses

Buses are parallel wire communications paths over which the CPU and the primary memory exchange data and control information. Some transfer information a byte at a time; others transfer multiple bytes at a time. The transfer rates are comparable to the primary memory access rates.

### I/O Channels

Input/output (I/O) channels typically interface peripherals with the CPU and primary memory. These peripherals include secondary memory devices such as disks and tapes, and input/output devices such as terminals, printers, and external communications devices. These channels generally satisfy interface standards such as RS 232C and IEEE 488. Usually the I/O devices are connected to the I/O channel through an I/O controller (IOC). Information is usually transferred across I/O channels a full byte at a time.

Information transfer rates through the I/O channels range from ten to hundreds of million-bytes/second. The speed of the I/O controller must be compatible with the number, types, and transfer rates of devices that can be connected to it. Locally connected terminals are attached through terminal and cluster controllers. The terminals typically transfer their information at speeds ranging from hundreds of bytes to thousands of bytes per second.

### External Communications

Computers are connected to remotely located terminals and other computers through external communications. These communications channels typically transfer information serially (a single bit at a time) at rates ranging from 100 bits/second to several hundred thousand bits/second. These bits are either aggregated into single characters or into a larger collection of bits and/or characters, generally called *packets*. Single characters can be transmitted either asynchronously (no synchronization provided between individual transmitted characters) or synchronously. For larger packets, the transmission is always synchronized.

PCs, workstations, and larger computers located in the same building or building complex, a few miles apart, are connected by a local area network (LAN). Twisted wire pair, baseband cable, broadband cable, and fiber optic are all used as LANs. Fiber optic has the largest capacity, typically ranging from ten to a hundred million bits/second. Fiber optics are generally used for larger LANs when the distances and number of units is large, and therefore large capacity is needed. Twisted wire is the slowest medium, but with recent advances it is capable of one to ten million bits/second. When the network extends over an entire metropolitan area it is called a MAN (Metropolitan Area Network).

For communications over wider areas, hundreds to thousands of miles, the transmission media used are cable, satellite, and microwave. As workstations become capable of communicating through richer multimedia interfaces, the need for integrated voice, data, and video communications at the terminal or workstation increases. Integrated Services Digital Network (ISDN) addresses this need through a single networking scheme. ISDN promises to become an important concept in communications.

### Software

Computers need instructions that can tell them what to do. Collections of these instructions form computer programs. *Software* is anything other than hardware. It includes computer programs, documentation, and manuals.

A computer program generally deals with data. It is concerned with prompting the user for data, retrieving data from memory, transforming or manipulating data, storing it in memory, and presenting results to the user. This is why software is often described in terms of the input-process-output model. In other words, software can generally be described in terms of the instructions it provides the computer with respect to inputting data, manipulating and transforming, or processing, the data, and outputting the data either to memory and/or for presentation to the user.

Recently, with the advent of expert system technology, another software model has been proposed that is believed to more closely match the human processing model. In this model, knowledge is stored and manipulated. The knowledge base is composed of a collection of generic facts or data associations, context-sensitive rules (conditional linking of data and facts), and data-invoked procedures. This knowledge is acquired from human experts, usually through an interactive dialogue. The manipulation of this knowledge is achieved by running an inference engine.

The system is activated when the user inputs a problem statement. Once activated, the inference engine repeatedly cycles through the knowledge base, inferring new facts and searching for a solution. The inference engine applies a control strategy to determine which rules to try, and in what order. When a solution has been found, the results are usually sent to a special module called an explanation module, whose job it is to prepare a presentation of the solution, with a satisfactory explanation, to the user.

## SOFTWARE CATEGORIES

Software can be divided into the following categories:

- System software
- Real-time software
- Business software
- Engineering and scientific software

- Embedded software
- Personal computer software
- Artificial intelligence software

## System Software

System software consists of:

- Language compilers (which translate higher level computer languages into lower-level instructions the machine can understand)
- Operating systems (which schedule and manage multiple user processing tasks)
- Editors (which support the manipulation, search, insertion, deletion, and change of text and program files)
- File management utilities (which manage the storage, retrieval, and update of data and text files in secondary storage, and interface with and control the various storage devices)
- Database management systems (which serve as a single interface between users and user applications and the file management utilities, allowing multiple users and user programs to share the same set of files concurrently, handling data integrity, user contention, data access and update security, and allowing each application to look at and treat the data from a different viewpoint
- I/O drivers (which interface and control the various I/O devices)
- Telecommunications processors (which control the communications devices and manage the external communications transmissions and protocol).

## Real-Time Software

Real-time software typically receives and processes input data (often received from sensors as well as people), producing an output action, under tight time constraints, typically seconds or subseconds. Failure to take action within a specified timeframe in a real-time system usually has disastrous results; e.g., a manufacturing process going out of control, a bomb exploding, a plane crashing. Manufacturing process controls, military command and control, and airport traffic control are examples of real-time systems. As computers are increasingly used in roles more directly associated with the daily operations of the organization, the number and variety of real-time software is begining to proliferate. Real-time systems have unique scheduling, resource allocation, and conflict resolution requirements.

## Business Software

Business software represents the largest simple set of software applications. The applications include payroll administering, management of accounts receivable/

payable, inventory management and accounting, management information systems, point-of-sale data capture, and transaction processing.

### Engineering and Scientific Software

Engineering and scientific software is normally associated with mathematics and heavy number crunching. Recently, it has grown to include computer-aided design (CAD) and system simulation applications. These applications not only require heavy number crunching, but also have many of the characteristics we find in real-time system and graphics software. These are often hosted on powerful personal workstations.

### Embedded Software

Embedded software is software destined for computers that are embedded in and form a part of a larger system. Examples include the computer that provides the keypad control for a microwave oven and the computer that controls the digital functions in an automobile, such as fuel control, dashboard displays, and braking systems. Similar uses are found in aircraft and other vehicles. The computer hardware and software in embedded systems must often operate under severe hostile environments, such as extreme vibration, temperature, and humidity. The computer systems, once installed, cannot be easily upgraded and changed.

### Personal Computer Software

Personal computer software has some of the most innovative software. It includes word processing, spreadsheets, computer graphics, entertainment (games), database management, computer networking, and business and financial applications. Much of this software has migrated to larger machines and many of the other application categories just discussed.

### Artificial Intelligence Software

Artificial intelligence will eventually be integrated into most of the other categories. It is highlighted because of its relative newness and uniqueness. Artificial intelligence software, which includes expert system technology, is concerned with the representation, storage, and manipulation of symbols, ideas, concepts, and their relationships (often uncertain and tentative), rather than numbers.

## EVOLUTION OF COMPUTER SYSTEM APPLICATIONS

As computer systems have grown in processing power and the base of existing applications has expanded, the focus and nature of their use has changed greatly. They have evolved to assume a more central and strategic role in business.

## Batch

The first computer systems applications were *batch* jobs. These jobs were usually submitted by data processing personnel to the computer center, where they would be scheduled, loaded, and run, often overnight. Typically, these applications were custom software, specially written for a specific user, with little applicability to other users. These types of jobs dominated the computing scene from 1950 through the mid-1960s, when magnetic tape was still the dominant secondary storage medium.

## Transaction Processing and Product Systems

By the 1960s, a new type of application emerged. The first of these applications were the Air Defense SAGE system, and the American Airlines reservations system. These two specific implementations actually appeared in the 1950s, but it was not until the mid-1960s that these sorts of applications began to appear in significant numbers. The applications were designed for simultaneous, interactive use by multiple end users. Many of the systems required real-time responses. Many made heavy use of large databases.

This was also the time when we began to see the development of product software. *Product software* is software targeted for sale to a large number of users. Typically, this software is based upon a successful product in a mature application area that was made more general for broader appeal.

## Computer Networking and Distributed Processing

The early 1970s through the early 1990s have seen the rise of computer networking and distributed processing. With the increased availability of low-cost hardware, computers have proliferated to departments, individual desks, and homes. Closely coupled with this wider distribution of computers has been the growth of the technology associated with connecting these computers both locally, between floors and neighboring buildings, through local area networks, and across vast global distances, through wide area computer networks. A few early versions of these networks, such as the Department of Defense's ARPANET, actually appeared in the 1960s. These networks allow users and distributed computers to share data and processing in support of their real-time processing needs. This time frame, with the advent of the personal computer, and with the introduction of embedded "intelligence" in a myriad of consumer products ranging from cars, to toys, to washing machines, also saw the first real impact of computers on the general consumer.

## Future Trends

Today we are seeing many new computer advances, notably new computer architectures and more sophisticated human-machine interfaces. Some of the advances in computer architecture include RISC (reduced instruction set complex) designs, which have resulted in significant improvements in cost and performance; megaprocessors constructed with thousands to hundreds of thousands of tightly coupled processors working in parallel; specially designed symbolic processors; voice recognition and voice synthesis processors; and specialized image processors. There has been a growing trend toward hardware and software standards (for example, greater acceptance of common operating systems such as UNIX; common database commands, such as the relational data query language SQL; common communications protocols, such as the OSI standard; and common standard user interface such as X Windows).

New software initiatives, such as object-oriented programming, promise to improve software productivity and reusability. We are beginning to see a new wave of applications that take advantage of advanced technologies such as expert systems, neural networks, advanced graphics processing, and complex real-time simulation models. These trends are certain to introduce a new wave of computer systems applications in the future.

A continuing trend in the evolution of computer systems has been the wider distribution of computers and computer products to a larger and broader universe of users, hosting applications requiring little or no computer literacy. Building on a substantial and still growing software base, these applications are designed for use as part of the overall daily work (and play) flow. And they are increasingly being directed toward improving effectiveness rather than efficiency.

# Appendix 7

## The Human Computer

The human processor can be modeled as three cooperating systems:

- *Perceptual system:* consists of our sensors and their buffer memories, such as our visual image store and our auditory image store
- *Cognitive system:* receives symbolically coded information from the perceptual system, which it then processes and stores
- *Motor system:* carries out responses to stimuli and our decisions

Human cognition is centered around our senses and our brain. We will concentrate here on the perceptive and cognitive systems, as they bear the closest relationship to the computer. We need to understand the physical and cognitive constraints on the human sensors and brain in relation to the attributes of the contemporary computer in order to understand how best to interface computers with people.

Human information processing differs from contemporary computers in many respects. Neural network computers are a recent technology that attempts to more closely parallel the human processing architecture (see Chapter 3.) Human processors and communications are slower, but they utilize parallel processing and pattern recognition to a much greater extent. Moreover, the human memory is larger and more richly interconnected than a computer's primary memory, although not as large as a computer's secondary memory. Pencil and paper have served as human archival memory for centuries. Now, however, computers, with their massive secondary memory capacity, are increasingly being used to serve in this area. This function represents one of the most accepted and successful human-machine symbioses. It extends and amplifies mental capacities and accomplishments, much as earlier industrial machines, such as the motor, have amplified human muscle in such fields as manufacture and transportation.

## PERCEPTUAL SYSTEM

The perceptual system receives and processes sensory data (visual, auditory, tactile) and enters them into a "buffer" of limited size for a limited length of time. Each sensor has its own buffer: the visual image store, the auditory image store. These buffers store information obtained from external stimuli. The information is physically coded; that is, the codings are unidentified and nonsymbolic (they deal with color, orientation, movement, size, shape, intensity, curvatures). This system consists of a lot of specialized processors, each producing a physical code to be stored in buffer memory; many are processed in parallel. These physical signals are stored in buffer memory for further processing, such as symbol recognition. Once symbols are recognized, they are transferred to the cognitive system's working memory (called the short-term memory). Perceptual memory buffers have a limited capacity. Signals physically encoded and stored in this buffer memory will eventually fade, allowing the buffer to be reused. For example, visual store has a half-life of about 200 milliseconds with a capacity of about 17 letters, and auditory store has a half-life of about 1500 milliseconds, with a capacity of about 5 letters (Card 1983, p. 3). When signals come in faster than they can be processed for recognition, they become blurred. For example, visual perceptual events occurring within about 60 to 100 milliseconds (the time varies inversely with the intensity of the stimulation) are combined into a single perception.

## COGNITIVE SYSTEM

The brain's memory is divided into a long-term memory (LTM) and a short-term memory (STM). The short-term memory (the brain's working memory) receives symbolically coded information from the sensory image stores and uses this information in combination with previously stored information in long-term memory. The cognitive processor works in recognize-act cycles (Card 1983, p. 40). The contents of working memory (STM) initiate associatively linked actions in LTM, which in turn modify the STM, setting the stage for the next cycle. The recognition phase is a parallel operation, and the action phase is a serial operation. (Card 1983, p. 42). Thus we can be aware of many things at once, but we cannot do more than one deliberate thing at a time. The brain's working memory (STM) holds the intermediate products of thinking as well as representations produced by the perceptual system. The short-term memory is a subset of elements in long-term memory that have become activated.

## DECAY RATES

Each of these memories has a different rate of decay of stored information. Perceptual memory, for example the visual image store, has a decay time of about 200 milliseconds; STM has a decay time of about 7 seconds; and LTM has an infinite decay time. We never really lose information in LTM; the strength of the associative links just get weaker.

## CHUNKS

The activated elements consist of symbols called *chunks*. The information can be coded in many different ways, but in STM, the use of symbolic acoustic codes is especially common. Visual codes are also possible. When a chunk is activated, the activation spreads to other chunks in LTM through connecting pathways that have become established through past experiences (these associations are a form of semantic encoding). Older chunks become less accessible as newer chunks become activated; the new interferes with the old. An activated chunk has a half-life (the time a chunk remains easily accessible; it effectively loses all accessibility after double the half-life).

The half-life varies with the number of chunks currently activated (recalled). For example, the half-life of a single chunk is 73 seconds, whereas the half-life decay of a chunk in working memory with three chunks already recalled is only 7 seconds (Card 1983, p. 39). Working memory can retain only three or four chunks for more than a few seconds. When augmented by the use of LTM, this increases the effective short-term memory recall capacity to approximately seven chunks, plus or minus two chunks (Card 1983, pp. 38–39). Of course the information contained in a chunk can vary greatly with the coding. For example, for one person, "CBSIBMRCA" represents nine chunks (in this case, nine letters), whereas for another person it could be coded as "CBS IBM RCA" which can be thought of as only three symbols, or chunks (Card 1983, p. 37).

## REACTION TIMES

Knowledge in LTM forms the basis for learned response to stimulus and ideas. Information is stored in both semantic and syntactic form, although semantic code is the predominant code type in LTM. LTM is accessed in 25 to 170 milliseconds, about 70 milliseconds on the average. This constitutes a cognitive processing cycle of about 0.1 second. There is a timing asymmetry in LTM because it takes about 7 seconds to store a chunk in LTM, whereas it takes only 70 milliseconds to access a chunk from LTM. Thus, the human brain has a relatively fast read (although much slower than a computer RAM), and a slow write. Compared to a 7 second write, the 70 millisecond read time seems fast.

The reaction time for a simple decision is about 100 to 400 milliseconds. But this decision time increases with uncertainty about judgments. For example (Card 1983, p. 72):

$$T = I_c H$$

where

$T$ is the decision time

$I_c$ is a constant

$H$ is the information theoretic measure of uncertainty (entropy) in our decision

The more frequently we perform a task, the better we get at it; our associations get richer, stronger, and more direct. For example, the time to perform a task on the $n$th trial can be shown to follow a power law of practice (Card 1983, p. 57), or:

$$T_n = T_1 n^{-a}$$

where

$T_n$ is the time to perform a task on the $n$th trial
$T_1$ is the initial time to perform the task
$a$ is a constant

## A MACRO VIEW OF HUMAN COGNITION

We can think of the human processor as ideally obeying the "rationality principle," although we know that this is only an approximation and that people can exhibit irrational behavior. The rationality principle states that

> A person acts so as to attain his or her goals through rational action, given the structure of the task and his or her inputs of information, bounded by limitations on his or her knowledge and processing ability. In other words: Goals + Task + Operators + Inputs + Knowledge + Process-limits → Behavior. (Card 1983, p. 86)

This rational behavior, for certain classes of tasks, can often be shown to reduce to a more precise procedure which follows the rules of symbolic logic, namely the "problem space principle," which states that:

> The rational activity in which people engage to solve a problem can be described in terms of (1) a set of states of knowledge, (2) operators for changing one state into another, (3) constraints on applying operators, and (4) control knowledge for deciding which operator to apply next. (Card 1983, p. 87)

## PERFORMANCE COMPARISON: PEOPLE AND COMPUTERS

A comparison between some of the key processing performance parameters of digital computers and humans is provided in Table A7.1 (Schutzer 1987, Fig. 6–9). We see that the brain has more memory capacity than a computer's primary memory, but recalls at slower speeds. However, it is a more richly interconnected memory, and it is accessed and processed in a more parallel fashion. Digital computers can perform logical and numerical computations and data reads and writes more rapidly; however, they must perform all operations serially. Furthermore, only the larger and more expensive computers can store and retrieve much larger quantities of data than the human brain, and they need to employ secondary as well as primary memory to achieve these capacities.

These constraints limit the contemporary digital computer's effectiveness, par-

TABLE A7.1. PERFORMANCE PARAMETERS OF DIGITAL COMPUTERS VERSUS HUMANS

| Digital computer | Human brain |
|---|---|
| *Primary memory* | |
| Cache: 10 to 100 bytes | STM: 5 to 9 chunks (about 9 to 10 bytes maximum) |
| RAM: 3 to 100M bytes | LTM: 100 billion neurons (only 10–30% useful for cognition; therefore about 10 to 30 billion bytes are useful for problem-solving) |
| *Secondary storage:* | |
| 100 Mbytes to G bytes | Nothing comparable |
| *Connectivity:* | |
| 3 or 4 inputs per logic gate | 1000 to 10,000 inputs/neuron |
| Single or duplexed common bus (newer parallel processors like the Thinking Machine have $10^9$ to $10^{10}$ interconnects) | 100 trillion interconnects |
| *Switching & transmission speeds:* | |
| $3 \times 10^7$ meters/sec (speed in silicon of signal transmission; upper limit speed of light in a vacuum, $183 \times 10^8$ meters/sec) | 10 mph (approx. 6 meters/sec) |
| *Processing speed:* | |
| 1 or 2 M flops* to B flops/sec. (supercomputers are approx. 100 B flops) | 10 to 100 processing cycles/sec (If we consider a processing cycle to be equivalent to a logical inference, then this equates to 10,000 to 100,000 processing cycles/sec) |
| *Size:* | |
| Varies from suitcase to a large cabinet | Smaller than a basketball |

*Flops = floating point operations/second.

ticularly in performing more qualitative, nonnumeric types of reasoning involving the manipulation of large numbers of symbols.

Consider the following simple examples. Suppose we wished to give a computer a minimal knowledge of the English language—specifically, a working knowledge of a 10,000 word vocabulary. (10,000 words is a very minimal vocabulary. A typical high school student has at least forty to fifty times this vocabulary. In fact, IBM and other researchers believe that an effective speech recognizer for applications like a "smart" dictation machine would have to master at least 100,000 words to be successful.) To be able to understand a word properly, we need to maintain and use semantic information associated with that word. A minimal set of semantic information could be represented by 150 bytes of definition, and 10 to 100 semantic relationships, or associations, connecting this word to other words and external stimuli. Just to maintain this minimal semantic information for 10,000 words requires storing anywhere from 100 million to 1 billion bytes of information. Thus relatively large memories are required to endow a computer with a capability for semantic reasoning, even for this simple, fundamental example.

Furthermore, retrieving and processing information within acceptable time frames from such large memories in response to pattern-invoked stimulus would prove stressing for today's serial computers. To illustrate this processing bottleneck, consider the following example. Human experts have been estimated as utilizing about 70,000 chunks of information, give or take a binary order of magnitude (+ or − 20,000), to solve a significant problem (Reddy 1988, Schutzer 1987). In expert system technology, we attempt to simulate a chunk and its associated activations by matching (firing) an "if-then" production rule. Matching a production rule produces a logical inference. This operation has been shown to require the execution of about 1000 machine instructions per rule. Making a decision using this production rule set requires cycling several times through the set: first, matching the input stimuli to the set of rules, and then recycling through the rule set, attempting to match the outputs of activated rules to other rules in the rule set. A simple decision typically requires cycling through the production rule set three or more times.

A simple decision on a 50,000 rule set with only three cycles could require attempting to match as many as 150,000 rules. This equates to over 150 million instructions. A 1 MIPS (millions of instructions per second) personal computer would require over 2 minutes to perform this computation; a high-powered 20 MIPS workstation would take at least 7 1/2 seconds to complete it (which is a marginally acceptable performance), and a top-of-the-line 100 MIPS mainframe would require a minimum of 1 1/2 seconds. Top-of-the-line contemporary serial digital computers (excluding supercomputers) are only marginally capable of handling this class of problems. Furthermore, digital computers of acceptable size and reasonable cost will generally prove inadequate for these tasks. However, structuring of rules into rule sets, frames, or objects, and/or using efficient A.I. pattern-matching algorithms, such as the Rete algorithm, can sometimes improve these processing times by an order of magnitude.

Many currently fielded commercial expert systems, however, contain only 100 to 10,000 rules. But as more ambitious problems are attempted, we will reach current performance barriers, without either dramatic increases in the computer's performance/cost envelope and/or the introduction of new specialized parallel processors. One such parallel processing architecture is neural networks modeled after the way we believe the human brain does its parallel processing (see Chapter 3). We know that humans must do parallel processing for activities such as scene analysis, speech recognition, and commonsense reasoning, because these activities require processing symbolic programs that would have to execute thousands of steps. Humans can be observed to perform these activities in a half-second time frame. Yet experimental evidence from cognitive psychology and neurophysiology (Bosurgi 1988, pp. 18–19) indicates that the mind cannot process a "program" of greater than 10 to 100 steps in the time frame of 1 second, even at the perception system level. So in order to respond as rapidly as humans do, some form of subsymbolic parallel processing must take place to account for the intelligent behavior that occurs within the first half-second horizon.

## CONCLUSION

Both humans and computers have their own strengths, weaknesses, and limitations, and there is opportunity for mutual support and augmentation of their respective effectiveness. Computers can perform repetitive logical operations in a consistent manner, at remote, relatively inaccessible locations, twenty-four hours around the clock. They never get bored or overwhelmed. They can perform serial computations faster than humans, and with the help of secondary memory, can store and recall greater volumes of information faster. Humans are better at learning and adapting; at properly including qualitative considerations; at identifying patterns and contributing facts; in dealing with beliefs and conflicting objectives; and in performing inductive reasoning. With recent dramatic improvements in performance and reduction in cost, the intelligent computer assistant is becoming an addition to the executive's staff, augmenting, and perhaps even replacing, one or more of the executive's human assistants.

# Appendix 8

# Expert Systems

## THE PROBLEM-SOLVING PROCESS

One way to think about problem-solving is in terms of the *problem space,* which consists of a set of knowledge states and a selection of operators (or rules) that can be used to transform states. A problem is defined in terms of an initial state(s) and goal state(s). Solving the problem involves finding a sequence of operators (a path) by which to transform the initial state(s) into the goal state(s). Thus problem-solving is a matter of searching the problem space on the basis of partial knowledge of how to proceed (what operator to select). This knowledge guides the search through the space. The difficulty of performance in the space, and the skill of the expert, can be assessed according to the extent to which the search control knowledge available constrains behavior.

In gaining expertise, the problem-solver amasses search control knowledge which he or she generalizes for a class of problems from a collection of individual instances to a task-solving search structure. This knowledge, when compiled into integrated procedures or packages of operators structured for efficient performance, suffices in most situations to enable the problem-solver to go straight to the desired goal, with relatively few false steps and relatively little need for backtracking, undoing earlier conclusions, and partial solutions (Card 1983). When a class of problems can be solved by a control strategy composed of fixed procedures requiring no search at all, we generally describe the solver's ability as a cognitive skill rather than as an expertise.

Once a cognitive skill or expertise is learned, the expert devotes little conscious attention to the search control strategy and therefore is usually poorly prepared to explain the control strategy to others. This is what makes it particularly difficult for the knowledge engineer to uncover and codify the expert's knowledge in an expert system, especially the control or procedural logic.

An important aspect of problem-solving is the way in which the problem states and knowledge are represented and reasoned about. Some popular reasoning representations include:

- Goal-directed reasoning: Reasoning from a goal or hypothesis one wishes to prove or disprove
- Data-driven reasoning: Reasoning from a set of known facts
- Case-based reasoning: Reasoning from previous cases or situations
- Template-based or object-based reasoning: Reasoning about objects and templates by filling in missing slots (object values) or using a default value or stereotype object
- Model-based reasoning: Reasoning in terms of a model (a circuit diagram for reasoning about electronic circuits, or a spreadsheet model for reasoning about company cash flows)

## EXAMPLES OF EXPERT SYSTEMS APPLICATIONS

- Text browsing and understanding
- Monitoring the news
- Human-directed interactive news or text browser (Perform searches; retrieve documents or headlines, point to articles that one likes as examples. Then continue, new refined search.)
- Intelligent front-end to multiple databases (American Express credit card authorization system interfaces to multiple IBM IMS files, and reduces 12 screens to 1 or 2 with recommendations and explanations and inconsistency resolution.)
- Smart financial statement analyzer (Reads and interprets financial statements like SEC's ELOISE project.)
- Trader's dealing system uses natural language to read electronic messages and to build trade ticket
- Natural language queries and message repair and interpretation
- Natural language reading of money transfer wires
- Smart spreadsheet (Each time data update is made, the system makes logical deductions and recalculates; useful for stock market monitoring.)
- Smart interfaces to financial analytics and statistical analyses (prepares input, interprets output, suggests sequencing)
- Interactive simulation (Models behavior of products and commodity prices and supply/demand under different situation scenarios.)
- Business planning and forecasting and competitive assessment analysis
- Sales advisor
- Intelligent customer service assistance
- Customizing customer catalogs and sales campaigns, with link to inventory management systems to identify slow movers, obsolete prod-

ucts, and nonstandard products; suggests when to apply discounts and extra labor
- Sales and marketing prospecting and profiling for customized targeting
- Customized service (Based on prototypical stereotype/behavior and past responses and buying habits of customer, determines what to send and solicit to whom.)
- Custom investment advisor
- Assessment of workers and departmental performance; e.g. sales performance checking
- Financial planner
- Personal tax planning advisor
- Tax audit planning and assistance
- Trader's assistant
- Portfolio management advisor
- Portfolio optimization scenario analysis and impact of current rumors
- Automated trading
- Financial engineering ideas generation
- Market minder, real-time intelligent market information filtering, or real-time trade or transaction monitoring
- Analysis of merger and acquisition candidates
- Hedging and portfolio risk assessment (bonds, stocks, futures, options)
- Pattern detection (trading patterns)
- Interest rate and stock price forecasting
- Corporate credit analyzer
- Risk assessment (of trading portfolios, commercial loans, insurance underwriting, credit risk scoring)
- Insurance underwriting advisor
- Credit card authorization
- Fraud detection
- Monitoring and policing trades on exchanges
- Automated order processing
- Intelligent equipment leasing analyzer
- Expert system for residential appraisals
- Health claims adjustment
- Office relocation planning
- Graphics selection
- Smart message center
- Records management

## EXPERT SYSTEM SHELLS

The following list gives some of the currently popular expert system shells. In addition, many AI developers program directly in one of the AI languages.

- Knowledge Base Management System (KBMS), from AI Corp.
- Aion Development System (ADS), from Aion Corp.

- FFAST, from Coopers and Lybrand
- Goldworks, from Gold Hill Computers
- Automated Reasoning Tool (ART), from Inference Corp.
- Knowledge Engineering Environment (KEE), from Intellicorp.
- Nexpert and Nexpert Object, from Neuron Data, Inc.
- Level 5, from Information Builders
- TIRS (The Integrated Reasoning Shell), from IBM
- KnowledgeTool, from IBM
- OPS 5, from Carnegie Mellon
- Copernicus, M1, S1, from Teknowledge
- Personal Consultant, from Texas Instruments
- KESII, from UNISYS

## COMMERCIALLY AVAILABLE FINANCIAL AI APPLICATIONS

- Intellect (smart natural language front-end to databases), from AI Corp.
- Personal Financial Planner, from A. D. Little
- Trader's Assistant, from A. D. Little
- Forecast Pro, from Business Forecast Systems
- Intelligent Bank System (natural language front-end for funds transfer and letter of credit telex messages), from Citicorp
- Consumer Lending System (evaluates credit worthiness for loans), from Cogensys
- Mortgage Underwriting System (evaluates credit worthiness for mortgages), from Cogensys
- Atrans and Aclass (natural language front-end for unformatted money transfers), from Cognitive Systems
- ExperTax (automates auditors and tax questionaire process), from Coopers and Lybrand
- Decision Expert (cross-selling and loan evaluation), from Innovative Microsystems
- Market Expert (accessing and analyzing customer base), from Innovative Microsystems
- The Lending Advisor (evaluation of commercial loans), from Syntelligence

# Appendix 9

# Object-Oriented Programming

## OBJECT-ORIENTED PROGRAMMING CONCEPTS

Object-oriented programming (OOP) is a popular language for artificial intelligence programming. In any computer language there are two types of constructs, declarative and procedural—data versus functions. Object-oriented programming gives ownership of the procedural constructs to the declarative ones and treats each package as an object. The data to be worked upon are bound together with the instructions on how to accomplish the work. The "what" is directly linked with the "how" in predefined objects. In contrast, conventional programs have evolved in a different direction. They generally treat the declarative constructs as distinct and independent items that are callable by the procedural constructs; they separate the what and the how (Amir 1989). One example is the growth of the independent database management system.

Another common feature of object-oriented programming is *object uniformity,* which means that no type checking or global knowledge of the different object types is necessary. The objects themselves will determine the proper actions. A Treasury bill object knows to compute its yield from its quoted discount rate, while a Treasury bond object computes its yield from its quoted dollar price.

Each object can be viewed as an abstract record structure that contains multiple slots and a message table. Slots hold values and represent the internal state of the object. The message table is a map between message names and functions to be executed in response to those messages. Different object-oriented programming systems implement these abstract records in different ways.

Objects have two major modes of inheritance: static and dynamic. With *static* inheritance, classes are first defined, and then objects are created from these classes. The newly created object is fixed as a member of the class. With *dynamic* inheritance, the classes are treated as objects. Each time an object is instantiated, it gets a copy of all its parents' slots. The parent hierarchy is searched each time a message is received. This adds processing overhead, but the advantage is that objects can change classes and message actions can be changed at run time. One feature of object-oriented programming is that we can define a new object in terms of how it differs from an existing one. This is a kind of programming by successive refinement. Another feature, called *delayed binding,* allows substitution of an equivalent object while the program is running. This provides the user with more flexibility.

## OBJECT-ORIENTED LANGUAGES

Some object-oriented languages are Smalltalk 80 from Parc Place Systems, a spinoff of Xerox (the original Smalltalk, developed at Xerox, was the first object-oriented language. It was inspired by a program language called Simula, which was used for computer simulations); $C^{++}$, developed by AT&T; Objective C, by Stepstone; VBase, by Ontologic, Inc.; and Gemstone, by Servio Logic. Unfortunately, there is not yet a commonly accepted standard for expert systems. The closest thing to a standard is CLOS (Common Lisp Object System).

# Appendix 10

# Intelligent Databases

## SEMANTIC NETWORKS

Semantic networks can be thought of as a series of nodes connected by arcs, where the nodes represent classes or concepts and the arcs represent relationships. When a node represents a specific value, such as "John J. Jones," it is referred to as a *concept;* when it represents a category of data, it is referred to as a *class* ("employee") The arc can be used to represent an assertion about the relationship: John J. Jones is an employee. In some systems the length of the arc indicates the strength of the relationship. Semantic systems resolve multiple relationship problems through a technique called *partitioning:* Only those relationships that apply to the current application are viewed by the database system. Semantic networks may be built on top of any traditional database, be it hierarchical, network, or relational. Most work, however, has concentrated on the development of semantic systems on top of relational database systems because of their strong mathematical and logical base and because, like semantic systems, they are nonprocedural in design.

## PRODUCTION RULES AND DEMONS

Two other techniques for imparting intelligence to the database are to store production rules and procedural demons along with the data items. *Demons* are embedded procedures that are triggered by queries, retrievals, or updates. Both approaches capture, manipulate, and store knowledge about the application and meaning of the data. These smart databases offer the advantage of a system capable of understanding more flexible queries, responding to words and their meanings within the context of the task and immediate needs.

## INDUCTION

IXL by Intelligence Ware is an unusual example of the marriage of artificial intelligence and extremely large databases. It subjects data to a comprehensive statistical analysis and then uses machine learning algorithms to find patterns and rules (Mahnke 1988). It was originally designed to run on a PC and was marketed in the Spring of 1987 for $490. It worked with ASCII, dBase, and Lotus files. A version is now available on the VAX under the VMS operation system for $7500 that reads ASCII, Oracle, and DEC's DB2. A version is also scheduled for IBM under VM for the DB2, Oracle, and Cullinet databases. Users utilize windows and menus to specify which databases and fields to search. The system can search through multiple databases concurrently. It then searches for patterns and relationships and generates easy to understand rules. The user works interactively with the system in assessing results and refining criteria.

Dr. Parsaye, president of Intelligence Ware and one of the developers, has cited the following successes using this product (Mahnke 1988): a recent medical discovery that found male and female patients react differently to enzymes used to detect lead poisoning; a solution to an elusive wiring problem at an automobile manufacturing plant; tracking down a recurrent quality control problem in disk drives to an employee in need of retraining in one phase of assembly; helping an insurance company find a pattern of fraudulent claims; supporting a network utilization analysis used by UCLA to optimize computer usage; supporting a financial analysis used in discovering indicators of a company's health; and helping direct marketing managers to discover new consumer buying patterns.

# Appendix 11

# Text-Based Management Systems

## AGENDA

There are three building blocks in an Agenda information base: items, categories, and notes. Any piece of information can be entered as an item. The maximum length of an item is 350 characters. Items can be assigned to categories implicitly or explicitly. The user can make an explicit assignment by adding a column to the display and making category entries in this column. Explicit assignments can be made by marking each category item to be assigned. Agenda makes implicit assignments by identifying matches between words in the item text and a category name, or by creating conditions and actions. Users can assign any item in the file to one or many categories, and categories can be arranged in hierarchical sequence. Agenda's notes provide a means for attaching additional information on a category or an item. A note can contain up to seven pages of double-spaced text for storing descriptive information. For a single file, a user can create and save many views. Agenda supports special views that show dependencies of items or prerequisites—for example, items with a specified data range.

A special group of instructions similar to functions in a spreadsheet allows custom processing of all types of data. Using these instructions, a user can search for specific characters, words, or phrases, and treat the text that follows as an item, note, or category. There are two ways to export data from Agenda: print a copy of related information, or save to a file in standard ASCII format. Users can also write a selected portion of an Agenda file to disk, stored in Agenda's STF format.

## OTHER TBMS

Some text retrieval programs, such as the PC-based Search Express/Objects can perform boolean "and/or" searches. They can be accessed directly from word processors, spreadsheets, and other programs. Another PC-based product, ZyIndex from Zylab, can search and retrieve free-form text, spreadsheets, or structured database entries. It can be used with over fifteen different word processors, or with files downloaded from public databases. Saztec International uses "image capture" to convert images into computer-readable format for management as part of the information base. The future probably lies with companies that integrate TBMSs with DBMSs. Examples include Software AG's Adabas 5, which incorporates both text and document processing, and Computer Corporation of America, which has integrated its Text/204 TBMS with its relational database. The oldest TBMS, and still the largest seller for mainframes, is IBM's Stairs.

# Appendix 12

# Hypertext Systems

## HYPERTEXT CONCEPTS

Almost all hypertext systems share the following three basic concepts: the information is held as chunks; the chunks are linked; and links are activated via screen buttons. Some systems, such as Xerox PARC's NoteCards and Apple's Hypercard, constrain a chunk to fit on a display screen. They use the box of file cards as the basic metaphor. Other systems allow the chunk to file many screens, allowing the user to scroll through the pages. In most hypertext systems, the links can be traversed in both directions.

There are viewing filters that suppress the detail, so users can scan rapidly through the data until they find the area of interest. Many systems permit users to create inverted files, retrieve on keywords in the context of the particular data or task, perform boolean searches, or establish hierarchical and content-based indexes.

Two types of nodes can generally be encountered in a hypertext system: type (or labeled), and untyped. *Typing* nodes makes it possible to define specialized operations by node category. An example of a typed system is the Graphic Issue-based Information System, gIBIS, from MCC and Computer Technology Corporation.

Most hypertext systems also allow the user to form composite nodes. Composite nodes can be treated as a single object or they can be broken out to create icons to reflect the individual contents of each of the elements that make up the composite node.

An emerging hypertext standard is the Standard General Markup language, SGML. It allows users to create links across applications. To use this system, the user must parse information into small, discrete units or nodes that consist of a concept or an idea.

## THE DEVELOPMENT OF HYPERTEXT

The idea for hypertext actually began in 1945 when Vannevar Bush, then the U.S. Presidential Science Advisor, proposed a project to organize scientific literature. The next milestone occurred in 1963, when Doug Englehart proposed a super-integrated office automation system called II-LAMT. By 1968, the NLS system, based on Englehart's work, and the Hypertext Editor by NASA had been built. In 1987, Apple's Hypercard was introduced, and it led to a flood of new products.

Many of the original ideas have still not been achieved with the present technology.

We can categorize the current hypertext implementations in terms of the type(s) of application they have been optimized to address:

- On-line help
- Problem resolution
- On-line browsing
- Library or literary exchange, and interactive publication
- Personal knowledge organizers
- Work group collaboration
- Multipurpose/Hyperverse

Hypertext is a good way of providing on-line help. If a user encounters a problem, the user can ask the system for relevant help. Hypertext-based help systems exist on the Symbolics and Tektronix workstations and Apple Macintosh, and are an integral part of Hewlett-Packard's New Wave operating environment for MS-DOS and OS/2 PCs. Hypertext aids in problem resolution by providing a framework for constructive discussion. Users can present issues, argue, and take positions which can be attached to these issues through pointers or links.

Hypertext supports browsing by letting a user freely explore the data, navigating along uncharted paths and exploring links at will, or alternately, by following a default path.

Hypertext is designed with the management of large databases in mind. Hypertext technology makes it easy for the user to use great libraries of information like those available in high-density storage devices like CD ROM. Hypertext is well suited to take advantage of the unique characteristics of CD ROM technology. The huge storage capacity means that various types of information—data, text, pictures, even music—can be held on the disk and linked. Moreover, it is easy to add items and links to CD ROM, but difficult to reorganize or delete data from it. Hypertext allows information to be organized so it can be assessed in different ways by different users for different purposes. Hypertext can do this because it separates information (chunks) from the structure (links), allowing several different structures to be applied to the same set of information. One caution is that constructing a CD ROM is a major undertaking. It comprises tens of thousands of frames of information and requires considerable skill to construct the links in a way that makes navigation easy. At present, this is an art without any established principles.

Hypertext can be used as a personal knowledge organizer to help keep track of and integrate the many small files generated by the typical business PC user. Links can be established, for example, between a spreadsheet that contains a cost model for a particular client and the text file that contains the report where the costs were presented to the organizer.

People work in groups in most organizations, and hypertext can be structured to support work group collaboration. This means that the tools need to support both messaging and the construction of knowledge structures which allow members of the group to file and retrieve information in a way that is natural and supportive of the activities of the group. An example is the hypertext system called ZOG used in the *USS Carl Vinson*. ZOG was built by Carnegie-Mellon, ran on a network of 28 PERQ workstations, and supported on-line manuals, a task management system, and an interface to an expert system.

Hypervers is an all-embracing system for organizing knowledge. It is a generalization of work group collaboration that goes beyond a single group. There are problems to be overcome before Hyperverse can become a real commercial success. The problems include the difficulties encountered when trying to deal with the sheer volume of published material.

## EXAMPLES OF HYPERTEXT SYSTEMS

Examples of hypertext systems include: Xerox's NoteCards, Apple's Hypercard; Owl International's Guide; Textnet; CREF; and For Comment.

NoteCards allows many cards to be displayed on the screen simultaneously. NoteCards is based on a hierarchical storage-and-retrieval system in some ways similar to videotext, but with sophisticated display facilities.

Apple's Hypercard allows the user to display only one card at a time. It provides facilities to backtrack through previous cards or to return to the home card. Hypercard has an embedded programming language called HyperTalk that allows actions of almost unlimited complexity to be associated with the buttons, not just bringing up another card.

Guide, by Owl International, is an example of a scrolling hypertext. In HyperCard and Guide all the links between chunks are of the same kind. In many other cases, the links imply specific relationships between chunks (e.g., evidence for, summary of, supersedes, refers to, qualifiers, implication of). The Textnet system, which is used for literary criticism, has 80 different types of links, including "refutation," "support," and "irrelevant point." A critic can link a chunk as a support point, or a refutation, and so on. The CREF system, which is used for research analysis, has four types of links: "refers to," "summarizes," "supersedes," and "precedes." For Comment, by Broederbund, allows users to share text on a network.

Others systems include ZOG, now available commercially under the name KMS (Knowledge Management System), from Knowledge Systems; Ask Sam, by Seaside Software; Black Magic, by Nvergaid; Cross Paint, by Cross Information; Hyperties, by Cognetics; Infosift, by Seaside Software; Test Pro and Knowledge Pro, by Knowledge Garden; Neptune, by Tektronics; Search Express, by Executive Technologies; Window Book, by Box Co.

# Appendix 13

# Neural Networks

## NEURAL NETWORK CONCEPTS

Although in research for over 30 years, neural network technology is still in its infancy. It was originally associated with work in artificial intelligence. In fact, Marvin Minsky, one of the founders of artificial intelligence research, was also one of the first to build a neural network. In 1965, after much study, Minsky issued a denunciation of neural network technology. He pointed out what he thought were many serious limitations—for example, that neural networks were incapable of solving the "exclusive or" class of problems. As a result, a neural network "winter" set in. Funding and research shifted to symbolic processing and logic-based systems, where Minsky had shifted his interest. Some work continued in neural networks, but at a low level.

Recently there have been several important breakthroughs—in particular, Bernard Widrow's work at Stanford (where he made important advances in the 1980s with respect to a better understanding of neurobiological processes), and a revolution in computer technology. With the introduction of neural networks with a middle, or "hidden" layer, a neural network solution to the "exclusive or" problem was demonstrated (Touretzky and Pomerleau 1989). Since that time, work in neural networks has began to surge. In the summer of 1988, the Defense Advanced Research Projects Agency (DARPA) recommended a federal investment of nearly $400 million (Williamson 1989).

Neural networks use parallel pattern matching. They simulate the right side of the brain, based upon the left brain–right brain hypothesis, which suggests that the left side of the brain concentrates on logical, analytical, and highly structured functions whereas the right side concentrates on intuitive and imaginative activities. Although neural networks are built from rather simple individual units, they offer the opportunity for highly complex systems to arise, especially since the functions involved in the individual units are generally nonlinear and often stochastic. A digital computer's processing elements are basically binary switches with two states (1 and 0, or on and off); neural processing elements are more like resistors and amplifiers; their values range from 0 to 1 in minute decimal increments. Each neural processing element has a summation function which totals incoming signals above a set threshold, and a transfer function, which is generally nonlinear.

The processing elements are arranged in layers that may be fully or partially connected with each other. Signals may go only forward, or they may feed error and output signals backward. A neural typical network has at least three layers: an input layer, a middle layer, and an output layer. Generally the output layer produces symbols, but the symbols are not discrete or inert; rather, they are the result of the network of neurons attempting to settle into a momentary steady state. Neural networks are data-driven and self-organizing, and therefore their performance improves over time. And because the work in a neural network is carried out by many elements working simultaneously on the same data, they are intrinsically fault-tolerant.

The neural network learns by adaptation. A neural network's architecture and learning rules can be defined in terms of its number of processing elements, number of layers, signal strengths, thresholds, and connection patterns. If it is fed a series of training patterns, known as *input responses pairs,* and adjusts itself by changing thresholds and signal strengths, it is said to use supervised learning. *Back propagation* is an example of supervised learning. This method is not suitable for all problems; the system can get confused and bogged down when there are several ways to achieve the same output. Supervised methods work well where speed is not critical. A neural network based on unsupervised learning is called a *self-organizing system.* It looks at all the inputs and determines a way to combine them that makes most sense to arrive at an answer.

## NEURAL NETWORK ARCHITECTURES

Some examples of the different neural network architectural concepts and terminology are given below (Williamson, *Digital News,* January 1989):

*Adaline/Madaline (Adaptive Linear Neuron/Multiple Adaptive Linear Neuron).* A class of neural network configurations capable of solving problems involving linear separability. Every instance falls into one of only two categories. An example of this type is Bernard Widrow's adaptive echo-canceling filter.

*Back Propagation.* A learning rule for multilayer networks that facilitates learning by feeding error signals from the output processing elements back to input. It is a form of feedback.

*Convergence*. The state of a neural network after training, when it has arrived at a set of processing-element weights suitable for producing correct responses to unfamiliar inputs.

*Feedback*. The flow of signals bearing information from output to input to correct a processing element's errors and control network behavior.

*Feedforward*. The flow of signals bearing information from input to output.

*The Hamming Network*. An example of an associative memory network. An *associative* (content addressable) *memory* is a memory that returns stored information by associating it with an inexact or incomplete version of that information.

*Hopfield Network*. A type of artificial neural network in which elements are fully connected and error signals are fed back to element inputs.

*Layer (also Slab)*. An arrangement of processing elements, each of which may have a different weight, but all of which have the same transfer function. A neural network consists of one or more layers.

*Learning Rule (or Learning Algorithm)*. The mathematical equations that specify how the responses of processing elements to the input signals they receive will change over time.

*Processing Element (also PE, Processing Unit, Cell, or Node)*. The basic unit of the neural network, loosely analogous to the brain's neuron. It receives an input signal, modifies it according to the learning rule of its network, and sends the signal on to other processing elements or to the network's output.

*Reduced Coulomb Energy Network (RCE)*. The technology patented by Nestor, Inc., and used in its products to solve problems involving pattern classification.

*Threshold*. The threshold determines how strong an incoming signal must be to cause the processing element to fire. A threshold value is assigned to each processing element.

## NEURAL NETWORK APPLICATION EXAMPLES

A good example of the application of this technology is the NETTALK system, invented by T. Sejnowski of Johns Hopkins. NETTALK is a neural network that can be trained to pronounce English words. It uses about 300 neurons, arranged in three layers. The input layer reads the words, the output layer generates the speech sounds or phonemes, and the middle, or "hidden" layer, mediates. This network constitutes about 18,000 adjustable interconnections, or synapses, whose strength can be turned up or down. NETTALK was able to recognize 1000 words after a half day, and 20,000 words after a week.

Although the rules in a neural network are implicitly coded, the inventor was able to uncover the hidden knowledge through a mathematical analysis of the results. It turns out that the knowledge is very sensible. Vowels are represented differently from consonants. Things that sound similar are clustered together—

for example, the letters "p" and "b," and "a" and "e." Also, any ten randomly chosen neurons could be used as a "seed" to reproduce the entire coding scheme. The system has another big advantage: It performs like a hologram; no matter how small the network is cut (1/2, 1/4, 1/8), each piece contains the whole image, but with poorer resolution. Therefore, the system is not only effective, it is robust and will not easily fail.

Some special-purpose neural chips exist today, mostly in experimental form. They include the California Institute of Technology's silicon retina and cochlea, simulating sensory receptors in the eye and ear, and the Bell Laboratories chip, a neural network packaged on a chip that is reportedly 100,000 faster than a neural network simulated with software on a general-purpose computer (Cortese 1988). With such a chip, neural networks can add functionality to existing systems, not as a standalone.

[We are likely to see a] "plethora of neural network chips arising from a variety of sources in the near future, including traditional chip manufacturers such as Intel, Motorola, and Texas Instruments," says Ed Rosenfeld, editor of *Intelligence Newsletter,* which specializes in neural network coverage. In fact, many other companies and labs have been reported to be building special neural chips. They include: Oxford Computer of Oxford, CT; Jet Propulsion Laboratory; MIT/Lincoln Labs; Texas Instruments; University of Pittsburgh; University of Maryland; University of Arizona; Calgary University; IBM; Fujitsu; and Hughes Aircraft.

# Appendix 14

## Groupware

Examples of groupware include Timbuktu from Farallon, Perfect Timing from Imagine, Mark Up from Mainstay, For Comment from Deneba, and FullWrite Professional from Ashton-Tate. Timbuktu lets users watch or control what is happening on another computer screen. It presents a list of users on the network that allow guests. Once logged, the guest can observe or control the system, depending on the privileges granted. When observers are connected, an eye appears on the far right corner of the host's menu bar, so the host knows that someone is observing. If a guest with control privileges is connected, a hand is shown in the far right corner of the menu bar. The host can revoke any guest's privileges at any time.

Perfect Timing handles office scheduling. It keeps track of personal schedules, and room and equipment availability. Each user can see other's schedules as blocks of time that are available or unavailable. Users can overlay each individual's schedule until they find a time when everyone is free.

Mark Up is a group work processor. It lets several people review manuscripts and add comments. It has tools so that the reviewer can write on the document electronically, in a manner analogous to using a red pen.

For Comment lets a user attach an electronic version of Post-it™ notes to cells in a spreadsheet or words or phrases in a document. The user highlights the cell or word and then chooses the note from the comment menu.

FullWrite Professional has a Posted Note Facility for storing annotated comments and the name and time of the reviewer.

Other examples include The Coordinator, by Action Technologies; Notes, by Lotus; and Participate, from Eventures.

MIT's Professor Thomas Malone's Information Lens is a prototype intelligent information-sharing system designed to combine good user and organizational inferences for supporting problem-solving. It applies artificial intelligence to the daily clutter of electronic mail. Hewlett-Packard's New Wave creates a task-oriented environment that includes an agent, or personal assistant. For example, if you have a regular report to write each month, your computer assistant will pull the pieces together—the sales forecast, divisional goals. The report then becomes an object to be manipulated in an object-oriented database.

# Appendix 15

# CASE

## CASE CONCEPTS

CASE is a product of research stemming from structured requirements analysis and programming design, such as Warnier-Orr, Yourdon, Jackson, HIPO methodology, and Data Flow Diagrams, and from research in the fields of artificial intelligence directed toward automated programming, such as the Programmer's Workbench. CASE involves applying a standardized methodology to the process of software development. This adds consistency to the development process. It also makes it easier for users to develop and to port applications under unfamiliar environments; they do not have to be experts in the systems software.

CASE segments the software development process into requirements analysis, program development, system verification, results analysis, documentation, and maintenance. CASE includes features such as graphic analysis and design, central information repositories, integrated tool sets, prototyping, code generation, documentation generation and upkeep, and project planning tools.

## COMMERCIAL CASE PRODUCTS

Many commercial CASE packages are available. There are currently anywhere from 60 to 100 vendors marketing CASE products, and new products are being introduced every week. A study by Focus Research found that Excelerator, an analysis and design CASE tool from Index Technology, holds 40.4 percent of the market. Other leading tools include Arthur Anderson's Design/1, Nastec's Design

Aid, and CASE 2000, Knowledgeware's Information Engineering Workbench, McDonnell Douglas's Stradus/Draw, CGI Systems, Pacbase, Sage Sofware's APS, Transform Logic, Cortex, and EXSYS. Their costs vary from $1000 to $100,000.

## LACK OF STANDARDS

One drawback with the current state of the CASE technologies is the lack of industry standards that would allow various CASE tools to work together. The best-known model of an integrated environment with a shared repository is the Portable Common Tool Environment (PCTE) sponsored by the European Economic Community ESPIRIT project, and Emerande, a commercial implementation of PCTE. In the United States, DEC and Atherton Technology have started a committee to define a Common Tools and Applications Interface Standard (CATIS) that is supported by several workstation and CASE tool vendors.

# Appendix 16

# Communication Standards

## SYSTEM NETWORK ARCHITECTURE (SNA)

IBM's SNA is a seven-layer model:

1. Hierarchical PU 2.0 (the physical layer)
2. Peer PU 2.1 (the data link control layer)
3. Device-to-device (the path control)
4. Hierarchical LU 1 - 3 (the transmission control layer)
5. Program to program LU 6.2 (the data-flow control layer)
6. The presentation services layer
7. The applications or end-user interface layer

Layers 1 to 3 are concerned with the physical services, and layers 4 to 6 are concerned with the logical services. Traditional SNA tied together mainframes and dumb peripherals in a hierarchical relationship. With the proliferation of minicomputers and PCs, IBM found it necessary to transform SNA into an architecture capable of supporting a cooperative processing environment where remote intelligent devices could be linked with mainframes and each other peer-to-peer. The Logical Unit 6.2 and the Advanced Program-to-Program Communications (APPC) are used to establish logical communications between cooperating programs. The Physical Unit 2.1 makes possible point-to-point physical connectivity between peer nodes without mainframe involvement.

## OPEN SYSTEM INTERCONNECTION (OSI)

We will use the OSI vendor independent standard as the basis for further illustrating these concepts. OSI has seven layers: the applications layer; the presentation layer; the session layer; the transport layer; the network layer; the link layer; and the physical layer.

### *Physical Layer*

The physical layer deals with the lowest level (level 1), the physical level. It is concerned with the way one physically encodes, modulates, and transmits data across the physical links. It deals with the physical connections, (number of wires and pin connections), their functions (control, data), and the electrical characteristics (voltage levels and timing). The IEEE 802.2 standard pertains to this level. An example of the physical layer is the recent high-bandwidth fiber optic standard, the Fiber Distributed Data Interface (FDDI).

### *Link Layer*

The link layer, or level 2, provides for the point-to-point data transfer over the physical links. It is the layer concerned with establishing, maintaining, and releasing the link connectons. Ethernet, first developed by Xerox, covers both levels 1 and 2 for OSI, TCP/IP, and DECNET. The Ethernet is also incorporated into the IEEE 802.2 and 802.3 standards. The link layer part of Ethernet, known as carrier-sense multiple access/collision detection, or CSMA/CD, is covered by IEEE 802.3. The physical level is covered under IEEE 802.2.

Token ring is a multiple access method that allows transmission by a node only when it receives a circulating token. It is both an SNA level 2 standard and an IEEE 802.5 level 2 standard. Two other SNA protocols are synchronous data link control (SDLC), which covers both levels 1 and 2; and binary synchronous protocol (BISYNC), which also covers levels 1 and 2. There is also a token bus multiple access method which is addressed by IEEE 802.4 level 2 protocol. Like the token ring, the token bus requires a node to receive a token before transmitting.

### *Network Layer*

The network layer, or level 3, deals with defining the end-to-end route between two communicating systems (two computers, or a terminal and a computer). The CCITT packet switching standard, X25, covers levels 1, 2 and 3. The Internet protocol (IP) from TCP/IP covers the level 3 protocol.

### *Transport Layer*

The transport layer, or level 4, provides the logical connection from a process on one machine to a process on another. It includes end-to-end flow control, assurance of delivery of the message, error detection/correction, and message sequencing. The Transmission Control Program (TCP) of TCP/IP covers the level 4 protocol.

### Session Layer

The session layer, or level 5, provides the necessary protocol to access processes on other machines. It organizes and synchronizes the dialogue between two network nodes. It validates the identification and authorization of the calling party.

### Presentation Layer

The presentation layer, or level 6, ensures that all devices can understand one another at the application layer. Message compression, terminal standardization, and data encryption are all handled at this level.

### Application Layer

The application layer, or level 7, handles the application aspects of the communication. Standards generally exist for most of the standard user functions requiring a network interface, such as electronic mail. Examples of some of the standard protocols at this level are the File Transfer Access Method (FTAM), an ISO standard; Virtual Terminal Protocol (VTP), another ISO standard; the CCITT Virtual Terminal Protocol, X400; Sun's Network File System (NFS); the Department of Defense File Transfer Protocol (FTP), and transport protocols TP1–TP5; Telenet, the Department of Defense virtual terminal protocol; and the Department of Defense Single Mail Transfer Protocol, SMTP.

## COMMUNICATION DEFINITIONS

Some of the more commonly used communication standards terminology are given below.

- SNA, Systems Network Architecture (IBM)
- SDLC, Synchronous Data Link Control (IBM)
- BISYNC, Binary synchronous protocol (IBM)
- X.25, a packet-switched network protocol (CCITT)
- FTAM, File Transfer Access Method (ISO)
- VTP, Virtual Terminal Protocol (ISO)
- X.400, a virtual terminal protocol (CCITT)
- TP1–TP5 Transport Protocol, classes 1 through 5 (ISO)
- FTP, File Transfer Protocol (Defense Dept.)
- SMTP, Simple Mail Transfer Protocol (Dept. of Defense)
- TELNET, a virtual terminal protocol (Dept. of Defense)
- NFS, Network File System (Sun Microsystems; public domain)
- TCP, Transmission Control Protocol (Dept. of Defense)
- IP, Internet Protocol (Dept. of Defense)
- Ethernet, local area network architecture developed by Xerox and others, and later incorporated into the IEEE 802.2 and 802.3 standards
- IEEE, Institute of Electrical and Electronics Engineers
- CSMA/CD, Carrier Sense Multiple Access/Collision Detection; multiple-access method used by Ethernet and IEEE 802.3
- Token Bus, multiple access method used by IEEE 802.4
- Token Ring, multiple access method used by IEEE 802.5 and IBM

# References

Amir, Shawn. "Building Integrated Expert Systems." *AI Expert,* Vol. 4, No. 1, January 1989, pp. 26–37.

Aseo, Joseph. "But Does It Do Windows?" *ESD: The Electronic System Design Magazine,* June 1988, pp. 61–68.

Barron, James. "Struck Dumb by the Incredible: 1-800-NOTHING." *New York Times,* January 16, 1990, p. A25.

Belitsos, Bryro. "Can We Measure What We Do?" *Computer Decisions,* August 1988, pp. 60–63.

Berg, Eric N. "Board of Trade to Weigh Changes." *New York Times,* February 9, 1989, pp. D1, D5.

Bernstein, Amy, "MCI Wins Marketing Game With 'Expert' IS Strategy." *Computerworld Premier 100,* Sept. 11, 1989, pp. 18–19.

Bosurgi, Joe. "From Symbols to Signals: Getting Closer to Machine Intelligence." *The Scientist,* January 13, 1988, pp. 18–19.

Card, Stuart K., Moran, Thomas P., and Newell, Allen. *The Psychology of Human-Computer Interaction.* Hillsdale, NJ: Lawrence Erlbaum Associates, 1983.

Carrol, J. B., et al. *Word Frequency Book.* New York: American Heritage, 1973.

Cortese, Amy. "Bellcore Puts Neural Nets on a Chip." *Computerworld,* September 19, 1988. pp. 23–30.

Davis, Stephen G. "The Superconductive Computer in Your Future." *Datamation,* August 15, 1987, pp. 74–78.

DeLong, David. "Computers in the Corner Office." *New York Times,* August 21, 1988, p. 4.

Drexler, K. Eric. *Engines of Creation.* Garden City, NY: Anchor Press/Doubleday, 1986.

Duda, Richard O., Hart, Peter E., Rebhoh, Rene, Reiter, John, and Reach, Tore. "Syntel Using a Functional Language For Financial Risk." *IEEE Expert,* Fall 1987, pp. 18–30.

Edwards, W. "Reward Probability, Amount and Information as Determiners of Sequential Two-Alternative Decisions." *Journal of Experimental Psychology,* 1956 Vol. 52, pp. 177–188.

Eichenwald, Kurt. "The Day the Nation's Cash Pipeline Almost Ran Dry." *New York Times,* October 2, 1988, p. 11.

Einhorn, H. J. "Expert Measurement and Mechanical Combination." *Organizational Behavior and Human Performance,* 1972, Vol. 7, pp. 86–106.

Fama, Eugene. "The Behavior of Stock Market Prices." *Journal of Business* (38), January 1965, pp. 34–105.

Feder, Barnaby. "Computer Helper: Software That Writes Software." *New York Times,* May 8, 1988, p. 5.

Frank, Howard. "Leading the Network into the 1990's." *Networking Management,* January 1990.

Fuchsberg, Gilberto. "Hand Held Computers Help Field Staff Cut Paper Work and Harvest More Data." *Wall Street Journal,* January 30, 1990, pp. B1, B9.

Goldberg, L. R. "Man vs. Model of Man: A rationale, plus Some Evidence for a Method of Improving on Clinical Inferences." *Psychological Bulletin,* 1970, Vol. 73, pp. 422–432.

Goldberg, L. R. "Man vs. Model of Man: Just How Conflicting Is That Evidence?" *Organizational Behavior and Human Performance,* 1976, Vol. 16, pp. 13–22.

Goleman, Daniel. "Why Managers Resist Machines." *New York Times,* February 7, 1988, p. 4.

Gutierres, Ted. "Automate the Futures Exchange." *New York Times,* December 31, 1989, p. F2.

Hitch, Charles, "Sub-optimization in Operations Research." *Operations Research,* 1953, Vol. 1, pp. 87–99.

Hoggatt, A. "An Experimental Business Game." *Behavioral Science,* 1959, Vol. 4, pp. 192–203.

Hooper, Laurence, and Schlesinger, Jacob M. "Is Optical Computing The Next Frontier, Or Just a Nutty Idea?" *Wall Street Journal,* January 30, 1990, pp. A1, A2.

Kahneman, Daniel, Slovic, Paul, and Tversky, Amos. *Judgment under Uncertainty: Heuristics and Biases.* Cambridge, Eng.: Cambridge University Press, 1982.

Kaplan, Robert and Bruns, William. *Accounting and Management: Field Study Perspectives.* Cambridge, MA: Harvard Business School Press, 1987.

Lane, Morton, " 'Open Outcry' Works Well and Cheaply" *New York Times,* December 31, 1989, p. F2.

Lee, Ed. "Window of Opportunity." *UNIX,* June 1988, pp. 58–75.

Lewis, Peter H. "The Executive Computer." *New York Times,* August 21, 1988, p. 9.

Lewis, Peter H. "The Executive Computer," *New York Times,* December 25, 1988, p. 6

Lewis, Peter H. "IBM's New System Is Put to a Test." *New York Times,* January 1, 1989, p. 10.

Libby, R. "Man versus Model of Man: Some Conflicting Evidence." *Organizational Behavior and Human Performance,* 1976, Vol. 16, pp. 1–12.

Mahnke, John. "IXL Tool Discovers Database Problems." *Management Information Systems Week,* December 12, 1988, p. 27.

Markoff, John. "Now PC's That Read a Page and Store It." *New York Times.* August 17, 1988. p. D6. (a)

Markoff, John. "IBM and a University Plan Swift File Network." *New York Times,* August 23, 1988, p. D4. (b)

Markoff, John. "Supercomputer Pictures Solve the Once Insolvable." *New York Times,* October 30, 1988, pp. 1, 26. (c)

Markoff, John. "The PC's Brand New Potential." *New York Times,* November 30, 1988. (d)

Markoff, John. "Laser Device Could Be Key to Faster Computer." *New York Times,* January 30, 1990, pp. A1, D8. (a)

Markoff, John. "A Darwinian Creation of Software." *New York Times,* February 28, 1990, p. D9. (b)

Meltzer, Allan. "What Really Happened in the Crash?" *Corporate Finance,* October 1988, p. 25.

O'Leary, Meghan, "Rethinking the Organization." *CIO,* December 1989, pp. 44–50.

Pava, Calvin. "In Managing New Office Technology." Free Press, 1983.

Pepper, Bill. "Fast Forward." *Business Month,* February 1989, p. 25.

*Personal Computer World.* October 1988.

Pollack, Andrew. "New Chips Offer the Promise of Much Speedier Computers." *New York Times,* January 4, 1989, pp. 1, D6. (a)

Pollack, Andrew. "Servers Spurring on Evolution in Computing." *New York Times,* October 11, 1989, p. D7. (b)

Polya, G., *Patterns of Plausible Inference: Mathematics and Plausible Reasoning.* Vol. II. Princeton, NJ: Princeton University Press, 1968.

Preston, M. C., and Barrata, P. "An Experimental Study of the Auction Value of an Uncertain Outcome." *American Journal of Psychology,* 1948, Vol. 61, pp. 183–193.

Reddy, R. "Foundations and Grand Challenges of Artificial Intelligence." *Artificial Intelligence Magazine,* Vol. 9, No. 4 Winter 1988, pp. 9–24.

*Release 1.0.* December 30, 1987.

Roach, Stephen. *America's Technology Dilemma: A Profile of the Information Economy.* April 1987.

Rockart, John F., and DeLong, David W. *Executive Support Systems.* Homewood, IL: Dow Jones-Irwin, 1988.

Rothfeder, Jeffrey, and Bartimo, Jim, Therrian, Lois, and Brandt, Richard. *Business Week,* July 2, 1990. pp. 54–55.

Saffo, Paul. "Same-Time, Same-Place Groupware." *Personal Computing,* March 20, 1990, pp. 57–58.

Schatz, Willie, and Foley, Mary Jo. "Users Welcome New NSF Network with Glee and Caution." *Datamation,* September 1, 1988, pp. 33–34.

Schiller, Zachary. "Stalking the New Consumer." *Business Week,* August 28, 1989, pp. 54–62.

Schutzer, Daniel. *Artificial Intelligence.* New York: Van Nostrand, 1987.

Scodel, A., Ratoosh, P., and Minas, J. S. "Some Personality Correlates of Decision Making under Conditions of Risk." *Behavioral Science,* 1959, Vol. 4, pp. 19–28.

Scodel, A., Ratoosh, P., Minas, J. S., and Lipetz, M. "Some Descriptive Aspects of Two-Person, Non Zero-Sum Games." *Conflict Resolution,* 1959, Vol. 3, pp. 114–119.

Shellenberger, Sue. "CBOT, in a Sign of the Times, May Finally Join Electronic Age." *New York Times,* February 6, 1989, p. C1.

Siler, Julian Flynn. "Broker Study by Exchange in Chicago." *New York Times,* February 9, 1989, p. D5.

Simon, H. A. *Models of Man.* New York: Wiley, 1957.

Sullivan-Trainor, Michael L. "Unified Business Focus Drives American Express' Diversified Success." *Computerworld Premier 100,* September 11, 1989, pp. 58–60.

Touretzky, David S., and Pomerleau, Dean A. "What's Hidden in the Hidden Layers?" *Byte,* August 1989, pp. 227–233.

Treacy, Michael. "Survival: Automating Sales, Marketing, Distribution and Service." *The Consultant Forum,* Vol 5, No 1, p. 2.

Wang, Richard, and Madnick, Stuart. *Connecting Among Information Systems.* MIT Composite Information Series Project, Vol. 1, September 1988.

Wiggins, N., and Kohen, E. S. "Man vs. Model of Man Revisited: The Forecasting of Graduate School Success." *Journal of Personality and Social Psychology,* 1971, Vol. 19, pp. 100–106.

Williams, Tom. "User Interface Management System Steps Up Application Development." *Computer Design,* June 1, 1990, pp. 56–58.

Williamson, Mickey. "Neural Networks." *Digital News,* January 9, 1989, pp. 29–35.

Zachary, G. Pascal. "Artificial Reality: Computer Simulations One Day May Provide Surreal Experiences." *New York Times,* January 23, 1990, pp. A1, A9.

Zuboff, Shoshana. "Smart Computers: The Challenge to Smart Managers." *Business Month,* February 1989. pp. 61–62.

# Bibliography


Ackoff, Russell L. *Progress in Operations Research,* Volume I. New York: Wiley, 1966.

Adler, Berni J. *Special Purpose Computers.* New York: Academic Press, 1988.

Agristi, William W. *New Paradigms for Software Development.* New York: IEEE Computer Society Press, June 1986.

Agres, Ted. "Is HDTV America's Last Hope, or Much Ado about Nothing?." *Research & Development,* September 1989.

Amir, Shawn. "Building Integrated Expert Systems." *AI Expert,* Vol. 4, No. 1, January 1989, pp. 26–37.

Andrews, Edmund. "The Lure of Digital Television." *New York Times,* June 24, 1990, p. 9.

Anderson, Dana (ed.). *Neural Information Processing Systems.* American Institute of Physics, 1988.

Anderson, James A., and Rosenfeld, Edward (eds.). *Neurocomputing: Foundations of Research.* Cambridge, MA: MIT Press/Bradford Books, 1988.

Aseo, Joseph. "But Does It Do Windows?" *ESD: The Electronic System Design Magazine,* June 1988, pp. 61–68.

Barron, James. "Struck Dumb by the Incredible: 1-800-NOTHING." *New York Times,* January 16, 1990, p. A25.

Begeman, Michael L., and Conklin, Jeff. "The Right Tool for the Job." *Byte* October 1988, pp. 255–266.

Behan, "Overview of Financial Applications of Expert Systems," *WESTEX 87.* 1987.

Belitsos, Bryro. "Can We Measure What We Do?" *Computer Decisions,* August 1988, pp. 60–63.

Bender, Eric. "Workstations, PCs Collide." *PC World,* August 1989, pp. 57–58.

Berg, Eric N. "Board of Trade to Weigh Changes." *New York Times,* February 9, 1989, pp. D1, D5.

Bermant, Charles. "Integrating OS/2 and DOS 3.X." *Personal Computing,* April 1988, pp. 129–134.

Bernstein, Amy. "MCI Wins Marketing Game With 'Expert' IS Strategy." *Computerworld Premier 100,* Sept. 11, 1989, pp. 18–19.

Blackford, John. "The Story of 'O'." *Personal Computing,* June 29, 1990, pp. 83–86.

Blackford, John. "Resolving a Nasty Little War." *Personal Computing,* April 27, 1990. pp. 43–44.

Blair G. S., Mariani, J. A., Nicol, J. R., and Shepherd, W. D. "A Knowledge Based Operating System." *The Computer Journal,* Vol. 30, No. 3, June 1987, pp. 193–200.

Borrow, Daniel G. "The Object of Desire." *Datamation,* May 1, 1989, pp. 37–41.

Bosurgi, Joe. "From Symbols to Signals: Getting Closer to Machine Intelligence." *The Scientist,* January 13, 1988, pp. 18–19.

"Advanced Television Systems." *Broadcasting,* April 6, 1987, p. 32.

Brownstein, Mark, and Parker, Rachel. "HDTV Could Improve Computer-Video Link." *Digital News,* February 13, 1989, p. 8.

Bullis, David C., and Powell, Joe. "Using CASE Tools Speeds Functional Test Development." *Electronics Test,* January 1989, pp. 34–38.

"Television Makers Are Dreaming of a Wide Crispness." *Business Week,* December 21, 1987, pp. 108–109.

"The HDTV Picture Starts Coming into Focus." *Business Week,* September 19, 1988, pp. 38–41.

Campbell, Mary V. "New Software Idea Could Change Future's Agenda." *Wall Street Computer Review,* December 1988, pp. 80–82.

Card, Stuart K., Moran, Thomas P., and Newell, Allen. *The Psychology of Human-Computer Interaction.* Hillsdale, NJ: Lawrence Erlbaum Associates, 1983.

Carroll, Paul B. "Computers Cut Through Service Maze." *Wall Street Journal,* May 1, 1990, pp. B1, B5.

Carrol, J. B., et al. *Word Frequency Book.* New York: American Heritage, 1971.

Carroll, John M. *Interfacing Thought: Cognitive Aspects of Human-Computer Interaction.* Cambridge, MA: MIT Press, 1987.

Chikofsky, Elliot J. *Computer-Aided Software Engineering (CASE).* New York: IEEE Computer Society Press, December 1988.

National Research Council Committee. *Crossroads of Information Technology Standards.* Washington, DC: National Academy Press, 1990.

Corcoran, Elizabeth. "A Technological Fix." *Scientific American,* August 1989.

Cortese, Amy. "Bellcore Puts Neural Nets on a Chip." *Computerworld,* September 19, 1988. pp. 23–30.

"Customers Drive Image Processing, Forcing MIS to Move Quickly." *MIS Week,* June 25, 1990, pp. 1, 27.

Davies, D. W., Holler, E., Jensen, E. D., Kimbleton, S. R., Lampson, B. W., LeLann, G., Thurber, K. J., and Watson, R. W. *Distributed Systems-Architecture and Implementation.* Berlin: Springer-Verlag, 1983.

Davis, Lawrence. *Genetic Algorithms and Simulated Annealing.* Palo Alto, CA: Morgan Kaufman, 1987.

Davis, Roger. "Scientific Environments." *Sun Expert Magazine,* June 1990, pp. 81–85.

Davis, Stephen G. "The Superconductive Computer in Your Future." *Datamation,* August 15, 1987, pp. 74–78.

Dawson, Joseph. "Family of Models." *Byte,* September 1989, pp. 277–286.

Denker, John. *Second Annual Conference on Neural Networks for Computing*: American Institute of Physics, Proceedings, Vol. 151, 1986.

Dickson, Gary, W. and Wetherbee, James C. *The Management of Information Systems.* New York: McGraw-Hill, 1985.

DeLong, David. "Computers in the Corner Office." *New York Times,* August 21, 1988, p. 4.

Donaldson, Gordon, and Lorsch, Jay W. *Decision Making at the Top—The Shaping of Strategic Direction.* New York: Basic Books, 1983.

Doyle, J., and Sacks, E. "Stochastic Analysis of Qualitative Dynamics." *Eleventh International Joint Conference on Artificial Intelligence.* Vol. 2. Detroit, August 20–25, 1989, pp. 1187–1192.

Drexler, K. Eric. *Engines of Creation.* Garden City, NY: Anchor Press/Doubleday, 1986.

Duda, Richard O., Hart, Peter E., Rebhoh, Rene, Reiter, John, and Reach, Tore. "Syntel Using a Functional Language For Financial Risk." *IEEE Expert,* Fall 1987, pp. 18–30.

Dudek, Virginia. "SCO Eschew UNIX Battle; See Opportunity Aplenty." *Management Information System Week,* January 2, 1989, p. 26.

Dyson, Esther. "Why Groupware Is Gaining Ground." *Datamation,* March 1, 1990, pp. 52–54.

"Shimmer, Flicker, and Picture Tricks." *The Economist,* January 30, 1988, p. 71.

Eckmiller, Rolf, and von der Malsburg, C. (eds.). *Neural Computers,* NATO ASI Series. Heidelberg: Springer-Verlag, 1987.

Edwards, W. "Reward Probability, Amount and Information as Determiners of Sequential Two-Alternative Decisions." *Journal of Experimental Psychology,* 1956, Vol. 52, pp. 177–188.

Eichenwald, Kurt. "The Day the Nation's Cash Pipeline Almost Ran Dry." *New York Times,* October 2, 1988, p. 11.

Eichenwald, Kurt, and Markoff, John. "Wall Street's Souped-up Computers." *New York Times,* October 16, 1988, Business Section, pp. 1, 9.

Einhorn, H. J. "Expert Measurement and Mechanical combination." *Organizational Behavior and Human Performance,* 1972, Vol. 7, pp. 86–106.

Einhorn, H. J. "Decision Errors and Fallible Judgment: Implications for social policy." In K. R. Hammond (ed.), *Judgment and Decision in Public Policy Formation.* Denver: Westview Press, 1978.

Ernst, Christian J., ed. *Management of Expert Systems.* Reading, MA: Addison-Wesley, 1988.

Fama, Eugene. "The Behavior of Stock Market Prices." *Journal of Business* (38), January 1965, pp. 34–105.

Feder, Barnaby. "Computer Helper: Software That Writes Software." *New York Times,* May 8, 1988, p. 5.

Feldman, Len. "I Want My HDTV." *Video Review,* August 1989.

Fersko-Weiss, Henry. "The Battle for the Broker's Desk." *High Technology Business,* September 1988, pp. 30–35.

Fick, Goran, and Sprague, Ralph H. Jr. *Decision Support Systems: Issues and Challenges.* New York: Pergamon Press, 1980.

Fiderio, Janet. "A Grand Vision." *Byte,* October 1988, pp. 237–244.

Fisher, D., and McKusick, K. "An Empirical Comparison of ID3 and Back-propagation." *Eleventh International Joint Conference on Artificial Intelligence,* Vol. 1. Detroit, August 20–25, 1989, pp. 788–793.

Fisher, Lawrence M. "A New Approach to Programming." *New York Times,* September 7, 1988, p. D8.

Flint, David. "Hypertext." *Butlercos Foundation.*

Francett, Barbara. "Neural Nets Arrive." *Computer Decisions,* January 1989, pp. 58–76.

Frank, Howard. "Leading the Network into the 1990's." *Networking Management,* January 1990.

Freed, Peter. "Super Television." *Business Week,* January 30, 1989, pp. 53–63.

Freeman, Peter. *Software Reusability.* New York: IEEE Computer Society Press, February 1987.

Friedland, P. "A. I. and Space Exploration." *Eleventh International Joint Conference on Artificial Intelligence,* Vol. 2. Detroit, August 20–25, 1989, pp. 1676–1679.

Frisse, Mark. "From Text to Hypertext." *Byte,* October 1988, pp. 247–253.

Fuchsberg, Gilbert. "Hand Held Computers Help Field Staff Cut Paper Work and Harvest More Data." *Wall Street Journal,* January 30, 1990, pp. B1, B9.

Gardner, Anne Von der Lieth. *An Artificial Intelligence Approach to Legal Reasoning.* Cambridge, MA: MIT Press, 1987.

Gizanka, Len. "Image Processing Leaps into the 1990's." *ID Systems,* January 1990, pp. 51–56.

Ginsberg, Matthew L. *Readings in Nonmonotonic Reasoning.* Palo Alto, CA: Morgan Kaufmann, 1987.

Gleick, James. *Chaos: Making a New Science.* New York: Viking, 1987.

Goldberg, L. R. "Man vs. Model of Man: A rationale, plus Some Evidence for a Method of Improving on Clinical Inferences." *Psychological Bulletin,* 1970, Vol. 73, pp. 422–432.

Goldberg, L. R. "Man vs. Model of Man: Just How Conflicting Is That Evidence?" *Organizational Behavior and Human Performance,* 1976, Vol. 16, pp. 13–22.

Goleman, Daniel. "Why Managers Resist Machines." *New York Times,* February 7, 1988, p. 4.

Greenbaum, Joshua. "OSF Offers Consensus Interface." *Computer Systems News,* January 9, 1989, pp. 1, 6.

Grimson, W. E. L., and Patil, R. S. *A1 in the 1980's and Beyond.* Cambridge, MA: MIT Press, 1987.

Grizanka, L. "Image Processing Leaps into the 1990's." *ID Systems,* January 1990, pp. 51–56.

Grossberg, Stephen (ed.). Neural Networks and Natural Intelligence. Cambridge, MA: MIT Press, 1988.

Grossberg, Stephen. *Studies of Mind and Brain.* Reidel, 1982.

Gutierres, Ted. "Automate the Futures Exchange." *New York Times,* December 31, 1989, p. F2.

Gupta, L. C. *Financial Ratios for Monitoring Corporate Sickness.* Delhi: Oxford University Press, 1893.

Hand, D. J. *Artificial Intelligence and Statistics II.* J. C. Baltzer AG, 1990.

Harrison, Bradford T. "Servers Set the Stage." *DEC Professional,* p. 36.

Hecht-Nielsen, Robert. *Neurocomputing.* New York: Addison-Wesley, 1990.

Hellauer, Brian. "Software Begets Software: Getting Ready for the Age of Case." *Computers in Banking,* August 1988, pp. 43–48.

Helstrom, Carl W. *Statistical Theory of Signal Detection.* New York: Pergamon Press, 1960, p. 188.

Heymann, H., and Bloom, Robert. *Decision Support Systems in Finance and Accounting* New York: Quorum Books, 1988.

Hillis, Daniel. *The Connection Machine.* Cambridge, MA: MIT Press, 1986.

Hitch, Charles, "Sub-optimization in Operations Research." *Operations Research,* 1953, Vol. 1, pp. 87–99.

Hoggatt, A. "An Experimental Business Game." *Behavioral Science,* 1959, Vol. 4, pp. 192–203.

Hooper, Laurence, and Schlesinger, Jacob M. "Is Optical Computing The Next Frontier, Or Just a Nutty Idea?" *Wall Street Journal,* January 30, 1990, pp. A1, A12.

House, Arthur S. *The Recognition of Speech by Machine—Bibliography.* New York: Academic Press, 1988.

Jackson, Perter, Reichgelt, Han, and Harmelen, Frank von. *Logic-based Knowledge Representation.* Bradford Books, 1988.

Jander, Mary. "COBOL's Salvation." *Computer Decisions,* January 1989, p. 67.

Jenkins, Avery. "DEC Techies: 'Let's Get Visual'." *Digital Review,* December 5, 1988, pp. 47–48.

Johansen, Robert. *Groupware.* New York: The Free Press Division of Macmillan, Inc, 1988.

Johnson, R. Colin, and Brown, Chappell. *Cognizers.* New York: Wiley, 1988

*Journal of Object-Oriented Programming,* September–October 1989, Vol. 2, No. 3, pp. 11–17, 80–82.

Jurgen, Ronald K. "EIA Study Predicts Strong U.S. Production of HDTV Receivers." *The Institute,* February 1989, p. 8.

Kahneman, Daniel, Slovic, Paul, and Tversky, Amos. *Judgment under Uncertainty: Heuristics and Biases.* Cambridge, Eng.: Cambridge University Press, 1982.

Kaplan, Robert and Bruns, William. *Accounting and Management: Field Study Perspectives.* Cambridge, MA: Harvard Business School Press, 1987.

Kaverva, Pentti. *Sparse Distributed Memory.* Bradford Books, 1988.

Keen, Peter G. W., and Morton, Michael Scott. *Decision Support Series: An Organization Perspective* Reading, MA: Addison Wesley, 1978.

Keough, Lee. "Point, Talk, Write in, Even Type." *Computer Decisions,* January 1989, p. 72.

Keller, John J. "AT&T Calls Smart Phone the Future." *Wall Street Journal,* June 22, 1990, pp. B1, B4.

Kelly, Nancy. "OSF Picks DECwindows Tool Kit, Rejects its 'Look'." *Digital News,* January 9, 1989, p. 60.

Kerr, Susan. "IBM's NFS Alternative." *Datamation,* January 1, 1989, pp. 63–65.

Kerr, Susan. "Legal Laissez-Faire." *Datamation,* April 15, 1989, pp. 54–56.

Kim, Won. "A New Database for New Times" *Datamation,* January 15, 1990, pp. 35–42.

Kim, Won. "Architectural Issues in Object-Oriented." *Journal of Object-Oriented Programming,* Special Database issue, Vol. 2, No. 6, March/April, 1990, SIGS Publications, Inc.

Knight, Frank. "Risk, Uncertainty, and Profit." *London School of Economics and Political Science.* Series of Reprints #16, 1933.

Kodratoff, Yves, and Michalski, Ryszard. *Machine Learning: An Artificial Intelligence Approach,* Volume III. Palo Alto, CA: Morgan Kaufmann, June 1990.

Kodratoff, Yves. *Introduction to Machine Learning.* Palo Alto, CA: Morgan Kaufman, 1989.

Kokubo, Atsuro. "Japan's R & D Managers Confront the Challenge of High Tech." *R & D Magazine,* June 1990, pp. 83–86.

Kolata, Gina. "In a Frenzy, Math Enters Age of Electronic Mail." *New York Times,* June 26, 1990, pp. C1, C10.

Kohonen, Tuevo. *Self-Organizaton and Associative Memory,* Second Edition. New York: Springer-Verlag, 1988.

Kolodner, J. ed. *Proceedings of DARPA Case-based Reasoning Workshop,* Clearwater Beach, FL, May 1988

Kull, David. "The House of Games." *Computer Decisions,* August 1988, pp. 3–56.

Lane, Morton, " 'Open Outcry' Works Well and Cheaply" *New York Times,* December 31, 1989, p. F2.
Lawrence, Jeannette. "Untangling Neural Nets." *Dr. Dobb's Journal,* April 1990, pp. 38–44.
Lee, Ed. "Window of Opportunity." *UNIX,* June 1988, pp. 58–75.
Leibs, Scott. "The Ultimate Interface." *Information Week,* June 25, 1990, pp. 46–48.
Leibs, Scott. "They Do It with Mirrors." *Information Week,* pp. 30–31.
Leventhal, Naomi S., and Fink, Robert C. "Redefining the Systems Analyst." *Management Information Systems Week,* April 25, 1988, p. 44.
Levin, Forrest, Buehler, M., Whitcomb, L., and Koditschek, D. E. "Transputer Computer Juggles Real-time Robotics." *Electronic System Design Magazine,* February 1989, pp. 77–82.
Lewis, Peter H. "The Executive Computer." *New York Times,* August 21, 1988, p. 9.
Lewis, Peter H. "The Executive Computer," *New York Times,* December 25, 1988, p. 6
Lewis, Peter H. "IBM's New System Is Put to a Test." *New York Times,* January 1, 1989, p. 10.
Lewis, Peter H. "Bringing Microsofts 'Windows' to Critical Mass." *New York Times,* January 28, 1990, p. 27.
Libby, R. "Man versus Model of Man: Some Conflicting Evidence." *Organizational Behavior and Human Performance,* 1976, Vol. 16, pp. 1–12.
Livingston, Dennis. "Software Links Multivendor Networks." *Mini Micro Systems,* March 1988, pp. 43–63.
Lockwood, Russ. "UNIX." *Personal Computing,* February 1990, pp. 79–86.
Lytton, Nina. *Open Systems Advisor,* December 28, 1990.
Mahnke, John. "IXL Tool Discovers Database Problems." *Management Information Systems Week,* December 12, 1988, p. 27.
Mahnke, John. "CASE Momentum on a Roll." *Management Information Systems Week,* January 2, 1989, p. 29.
Markoff, John. "Virus Outbreaks Thwart Computer Experts." *New York Times,* May 30, 1989, pp. C1, C9.
Markoff, John. "American Express Goes High-Tech." *New York Times,* July 31, 1988 (a).
Markoff, John. "Now PC's that read a page and store it." *The New York Times.* August 17, 1988. p. D6. (b)
Markoff, John. "IBM and a University Plan Swift File Network." *New York Times,* August 23, 1988, p. D4. (c)
Markoff, John. "Supercomputer Pictures Solve the Once Insolvable." *New York Times,* October 30, 1988, pp. 1, 26. (d)
Markoff, John. "The PC's Brand New Potential." *New York Times,* November 30, 1988. (e)
Markoff, John. "Powerful Intel Chip to Be Introduced Today." *New York Times,* February 27, 1989.
Markoff, John. "Laser Device Could Be Key to Faster Computer." *New York Times,* January 30, 1990, pp. A1, D8.
Martin, James. "DSS Tools Help Build, Analyze Models to Make Decisions." *PC Week,* May 1989, p. 48.
McPartlin, John P. "At Bennetton, It Is Always in Fashion." *Information Week,* February 12, 1990, pp. 24–25.
McWalter, Kathy. "HDTV: Turning Point for Television." *Design News,* May 23, 1988.
McWilliams, Gary. "Banks, Network Providers Eye EDI." *Datamation,* November 15, 1988, pp. 77–78.

McQuillan, John M. "Networks, the End of Distance?" *Data Communications,* June 1990, pp. 77–86.

Mehta, Angeli. "The Fifth Generation Goes Soft." *Datamation,* May 1, 1989, pp. 80.5, 80.9.

Meltzer, Allan. "What Really Happened in the Crash?" *Corporate Finance,* October 1988, p. 25.

Michalski, Ryzsard. *Machine Learning.* Palo Alto, CA: Morgan Kaufman, 1983.

Michalski, Ryzsard. *Machine Learning.* Vol. II. Palo Alto, CA: Morgan Kaufman, 1983.

Mooney, R., Shavlik, J., Towell G., and Gove, A. "An Experimental Comparison of Symbolic and Connectionist Learning Algorithms." *Eleventh International Joint Conference on Artificial Intelligence,* Vol. 1. Detroit, August 20–25, 1989, pp. 775–780.

Morley, Richard E., and Leadbeater, Todd. "Real-time A.I. Creates 'Smart' Flight Simulators." *Defense Science,* November 1988, p. 36.

Morton, Michael E. Scott. "The State of the Art of Research in Management Support Systems." *Rise of Managerial Computing,* ed. John Rockhart and Christine Bullen. Homewood, IL: Dow Jones Irwin.

Mowrer, Williams. "Hi-Fi for Your Eyes" *High Fidelity,* May 1984.

Myers, Brad A. *Creating User Interfaces by Demonstration.* New York: Academic Press, 1988.

"Cablers Envision Multi-Standard HDTV Sets." *Newsletter Digest,* December 1988, pp. 38–39.

"The Television of the Future." *Newsweek,* April 4, 1988.

Nolle, Thomas. "Exchange Standards Are Emerging, but They're Not Always Easy to Implement." *PC Week,* February 2, 1988, p. C23.

Obermeier, Klaus K., and Barron, Janet J. "Time to Get Fired Up." *Byte,* August 1989, pp. 217–224.

O'Connell, Daniel R., "A Matter of Semantics." *Datamation,* December 15, 1988, pp. 51–54.

O'Leary, Meghan, "Rethinking the Organization." *CIO,* December 1989, pp. 44–50.

O'Malley, Christopher. "A New Decade for DOS." *Personal Computing,* April 27, 1990. pp. 88–96.

O'Malley, Christopher. "Unix, Tomorrow's Operating System." *Personal Computing,* June 1988, pp. 100–108.

Opper, Susanna. "Strength in Numbers: Groupware May Revolutionize the Way We Work." *Computerworld,* August 3, 1988, pp. 25–26.

Pace, Brenda. "TBMS's Take Charge of Text." *Edge,* January–February 1989, pp. 39–41.

Parsons, Andrew. "Watch Out for the Market Data Glut." *New York Times,* April 24, 1988, Business Section, p. 2.

Pava, Calvin. "In Managing New Office Technology." New York: Free Press, 1983.

Pearl, Judea. *Probabilistic Reasoning in Intelligent Systems: Networks of Plausible Inference.* Palo Alto: Morgan Kaufmann, 1988.

Penczel, Peter. "Wall Street Rolls Out CASE Technology." *Wall Street Computer Review,* February 1989, pp. 56–66.

Pepper, Bill. "Fast Forward." *Business Month,* February 1989, p. 25.

Peterson, Gerald. *Object-Oriented Computing,* Volume 1, *Concepts;* Volume 2, *Implementations.* New York: IEEE Computer Society Press, January 1988.

Pereira, Joseph. "Nintendo Looks to MIT for Brain-Teasing Video Games." *The Wall Street Journal,* May 15, 1990, pp. B1, B6.

Pinson, Lewis J., and Wiener, Richard S. *An Intro to Object-Oriented Programming and Smalltalk*. New York: Addison-Wesley, 1988.

Pollack, Andrew. "For Artificial Reality, Wear A Computer." *New York Times,* April 10, 1989, pp. 1, D5.

Pollack, Andrew. "New Chips Offer the Promise of Much Speedier Computers." *New York Times,* January 4, 1989, pp. 1, D6.

Pollack, Andrew. "The Move to Modular Software." *New York Times,* April 23, 1990, pp. D1, D6.

Polya, G., *Patterns of Plausible Inference: Mathematics and Plausible Reasoning*. Vol. II. Princeton, NJ: Princeton University Press, 1968.

Porter, Bruce, and Mooney, Raymond J. *Machine Learning: Proceedings of the 1990 Conference*. Palo Alto, CA: Morgan Kaufmann, June 1990.

Pressman, Roger S. *Software Engineering,* 2nd edition. New York: McGraw-Hill, 1987.

Preston, M. C., and Barrata, P. "An Experimental Study of the Auction Value of an Uncertain Outcome." *American Journal of Psychology,* 1948, Vol. 61, pp. 183–193.

Proceedings of the IEEE International Conference on Neural Networks. New York: IEEE Press, June 1987.

Proceedings of the IEEE International Conference on Neural Networks. New York: IEEE Press, July 1988.

Proceedings of the IEEE/INNS International Joint Conference on Neural Networks. New York: IEEE Press, June 1989.

Ranada, David. "Aspects of HDTV." *High Fidelity,* April 1989.

Ranada, David. "The Art of HDTV." *High Fidelity,* April 1989.

Reddy, R. "Foundations and Grand Challenges of Artificial Intelligence." *Artificial Intelligence Magazine,* Vol. 9, No. 4 Winter 1988, pp. 9–24.

*Release 1.0*. December 30, 1987.

Rissland, E., and Skalok D. "Combining Case-based and Rule-based Reasoning: A Heuristic Approach." *Eleventh International Joint Conference on Artificial Intelligence*. Vol. 1. Detroit, August 20–25, 1989, pp. 525–530.

Roach, Stephen. *America's Technology Dilemma: A Profile of the Information Economy*. April 1987.

Robertson, Jack. "ATV European Co-star." *Electronic News,* August 1, 1988., p. 10.

Rockhart, John F., and Treacy, Michael E. *Executive Information Support Systems*. Working Paper #65, Center for Information Systems Research, Sloan School of Management, MIT, November 1980

Rockhart, John F., and Treacy, Michael E. "The CEO Goes On-line." *Harvard Business Review,* January–February 1982.

Rockhart, John F., and DeLong, David W. *Executive Support Systems*. Homewood, IL: Dow Jones-Irwin, 1988.

Rothfeder, Jeffrey. "Neither Rain, Nor Sleet, Nor Computer Glitches. . . ." *Business Week,* May 8, 1989, pp. 135–137.

Rothfeder, Jeffrey, Bartimo, Jim. Therrian, Lois, and Brandt, Richard. *Business Week,* July 2, 1990, pp. 54–55.

Rudd, Kenneth F., and Levy, Joel D. "Winning the PC Shell Game." *Today's Office,* January 1989, pp. 8–14.

Rumelhart, David E., McClelland James L., and the PDP Reserach Group. *Parallel Distributed Processing*. Vol. 1: *Foundations*. Cambridge, MA: MIT Press, 1988.

Rumelhart, David E., McClelland James L., and the PDP Research Group. *Parallel Distributed Processing*. Vol 2: *Psychological and Biological Models*. Cambridge, MA: MIT Press, 1988.

Runyan, L. "Hot Technologies for 1989." *Datamation,* January 15, 1989.

Sacerdoti, E. D. "The Copernican View of Artificial Intelligence." *Sun Technology,* Winter 1989.

Saffo, Paul. "Same-Time, Same-Place Groupware." *Personal Computing,* March 20, 1990, pp. 57–58.

Salus, Peter H. "Specifications and Open Systems." *Sun Expert Magazine,* June 1990, pp. 47–49.

Samuelson, Paul. *Economics.* New York: McGraw-Hill, 1958.

Sanger, David E. "Japan's Scratch-Pad Computers." *New York Times,* March 26, 1990, pp. D1, D5.

Schantz, Herb. "Out of the Lab: Neural Optical Character Recognition." *ID Systems,* July/August 1990, pp. 26–29.

Schatz, Willie, and Foley, Mary Jo. "Users Welcome New NSF Network with Glee and Caution." *Datamation,* September 1, 1988, pp. 33–34.

Schatz Willie. "EDI: Putting the Muscle in Commerce and Industry." *Datamation,* March 15, 1988.

Schiller, Zachary. "Stalking the New Consumer." *Business Week,* August 28, 1989, pp. 54–62.

Schmidt, Lisa M., and Watanabe, June M. *Network Primer.* Kinetics, A Division of Excelan, 1988.

Schindleer, Paul E. Jr., "SNA Comes of Age." *Information Weekly,* November 16, 1987, pp. 24–30.

Schneiker, Henry. "Protecting a System from Bugs." *Digital News,* January 23, 1989, pp. 23, 26.

Schultz, Brad. "Penn Research Challenges Need for Network Protocols." *Datamation,* August 15, 1988, pp. 30, 34.

Schutzer, Daniel. *Artificial Intelligence.* New York: Van Nostrand, 1987.

Schutzer, Daniel. "Business Expert Systems: The Competitive Edge." *Expert Systems With Applications,* Vol I. New York: Pergamon Press, 1990.

Schwartz, Robert S. "HDTV: Keeping the Rabbit Ears Alive." *High Fidelity,* April 1989.

Scodel, A., Ratoosh, P., and Minas, J. S. "Some Personality Correlates of Decision Making under Conditions of Risk." *Behavioral Science,* 1959, Vol. 4, pp. 19–28.

Scodel, A., Ratoosh, P., Minas, J. S., and Lipetz, M. "Some Descriptive Aspects of Two-Person, Non Zero-Sum Games." *Conflict Resolution,* 1959, Vol. 3, pp. 114–119.

Scott, Karyl. "X.400 Pushes the Envelope for Electronic Messaging." *Data Communications,* June 1990, pp. 93–102.

Securities Training Corporation. *General Securities Lesson 1–12, series 7.* 1986.

Seymour, Jim. "Text Management and Retrieval: Software that Tracks Down Key Information." *Today's Office,* June 1990, pp. 15–18.

Sharp, Kevin R. "Toshiba Express Reader." *ID Systems,* July/August 1990, pp. 32–33.

Sharp, Kevin R. "OCR from A to Z." *ID Systems,* July/August 1990, pp. 34–39.

Shellenberger, Sue. "CBOT, in a Sign of the Times, May Finally Join Electronic Age." *New York Times,* February 6, 1989, p. C1.

Sherr, Sol. *Input Devices.* New York: Academic Press, 1988.

Shklar, Gene. "Spreadsheets Are More Efficient When Teamed Up With A DBMS." *Management Information Systems Week,* May 2, 1988, p. 40.

Shriver, Bruce, and Wegner, Peter. *Research Directions in Object-Oriented Programing.* Cambridge, MA: MIT Press, 1987.

Siler, Julia Flynn. "Broker Study by Exchange in Chicago." *New York Times,* February 9, 1989, p. D5.

Simon, H. A. *Models of Man.* New York: Wiley, 1957.

Simon, H. A. "Theories of Decision Making in Economics and Behavioral Science." *American Economic Review,* 1959, Vol. 49, pp. 253–283.

Sims, Calvin. "AT&T and Zenith in TV Deal." *New York Times,* March 1, 1989, pp. D1, D4.

Sims, Calvin. "Computer Failure Disrupts A.T.&T. Long Distance." *New York Times,* Tuesday, January 16, 1990, pp. A1, A24.

Smoliar, S. W. "The Challenge of Neural Darwinism." *Eleventh International Joint Conference on Artificial Intelligence,* Vol. 2. Detroit, August 20–25, 1989, pp. 1669–1672.

Snyder, A. "Encapsulation and Inheritance in Object-Oriented Programming Languages." *Proceedings of OOPSLA '86 Conference.* Portland, OR, September 1986, pp. 38–45.

Speed, Austin H. III. *Desktop Video: A Guide to Personal and Small Business Video Production.* New York: Academic Press, 1988.

Spurga, Ronald C. *Balance Sheet Basics: Financial Management for Non-Financial Managers.* New York: Franklin Watts, 1986.

Stamper, David A. *Business Data Communications.* Menlo Park, CA: Benjamin/Cummings, 1986.

Stefik, M., and Brobrow, "Object Oriented Programming: Themes and Variations." *The AI Magazine,* 1985, pp. 40–62.

Steinberg, Don. "Electronic Data Interchange Use Moves from the Few to the many." *PC Week,* December 15, 1987, pp. C2 and C4.

Sullivan-Trainor, Michael L. "Unified Business Focus Drives American Express' Diversified Success." *Computerworld Premier 100,* September 11, 1989, pp. 58–60.

Szuprourez. *Intelligent Systems Analyst.* 7: p. 14–16.

Tazelaar, Jane Morrill. "Hypertext." *Byte,* October 1988, p. 134.

Tcheng, D., Lambert, B., C-Y Lu, S., and Rendell, L. "Building Robust Learning Systems by Combining Induction and Optimization." *Eleventh International Joint Conference on Artificial Intelligence.* Vol. 1, Detroit, August 20–25, 1989, pp. 806–812.

Terry, Fred. "Cooperation by Computer." *MACazine,* February 1989, pp. 21–24.

Thorndyke, P. W. "High-Impact Future Research Directions." *Eleventh International Joint Conference on Artificial Intelligence.* Vol. 2. Detroit, August 20–25, 1989, pp. 1675–1676.

Touretzky, David S. *Advances in Neural Information Processing Systems.* Palo Alto, CA: Morgan Kaufman, 1989.

Touretzky, David S., and Pomerleau, Dean A. "What's Hidden in the Hidden Layers?" *Byte,* August 1989, pp. 227–233.

Tore, Risch, Reboh, Rene, Hart, Peter, and Duda, Richard. "A Functional Approach to Integrating Database and Expert Systems." *ACM,* December 1988, Vol. 31 No. 12, pp. 1424–1437.

Tracz, Will. *Software Reuse—Emerging Technology.* New York: IEEE Computer Society Press, September 1988.

Treacy, Michael. "Survival: Automating Sales, Marketing, Distribution and Service." *The Consultant Forum,* Vol 5, No. 1, p. 2.

Trautman, Peggy, "Integrating Text for TV Databases." *Datamation,* May 15, 1990, pp. 102–103.

Vella, Ray. "High-Definition TV Is Rallying a Digital Revolution." Business Week, January 30, 1989, pp. 64–66.

Vemuri, V. *Artificial Neural Networks: Theoretical Concepts.* Washington D.C., Computer Society Press, 1988.

Violano, Michael. "The Documented Success of Automated Documents." *Bankers Monthly,* January 1990, pp. 54–58.

"High-Definition Video Technology." *Vital Speeches of the Day,* February 1990, pp. 241–244.

Waibel, Alex, and Hampshire, John. "Building Blocks for Speech." *Byte,* August 1989, pp. 235–245.

Waibel, Alexander, and Kai-Fu, Lee. *Readings in Speech Recognition.* Palo Alto, CA: Morgan Kaufman, 1990.

Wald, Matthew L. "Experts Diagnose Telephone 'Crash.'" *New York Times,* Tuesday, January 16, 1990, p. A25.

Wang, Richard, and Madnick, Stuart. *Connecting Among Information Systems.* MIT Composite Information Series Project, Vol. 1, September 1988.

Wayner, Peter. "VLIW: Heir to RISC?" *Byte,* August 1989, pp. 259–262.

Wegner, P. "Dimensions of Object-Based Language Design." *Special Issue of SIGPLAN Notices* Orlando, FL, October 4–8, 1987, pp. 168–182.

Weiss, S., and Kapouleas. "An Empirical Comparison of Pattern Recognition Neural Nets and Machine Learning Classification Methods." *Eleventh International Joint Conference on Artificial Intelligence.* Vol. 1, Detroit, August 20–25, 1989, pp. 781–797.

Weiss, Sholom, and Kulkowski, Casimir. *Computer Systems That Learn.* Palo Alto, CA: Morgan Kaufman, 1990.

"What Caused the Meltdown." *The Economist,* December 19, 1987, pp. 65–66.

Whyte, Bert. "Too Hot to Handle." *Audio,* September 1989.

Wiggins, N., and Kohen, E. S. "Man vs. Model of Man Revisited: The Forecasting of Graduate School Success." *Journal of Personality and Social Psychology,* 1971, Vol. 19, pp. 100–106.

Williams, Daniel. "New Technologies for Coordinating Work." *Datamation,* May 15, 1990, pp. 92–95.

Williams, Tom. "User Interface Management System Steps Up Application Development." *Computer Design,* June 1, 1990, pp. 56–58.

Williams, Tom. "The Next architecture: Design for the '90s?" *Computer Design,* December 1988, pp. 27–28.

Williamson, Mickey. "Neural Networks." *Digital News,* January 9, 1989, pp. 29–35.

Zachary, G. Pascal. "Artificial Reality: Computer Simulations One Day May Provide Surreal Experiences." *New York Times,* January 23, 1990, pp. A1, A9.

Zachman, William. "OS/2 Extended Edition and IBM's PS/2 Strategy." *PC World,* June 1988, pp. 73–76.

Zachman, William F. "OS/2: Heard but Not Seen." *PC World.* August 1989, pp. 59–62.

Ziegfeld, Richard and Tarp, John. *Desktop Publishing for the Writer: Designing, Writing, and Developing.* IEEE Computer Society Press, 1989.

Zdonik, Stanley B., and Maier, David. *Readings in Object-Oriented Database Systems.* Palo Alto, CA: Morgan Kaufman, 1989.

Zuboff, Shoshana. *The Age of the Smart Machine.* New York: Basic Books, 1988.

Zuboff, Shoshana. "Smart Computers: The Challenge to Smart Managers." *Business Month,* February 1989. pp. 61–62.

# Index